MW00533685

THE KINKS

Tempo
A Rowman & Littlefield Music Series on Rock, Pop, and Culture

Series Editor: Scott Calhoun

Tempo: A Rowman & Littlefield Music Series on Rock, Pop, and Culture offers titles that explore rock and popular music through the lens of social and cultural history, revealing the dynamic relationship between musicians, music, and their milieu. Like other major art forms, rock and pop music comment on their cultural, political, and even economic situation, reflecting the technological advances, psychological concerns, religious feelings, and artistic trends of their times. Contributions to the **Tempo** series are the ideal introduction to major pop and rock artists and genres.

THE KINKS

A Thoroughly English Phenomenon

Carey Fleiner

ROWMAN & LITTLEFIELD
Lanham • Boulder • New York • London

Published by Rowman & Littlefield
A wholly owned subsidary of The Rowman & Littlefield Publishing Group, Inc.
4501 Forbes Boulevard, Suite 200, Lanham, Maryland 20706
www.rowman.com

Unit A, Whitacre Mews, 26-34 Stannary Street, London SE11 4AB

British Library Cataloguing in Publication Information Available

Library of Congress Cataloging-in-Publication Data

Names: Fleiner, Carey, 1965– author.
Title: The Kinks : a thoroughly English phenomenon / Carey Fleiner.
Description: Lanham : Rowman & Littlefield, [2017] | Series: Tempo: a Rowman & Littlefield music series on rock, pop, and culture | Includes bibliographical references and index.
Identifiers: LCCN 2016033939 (print) | LCCN 2016034764 (ebook) | ISBN 9781442235410 (cloth : alk. paper) | ISBN 9781442235427 (electronic)
Subjects: LCSH: Kinks (Musical group) | Rock music—England—History and criticism.
Classification: LCC ML421.K56 F54 2017 (print) | LCC ML421.K56 (ebook) | DDC 782.42166092/2 [B]—dc23 LC record available at https://lccn.loc.gov/2016033939

Printed in the United States of America

CONTENTS

SERIES EDITOR'S FOREWORD

The Kinks: A Thoroughly English Phenomenon

In 2017, the Kinks' timeless "Waterloo Sunset" reaches its fiftieth anniversary—a song ostensibly about the simple and the ordinary in people's lives, where the scene of a daily commute becomes a paradise. Ray Davies has remarked that a song he wrote about a Londoner now belongs "to everyone." With its serendipitous timing, I welcome this examination of the Kinks into the Tempo series fold, in which Carey Fleiner reminds us with her energetic, deeply informed examination of one of the more popular—and populist—British Invasion bands that it is thoroughly English to make the future keep up with a bit of the past. The Kinks knew how to do the backward glance, not only into the personal histories of its own Ray and Dave Davies but also into the historically home-front concerns that felt thoroughly English to the Davieses and, judging by their success, with fans: a sense of permanence, place, and self-rule for the ordinary man and woman, such that enough time in the day was preserved for having a bit of fun as well. Keeping these concerns central to any plan for the future felt right for the Kinks, and it found some sonic inspiration for a way forward in the traditions of American blues and rock. Challenging tides that must have felt they could wash out the ordinary, homely values of the commoner were part of the serious playfulness the Kinks specialized in, and because the Davieses got neither too precious nor too debauched to remain relevant, they persevered as an influence on popular culture and as a comment on what does, in fact, persevere.

Fans and scholars alike still find culturally relevant conversations buoyed by the Kinks and see in the wide-ranging musical styles in the band's catalog and in the Davieses' solo projects the accomplishments of artists. As popular music makes a space for gathering around shared feelings, memories, hopes, and dreams, it should also be where a critical examination of all those things takes place, which Fleiner does exceedingly well, bringing her understanding of the motifs of classical literature to bear on her appreciation of the Kinks. She looks beyond the heights of the Kinks' success to explore the quests each Davies brother found he had to take and how the vital themes of popular culture tie into the most personal of our quests. She helps us understand the epic in the ordinary in the songs and lives of the Davieses and in their art, which is their attempt to chart a course for fans through the 1960s and beyond, which were, upon reflection, as much of an era of change as every era, including right now.

Scott Calhoun

TIMELINE

Cultural events

The Kinks

September 1939: Britain declares war on Germany.

1940: Battle of Britain; evacuation of Dunkirk.

1942: The Beveridge Report lays the foundation of the welfare state in Britain (which includes the foundation of the National Health Service in 1948).

December 31, 1943: Pete Quaife was born.

February 15, 1944: Mick Avory was born.
June 21, 1944: Ray Davies was born.

May 1945: VE Day over Germany; Hitler commits suicide.
August/September 1945: surrender of Japan.
1945–1951: Clement Atlee (Labour), prime minister (PM).

Cultural events	*The Kinks*
Rationing continued throughout his tenure in office. Military conscription is revived, and Britain is drawn into the Korean War.	
ca. 1947–ca. 1991: the Cold War between the Soviet Bloc and Western powers	February 3, 1947: Dave Davies was born.
1948: Britain hosts the "Austerity Games"—the name given to the Olympics as rationing is still in effect.	
1951: The Festival of Britain, a morale booster for British confidence during the postwar era (Ray remembers visiting attractions on the South Bank of the Thames that were part of this). Winston Churchill becomes PM (until 1955), and rationing ends during his tenure.	1951: Ray attends Festival of Britain with his father; it has lasting influence on his love of the area of central London along the Thames near Waterloo.
1952: Elizabeth II becomes Queen of England. First televised coronation followed by street parties in celebration.	
1955: Rock-and-roll records land on the mainstream music charts. Chuck Berry releases rock-and-roll tracks featuring the guitar as the main instrument. Disneyland opens in Los Angeles.	
1956: Suez Canal Crisis (Antony Eden, PM). Britain invades Egypt after the country decides to nationalize the canal, was met	

Cultural events	*The Kinks*
with international disapproval, and withdraws. Egypt becomes independent of British rule.	
1957–1963: Harold McMillan (Conservative), PM. Key events during his term include England's application to the European Common Market (vetoed by the French), the Notting Hill Race Riots, and New Commonwealth immigration.	1957: Ray receives his first guitar from his eldest sister who dies of heart failure later that evening while out dancing. Her death contributes to his musical inspiration throughout his life.
1962: The Profumo affair rocks British politics. The ban is lifted off sales of *Lady Chatterley's Lover*. The Beatles sign a contract with Parlophone Records; by 1963, "Beatlemania" sweeps Britain and the rest of the world bar America.	1961–1962: The band that would later become the Kinks performs as the Ray Davies Quartet.
	1962–1963: Ray attends Hornsey Art School; he spends these years playing with various blues bands in London.
1963: Great Train Robbery; Richard Beeching closes many minor railway lines this year.	1963: Dave forms what will become the Kinks with Pete Quaife. The band performs gigs throughout the year as the Pete Quaife Band, the Boll-Weevils, the Ramrods, and finally the Ravens. Mick Avory auditions and joins the band as its permanent drummer in early 1964. Late 1963/early 1964: The band is renamed the Kinks by their new management and secure a three-record recording contract.

Cultural events

February 1964: The Beatles appear on *The Ed Sullivan Show* in the United States, ushering in the "British Invasion" of American popular music. They nearly don't make their second tour of the States in 1964 due to the American Musicians' Union's protest.

Easter 1964: Mods versus rockers at seaside resorts in Britain

1964–1970: Harold Wilson (Labour), PM. Events during his time in office include many social reforms including the abolishment of capital punishment and the decriminalization of homosexuality. The Open University is founded. Crisis of the trade unions over prices and incomes.

January 1965: Death of Winston Churchill; Mary Quant debuts the miniskirt.

1966: England wins the World Cup against Germany and

The Kinks

1964: After two failed singles (on Pye Records) and touring throughout Britain, the Kinks reach number one with "You Really Got Me" in August. *Kinks* is released in October.

1 June 1965: Kinks start their first US tour. Due to a contretemps between the band and the American Federation of Musicians, the band is banned from performing in the United States for four years.

Albums: *Kinda Kinks*; *Kink Kontroversy*; key songs: "See My Friends," "Well Respected Man," and "Dedicated Follower of Fashion."

1966: *Face to Face*; key songs: "Sunny Afternoon" and "Dead

Cultural events

continues to crow about it for the next fifty years.

1967: Summer of Love characterized by "Be-ins" in San Francisco; the release of *Sgt. Pepper's Lonely Hearts Club Band*; and the Monterey Pop Music Festival; the era of psychedelic rock begins.

1969: Concorde, the first commercial supersonic transport (SST), makes its maiden flight; it is an Anglo-French joint development.

1970–1974: Edward Heath (Conservative), PM. Events during his tenure include the Troubles in Ireland, the Three-Day Week, the introduction of the value-added tax (VAT), and problems from striking miners.

1971: Britain decimalizes its currency, replacing pounds, shillings, and pence.

The Kinks

End Street"; John Dalton fills in for Pete Quaife on bass.

1967: *Something Else by the Kinks*; key songs: "Waterloo Sunset" and "Autumn Almanac." Dave has a massive hit over the summer with "Death of a Clown." Pete Quaife rejoins the band. Pye release the live album *Kinks Live at Kelvin Hall*.

1968: *The Kinks Are the Village Green Preservation Society*; key songs: "Wonderboy," "Days," and "Picture Book." Quaife returns for *Village Green*.

1969: *Arthur (or the Decline and Fall of the British Empire)*; key songs: "Victoria," "Young and Innocent Days," and "Shangri-la." The Kinks tour America after the ban is lifted. Pete Quaife quits the band for good, and John Dalton takes over on bass through to 1976 (and briefly in 1978).

1970: *Lola versus Powerman and the Moneygoround, Part One*; key song: "Lola." John Dalton joins the band on keyboards. John Gosling joins the band as a keyboard player through to 1978.

1971: Last album on Pye/Reprise: *Percy*. The band sign with RCA. Konk Studios is founded. *Muswell Hillbillies* on RCA.

Cultural events

The Kinks

1972: *Everybody's in Show-Biz*; key songs: "Celluloid Heroes" and "Supersonic Rocketship."

1973: Britain joins the European Union (European Economic Community [EEC]); military coup d'etat in Chile leading to fears amongst certain conservatives in Britain that a similar dissolution of the constitution and government could occur there.

1973–1976: The Kinks enter a period of producing concept albums and lavish stage theatricals.

1973: *Preservation Act 1*. Ray adds a horn sections, backing singers, and dancers to the group.

1974–1976: Harold Wilson (Labour), PM. Wilson managed to end the miners' disputes. The Health and Safety at Work Act comes into force.

1974: *Preservation Act 2*. This is the first album created and produced at Konk Studios. Ray acts in *Starmaker* for Granada Television.

1975: *The Kinks Present a Soap Opera*, the studio version of Ray's *Starmaker* show; *Schoolboys in Disgrace*, the conclusion of the *Preservation* trilogy. The Kinks contribute to the holiday season with "Father Christmas."

1976–1979: James Callaghan (Labour), PM.

1976: The Kinks leave RCA and sign with Arista Records. The group is reduced in size to a five-man ensemble, and the group embarks on arena tours. Andy Pyle replaces John Dalton on bass through to 1978.

1977: Queen Elizabeth's Silver Jubilee.

1977: *Sleepwalker*. The Kinks begin a commercial renaissance in the United States where they remain more popular than in Britain for the next six years or so,

Cultural events

The Kinks

playing large arenas and producing album-oriented rock (AOR).

1978: Winter of Discontent. Van Halen covers "You Really Got Me," sparking renewed interest in the band (complementary to the covers by the Jam and the Pretenders of Kinks' material).

1978: *Misfits*; key song: "Rock 'n' Roll Fantasy." Jim Rodford takes over bass through to 1996. Gordon John Edwards takes over as keyboard player.

1979–1990 Margaret Thatcher (Conservative) is prime minister, the first woman to hold the office in Great Britain. Events include the privatization of many government-owned industries and a drastic cut in power of the trade unions.

1979: *Low Budget* earns the Kinks a gold album. Ian Gibbons replaces Edwards as keyboard player through to 1989.

1980: Recession in Britain.

1980: Dave releases *Dave Davies* (aka "the bar code album"). Live Kinks: *One for the Road*.

1981: Brixton riots.

1981: Dave releases *Glamour*. The Kinks release *Give the People What They Want*; key songs: "Destroyer" and "Better Things." The Kinks continue to enjoy international tours.

1982: Falklands War between Britain and Argentina.

1982: Dave releases his third and final solo album of this era, *Chosen People*.

1983: *State of Confusion*; key song: "Come Dancing"—the Kinks' biggest hit in the United States and first top twenty in the UK since "Lola." Ray writes and appears in *Return to Waterloo*,

Cultural events

1984–1985: Miners' Strike—one of the biggest strikes since the 1926 General Strike.

1994: The Channel Tunnel linking France and Britain is completed. Britpop becomes popular in the UK, sparking a third wave of interest in the Kinks, but they do not benefit commercially from the renewed interest in the band. 1994–2007: Tony Blair (Labour), PM.

The Kinks

without the Kinks. Mick Avory leaves the band.

1984: *Word of Mouth*; key single: "Do It Again." Two biographies of the Kinks are published: Jon Savage's and Johnny Rogan's works.

1986: The band sign with MCA Records. *Think Visual* released; key tracks: "Lost and Found" and "Working at the Factory."

1987: *Kinks Live: The Road*.

1989: *UK Jive*. Mark Haley replaces Ian Gibbons on keyboards through to 1993.

January 1, 1990: Kinks inducted into the Rock and Roll Hall of Fame.

1993: The Kinks sign with Columbia Records and release *Phobia*. Ian Gibbons returns as keyboard player through to 1996.

1994: *To the Bone*, on the Konk label, a live acoustic album in front of an invited audience. The Kast-Off Kinks are formed of various former members of the band (still active as of 2016).

1995: Ray publishes his autobiography, *X-Ray*.

Cultural events	The Kinks
August 1996: Princess Diana killed in a car crash in Paris.	1996: Dave publishes *Kink*. The Kinks play one last public performance in Oslo together as a group.
1997: Britain cedes Hong Kong back to China after ruling the territory for 150 years.	
2002: Queen Elizabeth's Golden Jubilee.	2002: Ray performs "Lola" at the *Party at the Palace* as part of the Golden Jubilee celebrations. Brian Wilson plays a four-song set—too right.
	2004: Ray is shot in New Orleans while chasing a mugger; he collects his CBE while still recovering. Dave suffers a debilitating stroke that keeps him from public performance for almost a decade (although he continues to compose and release new studio work).
	June 24, 2010: Pete Quaife dies.
2012: Queen Elizabeth's Diamond Jubilee; 2012 London Olympics.	June 2012: Ray Davies performs "Waterloo Sunset" in the closing ceremony of the Olympics.
	2013: *Sunny Afternoon*, Ray's musical (book by Joe Penhall) debuts in Hampstead, UK. It moves into London's West End in 2014 to critical praise and various theater awards; still running as of 2016. Dave returns to public performance in America in the autumn.

Cultural events

The Kinks

December 15, 2015: Ray joins
Dave on stage at Dave's show in
Islington, UK, to perform "You
Really Got Me."

2016: Queen Elizabeth's ninetieth
birthday. The UK votes on
whether to remain in the EU or
not ("Brexit").

ACKNOWLEDGMENTS

I wish to thank those who helped and supported this project, especially Rowman & Littlefield editors Natalie Mandziuk and Bennett Graff, and Tempo series editor Scott Calhoun. Many thanks, too, to the formidable copyediting work done on my behalf by Naomi Burns and Lara Graham at Rowman & Littlefield. Britain and America really are separated by a common language, aren't they?

I am also most grateful to the history department at the University of Winchester, as I was granted financial support and study leave. This support allowed me to create and present the conference papers that formed the basis of several chapters of this book as well as gave me time to finish writing and revising the text. My colleagues' support at the University of Winchester has been invaluable and much appreciated.

Thanks also go to the many people who patiently answered questions and discussed with me sections of the book-in-progress, especially Dave Emlen, Rebecca G. Wilson and Dave Davies, James Jordan, and Jayne Morgan. Without the amazing volumes compiled and published by Doug Hinman, I would have been lost before I started on this project.

I am indebted to Thomas Kitts for his advice, guidance, and patience while I worked on this project. Special thanks, too, to Kathy S. Cephas, who patiently proofread drafts in exchange for copies of British celebrity gossip rags.

Many thanks also must go to the many Kinks fans who answered my survey back in 2014; many of you went above and beyond and included a number of lovely personal stories, photos, and mementos. A special note of thanks here goes to Dave Titterton. Those who answered the survey include: A Dedicated Follower of the Kinks; Al Zeberlee; Another Dan the Fan; Barry Shalen; Bob "Flash" Fiegleman; Bob Gill; Brian Leonard; Clark Jensen; Curtis Roberts; D. Scott Craig; D. Skorich; Dave from Shangri-La; Dave C; Dirk Deerenberg; Frank Lima; Gerard van Calcar; Gregg Landis; Gregory J. Malis; Henny Stahli; Hillar Teetsov; Iñaki Garcia; James Schwartz; Jeff Geither; Jim from Pittsburgh; Joe Hedio; John Snell; Jonas 1; Jonathan Browning; Karl Leigart; Ken Ferri; Kevin Ford; Lauren from Dallas; Mark Gelbs; Michael Dawson; Michael Malone; Michael Precin; Mike McKay; Nanette Varian; Nicky Dublin; Nigel Mawdsley from Southport; Olga Ruocco; Olivier Durin from France; Paul L; Paula; Peter Bochner; Peter Smith; Randie Brazel; Rich Torrez; Scott Allardice; Sean O'Brien; Stephen James Evans; Steve Ferguson; Susan Cole; Survivor Steve; Tim from Pennsylvania; Tim Staab; Thomas Winn; Tony DH; Tune Waif Jane; and Wayne C. Apologies if anyone was overlooked—not everyone signed the survey! But all of your comments were taken on board and much appreciated.

Thanks and that to Darren Holdstock.

Finally, much respect and appreciation must go to my best friend Ellen "Lee" Melody, whom I miss and who deserved much better.

INTRODUCTION

It transpired the least lucrative song was "Motorcycle Emptiness" by the Manic Street Preachers, yielding a measly 32p. Surprisingly, Queen's classic "Bohemian Rhapsody" fared little better with an 86p return while the Kinks' apt "Waterloo Sunset" earned Dave [the busker] £1.50 and an out-of-date travel card.[1]

On June 2, 2012, the Theatre Royal, London, staged a revue of Ray Davies's *Come Dancing*. Based on the Kinks' 1983 hit single, the play was staged originally in full in Stratford, UK, in 2008. This 2012 revival was meant to be only a song performance, but that £15 ticket bought me a semistaged version of the play as well as "Himself" appearing as the narrator.

"Come Dancing" not only is a love letter from the band to the Davieses' sisters but also is meant to bring to the audience memories of postwar Britain. As so many Kinks songs are, the plot of the play is a mix of memories and fiction. *Come Dancing*, the musical, tells a fictionalized tale of Ray Davies's sisters, of 1950s London, and of the early days of rock and roll. In the play, we meet the narrator—usually played by Ray himself—and his family circa 1959. Kinks fans would be aware of references to Kinks and Davies lore in the drama: the disabled sister, the "spiv" (black-market wheeler and dealer) uncle, and the music-loving parents. The characters refer to an unseen little brother, and the adult Ray, invisible to the characters of the play, tells us that this little brother is he. Ray wanders about the action, linking together the scenes and explicating events not unlike a modern-day Ghost of Christmas

Past. He remarks at one point, wistfully watching as the action unfolds around him, "I wish I could speak to them." Only once in the play does he interact and become briefly visible to a character on the stage: when the youngest sister Julie, who represents a combination of his real-life disabled sister Peg and his real-life sister Irene, prepares herself for a night out dancing as Ray looks on, unseen—until she turns to him and asks him directly if she's beautiful, and with unaffected happiness, Ray tells her, "Yes."

There are elements in the play of racism and alienation as Julie, having been afflicted by childhood polio, lacks the confidence of her older sisters. She walks with a limp, but despite her disability she desires only to dance at the family-owned "danse palais" (dance hall). Julie is both too shy and too protected by her family to fulfill her dream. Initially her soul mate is an ex-Bristol boy who woos her by defending her honor and clobbering anyone who mocks her limp. Everything then changes for Julie with the arrival of newcomer Hamilton, a young, talented saxophonist from Jamaica, himself an outsider because of the color of his skin. The local boys are threatened when he and Julie bond. Too shy to take the dance floor in front of her family, Julie instead bravely ventures into the strange new world of the R&B jazz club where Hamilton plays, mesmerized by the new music and her newly found independence. Her parents fret; the local boys fume.

The play concludes with the characters explaining their fate: Julie's parents sort out their troubled marriage and loyally stay together even after a family secret is revealed. Sister Rosie and her husband emigrate to seek new opportunities in Australia. The local boys who so desperately wished to form a rock band (they had earlier auditioned at the danse palais by belting out a cruder—if that is possible—version of "You Really Got Me" that had horrified the adults) fail at their ambitions to become musicians; instead, they settle down with local jobs and local girls (very much reminiscent of Noddy Holder's character in the alternate 1970s universe of ITV's *The Grimleys*). Hamilton himself goes his own way, and it is implied that he thinks fondly of Julie for the rest of his life. After the characters thus speak, Ray, having spent the play as the spectral narrator, steps forward to tell us of Julie's fate. Fans know that much of Ray's drive as a musician is owed to his sister Irene, who gave him his first guitar on his thirteenth birthday. After showing him a few chords, she went out to dance at the local dance hall, defying medical advice to protect her weak heart, and she died that night on the dance floor "in the arms of a stranger." So when, in the play, he tells us of Julie's fate, and that she died young, it is a powerful moment. At this performance in June, a couple of weeks before Ray's sixty-eighth birthday, the other actors openly wept. The actor playing Uncle Frank could not say his lines. The audience sat silent and sorrowful. Ray, who had wandered about the stage in previous scenes, gazing at the actors and especially the actress who played Julie with such true happiness on his face as he watched these fictional shades of his childhood, stood alone and sad as he told the audience about Julie, who had stood in for his real-life older sister: "On that day, her life ended as mine began."

"Come Dancing" is a joyful song about the changes wrought upon material things, but it likewise describes the enduring spirit of people: the danse palais is gone, but the love of music and family happiness continues—the track's narrator grows up and joins a band because of the love of music given to him by his sisters, and the sister of the song consequently allows her own daughter the freedom to go out and immerse herself in music and dancing.

Come Dancing, the musical, touches on the themes that the Kinks and Ray Davies would wrestle with in their music and performance for nearly thirty years (fifty, if one counts life after the group's last concert). These themes include the safety and sanctuary of home and family, fear of change and of loneliness and isolation, solidarity and rebellion against authority, and a pervading Englishness overall, which encompasses humor and family solidarity at even the worst of times. These are themes addressed throughout this book. Despite the tragedy that shapes the plot of the play, that performance in June ended with a performance of the eponymous track that included audience participation. The audience was invited to get up and to join in—and indeed, in the original run of the play, the stage set extended into the audience with no clear distinction where the stage ended and the audience began—a distinctive characteristic of the relationship between the Kinks and their fans.

That evening, I went back down into central London to see another play staged at the National Theatre. This one was also about a rough-and-tumble family, the conflict between social custom and personal integrity, and the effects of hubris and human stubbornness in the face of authority. Sophocles's *Antigone* makes the Davies family look like *The Archers* (and the Kinks look like the Archies), but the two plays have fundamental similarities: family ties and familial conflict, misfits acting out against social convention, and rebellion against authority. Ray Davies, fortunately, is driven more by Homeric *nostos* than Sophoclean *hubris*—the Kinks may have been "angry young men" ignited by changing cultural convention and shaped by tragedy, but as Ray would comment years later, the Kinks were "a series of catastrophes [that turned] into glorious triumph."[2]

Stratford is a suburb to the north of London—not exactly the same part of north London whence came the Kinks, but nevertheless a local neighborhood away from the heart of the capital. The National Theatre sits at the foot of Waterloo Bridge, immortalized by the Kinks in "Waterloo Sunset." On that misty evening of June 2, 2012, down on the south bank of the Thames, happy crowds wandered along the pavement, brought into town by the folderol of the Diamond Jubilee, which was then reaching its apex. The London Eye soars overhead here, and on that evening it was colored red, white, and blue; Waterloo Bridge itself was bedecked along its length in all of the flags of the Commonwealth. As Ray notes in his current concerts when he introduces "Waterloo Sunset," it's not "his" song anymore. It belongs to London, to the English, and to everyone who has felt they are not quite like everybody else.

I

AROUND THE DIAL

As we were tuning up in the studio Dave played a chord which started to feed back through the amplifier . . . on top of the Vox (amp) was the little green amp that Dave had started using to get the fuzziness into the sound. The engineer, who was placing a microphone in front of Dave's speaker, jumped backwards. Dave smiled and played an even louder chord. This time . . . the feedback had a piercing whistle that made the engineer put his hands over his ears. Dave held the screeching guitar aloft to maximize the feedback. The engineer screamed and ran out of the building into the street, and as far as we know, he never returned.[1]

The Kinks: A Thoroughly English Phenomenon is not really a biography of the band—there are plenty of fine ones out there written by scholars, fans, and members of the band itself. This book takes a look instead at a number of cultural strands that affected and shaped the music and performance of the Kinks and ways in which the band itself has reflected the way people think about ordinary life—work, play, buying a house, driving a car, drinking tea, getting drunk, and getting laid. The band's music considers the ordinary and the absurd, confronting these things sometimes in anger and sometimes with self-deprecating humor. In the case of the Kinks, pick a topic, the band has got a song about it; name a musical genre, and they have got it covered. This book's chapters follow the band's trajectory more or less chronologically and cover themes such as growing up in postwar and 1950s Britain; the marketing, packaging, and exploitation that accompanied the explosion of bands during the "British Invasion"; "Brit wit" and humor in British rock and pop; sexuality and gender-bending in sixties and seventies rock music; social and political pessimism; the good times of family and home; and the legacy of fame and fandom. Because of Ray Davies's prolific song-writing and eye for social satire, the Kinks are both a mirror of and a counterfoil to nearly five decades of British and American culture. The book focuses primarily on the group itself, although sometimes various Kinks' afterlife activities will be mentioned—for example, the individual work of Ray and Dave's subsequent individual careers and experiences.

This chapter provides first a brief biography of the band. It is not a comprehensive narrative, but it provides foundation for the general reader (and perhaps tries the patience of the die-hard fan for leaving out his or her favorite part of the Kinks' legend). Much of the narrative in this section relies on previous biographies by Jon Savage, Johnny Rogan, Neville Marten and Jeffrey Hudson, Thomas Kitts, and Nick Hasted. Details are kept to a minimum as subsequent chapters will supply further information as needed for context. A literature survey follows the band's history as there are a number of works on the Kinks that range from autobiographical, encyclopedic, and academic analysis. There aren't *many* Kinks' books, certainly not compared to, for example, the myriad of Beatles-flavored books on offer, but those out there are intelligent and accessible. Next, to round out the discussion of the printed material on the band, is a brief discussion of film and theater related to the Kinks—works that not only celebrate the music but also reinforce the Kinks' *nachleben*, that is, the "afterlife" of the band and how they are perceived almost as folkloric characters rather than histor-ical persons, at least in terms of popular expectations of the band's reputation. Finally, this chapter concludes with a brief overview of the remaining chapters that follow.

MY NAME IS OF NO IMPORTANCE: A BRIEF HISTORY OF THE KINKS

Chapter 2 will look in some detail at the creation of the band, so suffice to say here, Ray and Dave Davies tend to dominate most accounts of the band's history. They are the most consistent members of the Kinks, and they were the band's lead singers and songwriters. Much of the

Kinks' music could be a diary of the Davieses' formative years, interests, and influences. The influence of family on Ray and Dave, as discussed in chapters 2 and 7, cannot be overstated. Their family and home life, closeness as well as feuding, shaped their music and colored the character of the Kinks, which in turn had an effect on the particular appeal they have on their followers, even nearly twenty years on after their last album as a band. One necessary caveat must be given to the reader: as the primary authors of the myth of the Kinks, Ray and Dave have woven over the years a story filled with contradiction. They can be fiercely private on the one hand and mischievous on the other, dropping enigmatic hints to the press about reunions and controversial comments concerning their own history, relationships, and credit for various achievements.[2]

Between 1963 and 1965, the Kinks were hard at work securing a recording contract. They eventually won a three-record deal with Pye Records, and Pye subsequently worked them to the bone pumping out records and traveling on tour packages. The average "life expectancy" of a pop group was about eighteen months, and music producers and promoters were determined to squeeze as much out of the latest sensation as they could before teen tastes turned fickle. The key albums to look at in this period include *Kinks* (1964), *Kinda Kinks* (March 1965), and *The Kink Kontroversy* (November 1965). There are no particular themes on these albums, although the music well embodies the band's blues and American rock-and-roll influences. Nevertheless, Ray's burgeoning world-weariness and character songs can be found in tracks such as "Where Have All the Good Times Gone?" and "I'm on an Island." If there is any particular characteristic during this breakout period, it is the raw desperation of the overdrive and distortion found in songs such as "You Really Got Me," "All Day and All of the Night," and "Til the End of the Day." These tracks underline that the Kinks were not only working class but also still in their teens (at least in Dave's case), and these protopunk songs express both teenage angst and desire for freedom. The Kinks demonstrated a thoughtful side during this early period too, with ballads such as "Stop Your Sobbing," "Something Better Beginning," and "Tired of Waiting."

In these early days of the band's history, they toured extensively, including the United States, and concerts were fraught with violence both on the stage and off—the latter a release of tension and frustration not only between the two Davies brothers but also between Dave and drummer Mick Avory. The Kinks' audiences were also caught up in the violence as frequently fights would break out among the fans who would subsequently destroy the venues in the melee. The Kinks were condemned for excessive sexual display as well as hedonic lifestyles: Dave Davies's exploits during this era are the stuff of legend. Ray, in the meantime, was caught between the antics of being a showman and the pressures of the record company. He found himself collapsing emotionally under the strain of demands to crank out records and went briefly on hiatus from the band as a result of a nervous breakdown. This early period ends with the Kinks' ban on performing in America for four years (beginning in the summer 1965) and the late summer release of "A Well Respected Man." The ban and this track indicate a new direction for the band; not only did they avoid the subsequent fads and trends of the pop music industry for the remainder of the sixties, but also "A Well Respected Man" demonstrates Ray's desire to pen more thoughtful, artistically merited songs reflective of his art-school days' interest in film and his desire to write more carefully constructed songs about the lives of ordinary people.

The so-called golden age of the Kinks comes between 1966 and 1972. During this period they produced some of their most pastoral and English music, and many of the tracks from this ensured Ray Davies's enshrinement in the twenty-first century by critics and fans as a national treasure and an icon of "Englishness." The band released a number of albums in this period that have since become critically acclaimed: the four key ones are *Face to Face* (1966), *Something Else by the Kinks* (1967), *The Kinks Are the Village Green Preservation Society* (1968), and *Arthur (or the Decline and Fall of the British Empire)* (1969). Each of these four albums and the ancillary singles have thematic cohesion that includes social satire ("Dedicated Follower of Fashion" and "Mr. Pleasant"), family remembrance ("Rosy Won't You Please Come Home" and "Picture Book"), nostalgia for the lost England ("Victoria" and "We Are the Village Green Preservation Society"), and political satire ("Dead End Street," "Yes Sir, No Sir," and "Victoria"). The period ends with a strong concept album on the pitfalls of the recording industry, *Lola versus Powerman and the Moneygoround Part One*, highlighted by the cheeky "Lola," a top-ten song about a transvestite.

Despite the success of the singles in this period, the LPs were commercial failures, and British audiences dismissed the band as a novelty act. Part of this was because of Ray's propensity to write his character songs in the musical-hall style he remembered fondly from his childhood—initially welcome during the brief fad in mid-decade for rock bands to produce jaunty celebrations of English life (in the vein of 1966's "Winchester Cathedral"). By the release of "Autumn Almanac" in 1968, a panegyric to gardening inspired by Ray's memories of his father working in his allotment, this jolly type of song had worn out its welcome in the face of the disillusionment of those protesting Vietnam and political strife in Europe. The counterculture did not want songs that seemed more in tune with the values of their parents and grandparents, the generation they blamed for the current political and economic distress. Nevertheless, while fans may have regarded the Kinks as no longer hip, the albums themselves were well appreciated by the Kinks' contemporary musical peers; Pete Townshend, for example, was inspired to write *Tommy* partly as a result of *Arthur*.

In 1969, the ban against the Kinks in America was finally lifted, and their new label, RCA (from 1970), signed them up for a five-record contract. On their return to the United States, the label promoted them in publicity materials as quaintly English, following on Pye's propensity to write whimsical copy that emphasized the Kinks' Englishness and eccentricity (see, for example, the liner notes on the sleeves of *Face to Face* and *Something Else*). The promotional campaign that preceded them urged that "God Save the Kinks," and copies of *Then, Now and In-Between* (1969, part of a promotional box set issued by Reprise, the Kinks' American label while they were on Pye) came with a Union Jack, Kinks badge and sticker, a *Village Green* puzzle, and a little baggy of plastic grass "from Daviesland"—the last of which, a bemused Ray Davies noted, fans tried to smoke at concerts, thinking it was altogether a different sort of herbal offering. Returning to America, they were indeed strangers in a strange land—not just from Britain to the States, of course, but also set apart from their musical peers as the landscape of commercial popular music had changed considerably since their last visit in 1965. Their long absence, too, had kept them obscure except from the most die-hard fans in the United States (thus ensuring that they maintain[ed] a legacy of an exclusive rather than mainstream band).

The first two RCA albums, *Muswell Hillbillies* (1971) and *Everybody's in Show-Biz* (1972), were successful enough that the Kinks purchased a small, disused factory in north London that was christened Konk; this became their dedicated recording studio (which remains as of 2016 a working studio and part-time art gallery). This era saw a lowered profile for the Kinks in general, however; they tended to play small venues and university campuses. It was a difficult period personally for the two Davieses, as Ray went through a divorce, and Dave found himself in a bad situation due to drug and alcohol abuse (although the latter was pulled out of his downward spiral after a spiritual epiphany). Performances were chaotic to say the least, with Ray spraying beer on the fans and stumbling about the stage drunk (or pretending to be, depending on whom one believes). The shows sometimes ended either when Ray fell over or the band gave up in disgust with one another. Despite suffering from depression (and having spent time in the hospital after an attempted suicide), Ray carried on composing. After a brief dalliance with country rock and a nod to the Kinks' American rock-and-roll influences (*Muswell Hillbillies* and to some extent *Schoolboys in Disgrace*), he turned his creative attention onto complex concept albums that the Kinks thus acted out on stage.

Into the next period between 1973 and 1977, the band went through a number of lineup changes, and Ray added musicians as Kinks shows grew more elaborately staged. Key albums in this period include the two *Preservations* (Act 1 in 1973 and Act 2 in 1974) and *Schoolboys in Disgrace* (1976). During this period, Ray almost became lost within his creations as he struggled to voice his obsession with what he saw as England's inevitable, dark decline, which he expressed through increasingly elaborate, dystopian comedies. In addition to the Kinks' stage plays, Ray acted on television. He played, for example, an obsessive pianist for BBC-TV's *Play for the Day* called *The Long Distance Piano Player* (1970). He then wrote and starred in another musical made for ITV (Granada Television) called *Starmaker* (1974), which was adapted for the Kinks as *The Kinks Present a Soap Opera*. Ray immersed himself in his flair for acting on stage, first as "Norman" in *Starmaker* (which was refashioned and released as a Kinks album called *The Kinks Present a Soap Opera* in 1975) and then becoming "Mr. Flash" in the *Preservation* trilogy (the third of the set being *Schoolboys in Disgrace*). The social commentary and playacting that had begun with "Well Respected Man" became Ray's main focus in the mid-1970s as Ray turned inward and struggled with his identity, leaving the other the Kinks to become extras in his projects. Increasingly, Dave and the rest of the band felt alienated by Ray's vanity pieces, and the critics were unkind. RCA let them go. Only the die-hard fans remained.

From 1977, beginning with *Sleepwalker* the band renewed itself with a new label (Arista); a new, trimmed-down sound; and, thanks to a younger generation of musicians, a new following, especially in America. Ray abandoned his propensity to use the band as a prop in his increasingly arcane concept albums and began to write more commercially orientated songs—albeit still maintaining his witty social commentary. Some fans and critics complained that in this period the Kinks became somewhat bland, slickly produced album-oriented rock (AOR) that blended in with any number of hard-rock acts on American radio stations. Nevertheless, thanks to energetic covers of sixties' Kinks tracks by newly established bands such as the Jam, the Pretenders, and Van Halen, a new generation of fans discovered the band. For the first time in years they had decent album sales, and for the first time they filled stadiums and arenas during their concert tours, primarily in the United States, as by the late 1970s, most of the Kinks' fan support was coming from America. From the late 1970s until 1995, the Kinks were almost completely ignored in Great Britain and were, for the most part, seen there as an oldies band. Contemporary British press ran hot and cold, sometimes praising the eccentricities of the group and sometimes withdrawing their support with weary exasperation.

Highlight albums from this period that show the Kinks' renewed commercial rise and success of the band include *Sleepwalker* (1977), *Misfits* (1978), *Low Budget* (1979), and *Give the People What They Want* (1982). The peak of the band's second wind came with *State of Confusion* (1983) and the standout single "Come Dancing," an example of Ray's ability to mix commercial success with his talents for bittersweet memories. Despite the revived fortunes of the band, however, it was chaos as usual behind the scenes: Ray, for example, was embroiled in a tempestuous relationship with Chrissie Hynde that both influenced and affected his work at the time. Dave, who had felt increasingly alienated from both Ray and the band over the past decade, nearly quit, forging a second attempt at a solo career (the first had been in the late 1960s) with three independent albums between 1980 and 1982. The band (and Ray) did not take advantage of their renewed fortunes; they missed opportunities and began another commercial decline in the wake of the success of "Come Dancing."

Between 1984 and 1996, the band did well but ultimately failed to capitalize on their success. While now a radio-friendly, popular arena-ticket draw, especially in the United States, they would begin another decline after *Word of Mouth* (1984). Longtime drummer Mick Avory quit the band around this time, as did other dependable members who could no longer take the stress. The band failed frequently to tour to support new work, and they entered another period of self-destruction. Dave was still concerned about his position in the group, and Ray was distracted by new acting projects (he penned, composed for, and starred in the film *Return to Waterloo* [1984] in this period, allegedly infuriating Dave by using as his backup band on the movie's soundtrack all of the Kinks except his younger brother). *Word of Mouth* itself was a competent album, and it included a strong contribution from Dave, "Living on a Thin Line," a track that would gain iconic status itself years later due to its inclusion on the soundtrack for the television program *The Sopranos* (1999–2007). Ray's own personal outlook was bleak during these years as reflected on the Kinks' next album, *Think Visual* (1986). This record seemed to be a return to Ray's dark brooding over the recording industry, and it failed to chart well in the United States. *Think Visual* was followed by a live album: it was released first in Germany, illustrating how far their popularity had fallen even in America. In 1988, they released *UK Jive*. The album yet again reflects the chaos within the band: Ray was involved in yet more outside projects, he and Dave were at each other's throats, and the band did not tour to help support the album (which charted neither in the United States nor in the UK). The next album, *Phobia* (1993), saw the Kinks on yet another label (Columbia) and poised to ride another wave of revival on the strength of the burgeoning Britpop scene—Blur and especially Oasis acknowledged the Kinks' influence on their own work. In the United States, Green Day was carving out their own niche by aping Kinks riffs and volume as part of the West Coast postpunk scene. Nevertheless, the band again did not capitalize on this third wave of interest; while their concerts were still well attended, commercially they were sinking fast. The Kinks' swan song was *To the Bone*, a stripped-down version of the Kinks and a return to their tight sixties-style ensemble. Released as first a live album (1994) and then a reworked studio album (1996), the collection provided a strong retrospective of the Kinks' thirty years in the industry (along with two new tracks). The Kinks' last concert was in 1996, and then the band went on hiatus. For the next twenty years, Ray would tease the press and fans about the possibility of a full-on Kinks reunion.

Much of the discussion of the Kinks between 1996 and 2016 tends to focus on Ray and Dave Davies's individual solo careers, as they have remained the most active creatively. Elsewhere, many former band members have formed a tribute band, the "Kast-Off Kinks," which includes original Kinks' drummer Mick Avory. This latter band is active mainly in the UK and Europe and is a staple at the British fan-club meetings. The original bassist, Peter Quaife, quit the band for good in 1968 and left the music business in the early seventies. Ray Davies went out on his own in 1995 with his *Storyteller* tour; initially simply a series of readings from his newly published "unauthorized autobiography" *X-Ray*, Ray performed acoustic versions of old Kinks songs as well as pieces penned for the tour. Ray continues to tour, write new material (currently to support his autobiography *Americana*), and tinker with the Kinks' back catalog (variously performing the songs as blues pieces, as elaborate choral arrangements backed by a forty-strong chorus, or as traditional rockers with younger rock bands such as the 88 in support). He has also seen come to fruition several stage shows including *Come Dancing* in 2008, and he has overseen the creation of the West End musical *Sunny Afternoon* (from 2014). New Year's 2014 kicked off with much excitement and speculation that the three surviving Kinks would at last reunite to celebrate the fiftieth anniversary of the band's first hit, "You Really Got Me." As usual, nothing came of it, but Ray did appear onstage to sing the track with his brother Dave at Dave's show in Islington, London, in December 2015. His appearance not only surprised those of us lucky enough to be in the audience but also allegedly surprised Dave himself.

Dave Davies was left floundering a bit in 1995 when Ray struck out on the *Storyteller* tour. He assembled his own backup band and toured the United States and then the UK, gaining confidence from playing smaller and grittier venues than Ray tended/tends to book. Dave put together his own autobiography (1996) and began releasing a rather substantial back catalog of songs as well as receiving critical praise for new solo projects such as 2001's *Bug*, all the while focusing energy on his spiritual practices and beliefs. He joined in the rumblings about reunions—each brother tends to accuse the other of being the one holding things up. (Dave has recently remarked that any Kinks reunion would be like a remake of *Night of the Living Dead* and that Ray seemed happy enough directing his own version of karaoke Kinks.[3]) Reunion plans were put on hold by necessity in 2004 when Ray suffered a gunshot injury from a mugger in New Orleans, and then Dave was struck down by a stroke. Nevertheless, both have recovered: 2013 saw Dave active and back on the road for the first time in almost a decade playing gigs in the United States, and he continues to release new material. Ray has incorporated the effects of being shot into *Americana* and into his stage shows. Despite the trauma, he addresses the issue with typical naughty humor, referring to the track as "You Really Shot Me" in recent performances.

SCHOOLDAYS: LITERATURE ON THE KINKS

Each chapter of this book includes suggestions for further reading that provides foundation and context for the relevant themes in the Kinks' music and performance. As for resources for the band itself, the list below is by no means comprehensive; for the sake of space and sanity, it is restricted to a selection of popular print and film biographies and academic studies on the Kinks and Ray and Dave Davies. Two early band biographies were released in the 1980s, both by well-known British music journalists: Johnny Rogan's *The Kinks: The Sound and the Fury* (UK title) and Jon Savage's *The Kinks: The Official Biography*. Both were groundbreaking for the time; Rogan, for example, explored the Kinks' career as would a detective rather than penning a fluffy rock annual piece. Both he and Savage, writing when the group was experiencing its renaissance as an arena band, gained access to the Kinks and Kinks' insiders, including close family members. Savage scored a coup by interviewing Ray and Dave's mother, who provided further insight on and images of the band. Around the same time, fan and music journalist John Mendelssohn wrote *Kinks Kronikles* (1985), part biography, part memoir. Other biographies have subsequently appeared from the 1990s. For example, Neville Marten and Jeffrey Hudson published

The Kinks: Well Respected Men (1996, revised in 2001). In 2008, Thomas Kitts published *Ray Davies: Not Like Everybody Else*, an academic study of the art and craft of Ray's oeuvre and place of the Kinks in the context of British culture, art, and national identity. Other recent biographies also focus on the Kinks within a cultural context, especially following Ray's CBE in 2004 and his contribution to Danny Boyle's very English set piece at the 2012 Olympic ceremonies. Nick Hasted, for example, has received excellent reviews for his 2011 biography of the band, *The Story of the Kinks: You Really Got Me*. Hasted's book is notable not only because it augments up through the Davieses' solo careers but also because he was granted rare interviews (and cooperation) from Ray and Dave. There are a few works on the Kinks outside of England and America: Alain Feydri published *The Kinks: Une histoire anglaise* (2013), the first biography of the band in French. Feydri's book is worth a look as he wrestles with the idea of Britishness of the band from an outsider (and non-American) point of view. In German are two worthwhile publications: the first is Peter Krause's charming *The Kinks: A Rock and Roll Fantasy* (2006), which is a fairly straightforward biography of the band. The other is a web-based collection of unusual essays compiled by then student, now journalist Helge Buttkereit, hosted on Dave Emlen's invaluable "Unofficial Kinks' Web Site" at http://www.kindakinks.net/. Created in 2004, *40 Years of the Kinks* is a collection of essays in both German and English translation that focus on lesser-discussed aspects of the band's influence and activities on the Continent.

The Kinks have also been the subject of academically orientated studies, and the group and both Davieses individually have been the subject of papers and panels at conferences in recent years. The versatility of the Kinks' oeuvre lends itself to a dynamic range of depth and study. Topics in published specialist studies that reference the work and performance of the band include musicology, family and popular culture studies, music hall and performance theater, spirituality, humor, national identity, music therapy, and aspects of British national identity. For example, the academic collection *Living on a Thin Line: Crossing Aesthetic Borders with the Kinks* (2002) considers topics ranging from the Kinks and the working-class experience to their theatrical productions and comparisons between them and other artists ranging from Brian Wilson to F. Scott Fitzgerald. In 2006, the journal *Popular Music*

Society published a special edition on the Kinks that provides further range and analysis of the group's performance and music in relation to their social and cultural influence in the context of social class, family relations, urban planning, postwar Romanticism, the music industry, spiritualism, and Japanese rock and roll. Other recent studies focus on the sound, poetry, and prosody of the Kinks' output. For example, J. Bellman discusses the Kinks' experimentation with droning tones and instruments in his "Indian Resonances in the British Invasion, 1965–1968" (1997). In 2003, M. Geldart took a literary approach to the study of the lyrics of the group's work in the Pye years in "Persona and Voice in the Kinks' Songs of the Late 1960s." Elsewhere, Gordon Thompson includes a section on Ray Davies as a songwriter in his *Please Please Me: Sixties British Pop, Inside Out* (2008), and Dan Le-Roy discusses Ray's obscure score for a stage version of Jules Verne's *Around the World in 80 Days* in *The Greatest Music Never Sold: Secrets of Legendary Lost Albums* (2007). The Kinks, especially Ray Davies, also feature in wider academic studies and collections that include chapters on British and English music, culture, and identity. For example, Iain Ellis looks at the Kinks in his discussion of British humor and the pop music scene in *Brit Wits: A History of British Rock Humor* (2012). Another scholar who folds the character and music of the Kinks into his work on cultural history and social class is Keith Gildart. In 2012, he published the article "From 'Dead End Streets' to 'Shangri-Las': Negotiating Social Class and Post-War Politics with Ray Davies and the Kinks." His recent monograph, *Images of England through Popular Music: Class, Youth and Rock 'n' Roll, 1955–1976* (2013), frames around the Kinks a discussion of class distinction and social mobility in early sixties Britain. My forthcoming examination of the signposts of Englishness found in the Kinks' music and character, "'Rosy, Won't You Please Come Home': Family, Home, and Cultural Identity in the Music of Ray Davies and the Kinks," will feature in *Mad Dogs and Englishness: Popular Music and English Identity*, edited by Mark Donnelly, Lee Brooks, and Richard Mills (forthcoming, 2017).

For aficionados who prefer the factual nuts and bolts of Kinks music, there is Johnny Rogan's *Complete Guide to the Music of the Kinks* (1998) a volume in Omnibus Press's Complete Works series. This little handbook covers chronologically the output of the Kinks with information about the creation and production of songs if not albums. There are also two formidable encyclopedias compiled by Doug Hinman: *The Kinks: All Day and All of the Night; Day-by-Day Concerts, Recordings, and Broadcasts, 1961–1996* (2004) and *The Kinks Part One: You Really Got Me; An Illustrated World Discography of the Kinks, 1964–1993* (1994)—indispensable for any detailed discussion of Kinks' music, releases, or performances. Hinman is a librarian and an archivist, and in these two works he has assembled an annotated chronology and discography from myriad contemporary and primary sources. On a smaller scale, *The Kinks Are the Village Green Preservation Society* is the subject of one of the 33 1/3 series. Here Andy Miller not only examines the album song by song throughout its production, but also provides along the way the relevant cultural and biographical context inherent in the album's tracks.

Then, of course, one has a selection of primary sources, as it were. In addition to the two principles of the group, bassist Peter Quaife published posthumously *Veritas* (2011), a fictionalized retelling of the Kinks' story up through the band's big break and early years of the band's fame. The as-yet-unpublished sequel continues on as an account of the band's 1960s ups and downs, a fictional mirror of the experiences and antics of the real-life band. Onetime Kinks' drummer Bob Henrit published his autobiography in 2013, and he includes tales from his time with the group as well. Ray and Dave have each written autobiographies, Ray's *X-Ray* (1995) and *Americana* (2013), and Dave's *Kink* (1996). Dave's autobiography, published in 1996, is a freewheeling tell-all of sexual exploits, destroyed hotel rooms, consumed substances, and spiritual revelations. Ray, on the other hand, has been writing his autobiography for the past fifty years, if one counts the songs, concept albums, Kinks stage shows, various film and television projects, and the stage shows and musicals. He has also written a number of short fiction stories (*Waterloo Sunset*), ostensibly creating little tales inspired by a selection of tracks from his days with the Kinks and as a solo act. Marten and Hudson note that Ray enjoys "romanticizing his own weirdness,"[4] and indeed, *X-Ray* is a complex telling of his own story—an "unauthorized biography"—set up as a story within a story and set in a dystopian future. He tells his story in the guise of two characters: the bitter, old "RD" who represents Ray and relates the autobiographical parts of the story, and the young, confused journalist who has been sent to interview RD by the faceless men in grey. The follow-up, *Americana,* published about twenty years later, is more prosaic in style as here Ray explores his long love-hate relationship with America and its culture. This volume continues more or less where *X-Ray* leaves off, and it is framed throughout by an account of Ray's attack and injuries in the New Orleans shooting in 2004.

The history of the band is not limited to print media. The story of the Kinks and their place in social and cultural contexts can be found in film, on television, and on stage. For example, in addition to appearing in numerous BBC Four productions on early sixties rock and roll and blues with the Kinks, Ray and Dave have each had a documentary made about them by director Julien Temple (2010's *Imaginary Man* for Ray and 2011's *Kinkdom Come* for Dave)—two diverse films that not only complement the personality of each Davies but also fit neatly together visually and sonically in describing them. There is extant concert footage of the band in varying degrees of quality; myriad bits and pieces once only available on bootlegged copies of copies of copies of VHS tapes circulated among fans can now be found on YouTube. The clips range from the Kinks' live performances on television shows around the world from between 1964 and 1996 to the full-length concert filmed at the Rainbow Theatre in 1972.

Ray's interest in film, drama, and acting from his art-school days has also resulted in a number of dramatic performances (in addition to the Kinks' 1970s concept albums–stage shows). There are, for example, his previously mentioned roles in *The Long Distance Piano Player* and 1974's *Starmaker*. Ray's interest in film and stage production of his own inner turmoil can also be found in the curious *Return to Waterloo*, a grim tale of 1980s London in which he plays only the small part of a busker. Completists might also search for *Absolute Beginners* (1986), a gem directed by Julien Temple. The script is adapted from Colin MacInnes's novel about life in late 1950s London, and how the main character, Colin, becomes involved in the world of pop music. Ray, who could certainly identify with the themes of the story from firsthand experience (which he himself touches on in *Come Dancing*), is cast as Colin's father in the film. The soundtrack feature "Quiet Life," penned and performed by Ray.

Finally, there are other stage shows besides the various concept albums performed onstage by the Kinks in the 1970s. Ray's *80 Days* failed to reach the stage in any significant way, but the music from a

1988 performance in San Diego was released. Another play that Ray collaborated on with Barrie Keeffe, *Chorus Girls* (loosely based on Aristophanes's *Lysistrata*), ran for five weeks at the Theatre Royal in northeast London. Sadly none of the music has been released.[5] Most recently are two autobiographical musicals, the aforementioned *Come Dancing* and the commercially successful and award-winning *Sunny Afternoon*, a retelling of the Kinks' early days from 1963 through to mid-1966. The latter is a collaboration of Ray (story and music) and Joe Penhall (book), and the themes of *Sunny Afternoon* underscore the themes of this book: the Kinks wrote a song for every occasion, and their output is so entrenched in English life and culture that it becomes difficult to tell fact from folklore. *Sunny Afternoon* takes its music from the Kinks' output between 1964 and 1973—not at all featured chronologically but instead fitted together to make the story a cohesive whole. The play celebrates the Kinks' legend rather than documenting in detail the absolute truth: fans revel not only in the songs (and there's a concert at the end) but also in the appearance of many well-known episodes of the Kinks' legend. Nonfans out for a night at a jukebox musical come away amazed at how many songs they knew (and didn't know the Kinks wrote, if the online reviews and blogs are any indication). Even if the play reflects the mythology of the band rather than the forensics, it also embodies the character and image of the Kinks that were promoted by the suits, embraced by the fans, and rooted in the Kinks' own make-up—their rebellion, humor, gender-bending, family solidarity, and Englishness.

AROUND THE DIAL: THE STRUCTURE OF THE REST OF THIS BOOK

Chapter 2 of this book, "Something Better Beginning," provides some context for the origins of the band's character, and it looks at the musical and environmental influences on the Kinks as they grew up in postwar Britain. Topics range from influential entertainment such as family parties, film, and television through to the diverse musical genres that influenced and appeared in the work of the band. Chapter 3, "Marketing and the Money-Go-Round," considers how the Kinks coalesced as a band, and how they succeeded in finding their own sound and image while becoming a part of the music industry in early 1960s London. Crunchy power chords put the Kinks on the map musically, and they were swept up in the wake of the Beatles' early success both in Britain and in America. As with so many other bands, the Kinks were exploited by their management and publishers; this chapter thus focuses on consumer consumption and the rock-and-roll market, with a featured case study of tracks from their 1970 album *Lola versus Powerman and the Moneygoround, Part One*. The Kinks exemplify how British Invasion bands were marketed and managed and the attitude of the recording industry toward both its product and its consumers. The band themselves were square pegs against the round holes into which the "imagineers" tried to place them.

Chapter 4, "Humor and the Kinks," considers the band in the context of satirical humor in late 1950s and early 1960s British popular culture, and the influence of humor on and expansion into British rock music. The Kinks were products as well as producers of the distinctive humor that defines the satire and comedy of the 1960s. Such humor gave British youth their outlet to rebel against the staid mores of traditional society and put a distinctively British stamp on rock and roll: Ray Davies and the Kinks, as well as others such as John Lennon, Pete Townshend, and Vivian Stanshall, illustrate the use of intellectual humor to criticize, satirize, and just in general revel in a strange whimsy that places certain aspects of British rock and roll within the tradition of Jonathan Swift or Oscar Wilde. And because the Kinks' humor is English, even their sharpest satire of traditional convention is self-deprecating.

Chapter 5 considers themes of sexuality and gender in the music of the Kinks. If the Kinks' humor has lent itself to argument and interpretation, the sexual ambiguity in tracks such as "See My Friends," "Little Miss Queen of Darkness," and "Lola" reinforce it. Between 1960 and 1963, an outspoken sector of British youth challenged the norms of sexual expression and power long held by older members of conservative society. The first challenge to the mainstream appeared in the theater before crossing over into the world of early 1960s popular music. The self-conscious and high-maintenance Mods became role models for male heterosexuals with their attention to the details of their hair, clothes, and styles of dancing, first in Britain and then slowly in the United States—a distinct change from the model set by the masculine rock stars of the 1950s. The Kinks provide a case study of members who expressed frequently both feminine and "gender-bending" traits in their lyrics, appearance, and behavior (on stage and off) from the early sixties through to the glam period of the early seventies. The feminine aspects of the music and performance of the Kinks are complex and multifaceted. Unlike their peers the Who and especially the Small Faces, who embraced the material culture, looks, and behavior of the Mods, the Kinks' expression of female traits was internalized and emotional, rather than externalized and material, perhaps because the Davieses grew up in a houseful of women.

Chapter 6 considers the question of the Kinks as a socially conscious band. Fans have long admired that the Kinks have come across as "genuine" and "ordinary guys" who represented the working class. This chapter focuses on the Kinks' part in the so-called willful pessimism that appeared in British popular culture of the 1970s. With numerous tracks beginning with "Dead End Street" and culminating in the elaborate stage shows of *Preservation*, Ray and the Kinks cut down to size those in authority. Ray's gloomy predictions and satire on the state of authority, education, and social welfare was mirrored by other artists: Pink Floyd and David Bowie each set Orwellian themes to music (*Animals* and *Diamond Dogs*, respectively). Grimness didn't sell, unfortunately; what was commercially popular was escapism—the music-hall singsong of glam, the ditz and glitz of disco, and the wild popularity of *Star Wars* (itself about triumph over a ruthless empire). The Kinks offered no solutions and suggested no action, and instead returned to their own musical roots at a time when the punks were demanding anarchy.

Chapter 7 complements 6: the Kinks found refuge and comfort in family and subsequently in the past, and they drew on the happy memories of the past as a way to improve one's present if not future situation. The Kinks weren't drowning in nostalgia nor suggesting one hide in the past. Ray has always insisted that he is not nostalgic and "longing for an England that never was" but that he has always been instead moved by the optimism of his parents and grandparents even at the darkest times. Their cheerfulness in the face of adversity and their solidarity as a family was and remains an inspiration for him. Initially, supporting the values of the older generation was not a popular attitude for a band to take during the heyday of the late-1960s counterculture: while the

Beatles told youngsters to flee the trappings of their consumerist parents, Ray urged runaways to look for strength in home and family, even as he and the Kinks recognized that the idyllic village green was a relic and a fantasy.

Finally, chapter 8 considers the Kinks' legacy particularly by discussing on the one hand trends in covers of Kinks songs and on the other the complications of fame and expectations of the fandom. Kinks fans tend to be fiercely loyal, if not defiant, individuals themselves; "I'm Not Like Everybody Else" suits well both the Kinks and their followers. The band remains rock music's favorite underdogs, always coming in "fourth," and snubs of the band and Ray Davies in polls and "best of" lists remain both a source of frustration and of pride for the fans. The Kinks strike a chord in their appreciation of the everyman and the misfit, the underdog, and the forgotten, as illustrated in tracks such as "Misfits." The band has expressed appreciation for the fans' loyalty, those who stuck with them even through the periods of their obscurity (hence the tribute to such fans collectively in "The Road" and "Rock 'n' Roll Cities"). Conversely, the band also considers the lesser desirable effects of being famous in tracks such as "Rock 'n' Roll Fantasy" and "Celluloid Heroes." Finally, as explored through words of the fans themselves in response to a survey conducted for this study, the Kinks' character as English, or British, comes full circle in this chapter. In song and on stage, the Kinks frequently break the fourth wall between themselves and their fans, and their working-class Englishness is admired for being "authentic" and familial. The kerfuffle following the American reaction to NBC's decision to cut the Ray Davies's performance of "Waterloo Sunset" from the tape-delayed transmission of the 2012 Olympics closing ceremony (theme: "A Day in the Life of Britain") in the States reveals much about how the band is perceived and defined fifty years on from the release of "You Really Got Me," and how they represent not only British culture and the definition of the British "self" but also what it is about the defiant "outsider" they represent to their fans and cultural analysts.

CONCLUSION

Across the chapters of this book, several themes emerge: the Kinks as teen rebels; the Kinks as champions of the "ordinary guy"; and the Kinks as a band whose Englishness becomes a metaphor of inclusiveness that inspires their followers to feel distinctive from the fans of other contemporary bands. Obviously, the Kinks did not exist in a vacuum, and the creation and shaping of their character and image was driven by a number of outside factors: the effects of their home environment, the marketing of the suits, and the expectations of the critics and fans. To accompany all of this is a prodigious number of songs, as Ray has proven a prolific composer, expressing his emotions, observations, and experiences through verse and music—all complemented by Dave's vicious and expressive guitar lashings. Each of these chapters is easily supported by Kinks songs—there are so many in fact that quite a few had to be left out only due to restrictions of space and of word count. One hopes readers will be inspired to fill the void with their own thoughts and conversations.

2

SOMETHING BETTER BEGINNING

The Creation of the Kinks

For me—with Ray's writing and my writing—it's very inspired by our family. It's a very big family. . . . I'm very thankful for that and I think it helped our music. My mum would have parties on weekends, and the music was a cross-section of everything from the Platters to Al Jolson. It's not surprising me and Ray got into music, it was a main-stay of growing up.[1]

This chapter looks at the formative influences that shaped the Kinks' sound and character. As fans who contributed to this project put it, the band's output was "a blend of different ideas and thought and imagery," and "if you like the Kinks, then it's as if you like 367 different bands."[2] In his study of English working-class youth through the lens of popular music, Keith Gildart remarks that there are distinct cultural strands that coalesce in English popular music in the 1950s and 1960s, including the music and values of Victorian and prewar Britain, music-hall performance and repertoire, and the hominess of family entertainment,[3] as well as the impact of American culture in popular media. Shaped by these influences, the Kinks evolved into a group admired by their fans and critics for their rebellious nature, working-class solidarity, and devotion to family and home. The era in which the Kinks grew up is a complex one as much changed quickly in British politics, economics, and culture. There are many studies on the shaping of the social and cultural contexts and the working-class experience in postwar Britain—

but what takes a scholar hundreds of pages to describe, the Kinks can evoke in about three and a half minutes.

THE KINKS FROM THE INSIDE OUT: WHAT MAKES A KINK?

In 1957, Harold Macmillan told Britons that they'd "never had it so good." Britain's postwar economy was improving, and as the fifties waned and the sixties began, a number of social changes affected British culture, especially in the lives of the working classes. It was a time of new prosperity as well as a period that saw the breakdown of social barriers; many societal changes were led by the younger generation. The Kinks' formative years straddle the line between traditional working-class lives set against a highly stratified, social class system and an era of new mobility—these opportunities didn't always signify the removal of class barriers, however, and sometimes the challenges to the social order sat uneasily with this brave new generation.

Nearly all academic study on Ray and Dave Davies's background point the reader to studies on the creation of the working classes published from the nineteenth century onward, and it is impossible to provide here more than a limited selection of general contextual reading. Earlier academic studies on the life of the working classes followed Marxist themes and examined the impact of Britain's changing economy on the working classes from the Victorian Age through to the postwar period.[4] Because they expressed themselves and their anger, passions, and experiences through music, a number of rock stars of the Kinks' generation are widely admired for their honesty and authenticity. One current trend in studies of cultural history of this period in Britain is to consider social history through the study of popular music of groups from the Kinks' era. None of these groups sat down to write their music with a Marxist manifesto in mind; instead, they drew off their own experiences and interests, and their songs more readily engage us in a dialogue about growing up in this period.[5]

It can be a challenge to study social history on a comprehensive scale, and one must be wary of making generalizations, especially as contemporary analysis of working-class and popular culture itself has been affected by social and economic changes over the past century.

Before one dives headlong into the weighty history and character of the English working class by Eric Hobsbawm or Asa Briggs, or even Dominic Sandbrook and Peter Hennessy, consider carefully. Most of the general literature out there that examines the Kinks' environment is written by the sort of people that the Kinks twit in their music: middle-class, well-educated academics who have been peering through a glass darkly at the working-class experience from the outside in.[6] So as popular music becomes a filter by which to study working-class culture and analyze the "true British experience" through their own words and expression, one should recall the lyrics to Ray's solo track "Stand Up Comic": "Jack the Lad has become Oscar Wilde."

THIS IS MY STREET: FAMILY AND MUSIC

The Davies family was solidly working class,[7] a large brood who ultimately settled in East Finchley, north London, by 1940 to avoid evacuating the children to the countryside at the start of the war.[8] Their street, Denmark Terrace, lies very close to Muswell Hill; the area is sometimes referred to as Fortis Green after the main road that connects it to East Finchley. The names and descriptions of these places, as well as nearby Holloway, appear in a number of the Kinks' tracks such as "Muswell Hillbillies" and "Holloway Jail." Other tracks such as "Berkeley Mews" evoke the hard life and grim economy in the 1940s; "Dead End Street" touches on the burdens of the austerity years and coping with personal hardship and loss.[9] Another track, "Oklahoma, U.S.A.," reflects the dreams of escaping the daily grind of postwar, working-class drudgery. The woman in the track's narrative "lives in a house that's near decay/built for the industrial revolution." She goes mechanically about her mundane life while her imagination is filled with fantasies of escape through Hollywood swashbucklers and musicals.

The large and noisy Davies brood was not popular among their neighbors as there were no other children in the area; subsequently, the family became very closely knit.[10] Such familial solidarity and class consciousness, according to social historian Asa Briggs, had taken a firm hold in Great Britain in the nineteenth century. Class solidarity came into its own especially during the war and the years afterward, when the gap between working class and upper classes, especially in London, became more pronounced. This gap was most obvious not only in terms of wealth and lifestyle but also psychologically. Postwar, Briggs notes, the working class developed a distinct awareness of their position.[11] Being working class provided them with an identity and even a sense of authority in a world that offered them very limited opportunities at the time, and it gave them a feeling of solidarity against the middle and upper classes.[12]

MUSICAL INFLUENCES FROM FAMILY

As did many working-class families of the time, the Davies indulged in homey entertainments: football, music hall, cinema, drives to the sea-side, going up the pub, and having a piano in the front parlor.[13] Ray and Dave were the only boys and youngest of eight children, with a spread in age of nearly thirty years between the oldest daughter, Rose, and Dave.[14] The sisters doted on their little brothers, and both men speak with great affection and pride about their female siblings. Ray notes as the first boy he was surrounded by teenaged mums who spoilt him;[15] then Dave came along and was also "spoilt and adored by my mother [and] sisters" much to Ray's irritation.[16] The number of people crammed into the five-room house in Denmark Terrace included ex-tended family, in-laws, and their broods. Ray and Dave themselves were not always physically close as children as at times they lived separ-ately with older sisters, but they did have many shared experiences.[17] The family had a great impact on all aspects of the Davieses' individual musical development and the inspiration for lyrics, including "Don't Forget to Dance," "Rosy, Won't You Please Come Home," "Come Dancing," and numerous tracks off *Arthur* (sisters and their families); "Get Back in Line" and "Autumn Almanac" (father); "I Go to Sleep," "Wonderboy," and "Art Lover" (Ray's children); and "Have a Cuppa Tea" and "Uncle Son" (respectively grandmother and uncle).

Ray and Dave grew up surrounded by not only recorded music off the radio and records but also homegrown music and performance as the family made their own entertainment. Both brothers describe the parties in the family front room on Saturday nights when extended family and friends crammed in to play piano, sing, and dance. Remarks

Ray in his autobiography *X-Ray*, he was singing before he could talk, and the happiest times of his childhood were memories of these house parties on Saturday nights after the pub closed.[18] These lively parties, which lasted until the wee hours,[19] had a major impact on Ray and Dave's individual childhoods. Ray has remarked that the songs performed and played at these times reflected the family's joys and tragedies; the sum of their emotions could be expressed through a wide range of songs. Each family member, he notes, had their own "theme song," and the boys' contribution was to update the family musical tastes by adding music from their own rock-and-roll heroes.[20] The diverse repertoire of these parties included musicals and music-hall tunes, traditional and Dixieland jazz, blues and bebop, and early rock and roll. The playlist is reflected in Ray's current preshow tape, which includes Chuck Berry's "Memphis, Tennessee" and "Maybelline," Hank Williams's "Your Cheatin' Heart" and "Honky Tonk Blues," Cab Calloway's "Minnie the Moocher," Bill Broonzy's "Hey," Sonny Boy Williamson's "Bring It on Home," George Formby's "When I'm Cleaning Windows," and Perry Como's "Magic Moments."[21] Many Kinks tracks recreate these Saturday night parties, and in concert, the group frequently encouraged audience participation with songs containing jaunty choruses and music-hall rhythms, including "Dedicated Follower of Fashion," "Cricket," "Harry Rag," and "Tin Soldier Man" to name but a few. The Kinks' set list included additionally nonrock numbers meant to engage the audience, such as "Baby Face" and "The Banana Boat Song"; evidence of early audience participation is captured in 1968's tumultuous live album, *Live at Kelvin Hall*.[22]

Ray and Dave's father, Fred Davies, influenced and supported the boys musically: for example, he provided the boys with their first gig at his local, the Clissold Arms, a pub opposite the family home in Denmark Terrace. Both sons overall have fond memories of him.[23] Ray has stressed that his father was supportive of his sons' musical pursuits, and he has remarked that he tended to write songs he thought his father would like.[24] One key aspect of Fred Davies's love of music was his showmanship. Ray notes that his father not only performed at these parties, that is, playing on banjo and singing—but also *performed*— frequently over-the-top Cab Calloway impersonations, his showstopper (sometimes literally if he'd had too much to drink) being an enthusiastic rendition of "Minnie the Moocher." Ray noted that his father was a "closet vaudevillian,"[25] as well as "an early bluesman in sort of many ways" who "moved brilliantly." Unlike the stiff and formal moves found among ballroom dancers, the Davieses' father could dance "almost like he was from Louisiana or somewhere."[26] Ray himself would incorporate alter egos into his subsequent song narratives and stage performance, especially for the performances of the band's concept albums and stage shows in the seventies. Still assuming a stage persona during shows in the twenty-first century, Ray struts and dances across the stage as if in a comedy cabaret, as he pulls faces, strikes poses, and cups one hand behind his ear in an exaggerated "I can't hear you!" pose. The audience is expected to join in and become, if only for a little while, part of a raucous party, hoping, as the Davieses' family did in Denmark Terrace, that the police wouldn't be called "again."[27]

Similar showmanship is found within English rock and roll and reflects the impact of such homey influences in general. Even the most outrageous pop-music acts of the twentieth century, punk and heavy metal, have regarded themselves as showmen or performers rather than artists or musicians.[28] For example, the Sex Pistols, considered by Americans (if not middle-class Britons) as harbingers of the collapse of Western civilization, were created by Malcolm McLaren deliberately (in part) to outrage middle-class society. Most Pistols fans, as were the Kinks, were middle-class teens wanting an outlet to rebel against their parents; even as they broke social taboos, the band members themselves maintained solidarity with their working-class roots. In Julien Temple's film *Never Mind the Baubles*, for example, John Lyndon reflects on the Pistols as "pure music hall" as the band are shown entertaining children at a Christmas party.[29] Ozzy Osborne, who horrified parents and critics as the front man for Black Sabbath, once retorted in response to criticism of his band's darker output that he was a performer not a musician.[30] In both of these cases, the performers' working-class character is at the heart of their attitudes: the Pistols' kiddie audience were the offspring of striking firefighters; and Sabbath came from the industrial steel-mill city, Birmingham, and their sound reflected the rhythm of the foundries that the band had escaped.

Music-hall performances allowed escape from the stress of work or everyday life in the form of physical pratfalls, corny jokes, and sentimental songs, and perhaps such silly humor seems at odds with the Kinks' violent reputation in light of the mayhem that accompanied their early concerts. But as with music-hall performers, the Kinks' down-to-earth and "authentic" use of humor complemented their anger and expressed commiseration with their audience on the absurdities of everyday life. For example, on first meeting the comedian Ronnie Corbett in the mid-1960s, John Cleese recalls that Corbett had a "background . . . in cabaret and some music hall. He could go out in front of an audience as himself, without needing to be in character . . . he had a highly tuned bullshit detector, and behind some of his funny remarks there was often a wickedly accurate observation."[31] Working-class folks didn't get their editorials from highbrow newspapers; they came from their comedians with whom they could identify in class and outlook. Frankness made them trustworthy and believable; humor kept them from sounding whiny or entitled. What was expressed in the music halls of the nineteenth and early twentieth centuries was found equally at home on the concert stage of the 1960s, the 1970s, and beyond.

"Low Budget," off the eponymous 1979 album, not only exemplifies the style of the musical-hall performer found in the Kinks' (especially post-1960s) performances but also illustrates the band's working-class attitude. Ray sings the track in a grinding vocal while prowling the stage as if in a strip-tease burlesque, turning the microphone toward the audience to join in on the chorus. Forced into austerity and living on the cheap, the hero of "Low Budget" wears ill-fitting clothes several sizes too small; he's been forced to economize and buy the cheaper goods. As with the hero of "Sunny Afternoon," Low Budget man has fallen from grace: he's had to trade in his champagne and cigars for brown ale and Polo mints. But as with "Sunny Afternoon," the narrator of "Low Budget" makes the best of what he's got and scolds people for judging him. He might currently *look* like a tramp, but he used to be a member of the upper classes, or "a toff"—even if the only things he possesses not on "permanent loan" are his teeth and hair. He finishes out the verse by admonishing the listener that everyone is in the same state. He reminds the listener that the trappings of wealth are superficial. What one is born with is all one is left with at the end of the day: possessions are transitory—only personal integrity remains.

Even when the Kinks focus on their class as a whole, however, there are personal elements from their family life that shape the music. Dave notes, for example, that while elements of "We Are the Village Green Preservation Society" was about the greater whole of mourning for the lost England, the song also recalled memories of his mother and her perseverance in making a good life for the family out of virtually nothing. Annie Davies was a well-respected woman among the family and neighbors, and she had faith that others would do her the same regard.[32] She was supportive of her sons and the band in their early days as she saw music and art as their means out of poverty. For example, she bought Dave his first guitar, laying down £7 on a £40 Harmony Meteor (the guitar featured on "You Really Got Me," and, noted Dave, despite the cost to his mother, the instrument was eventually paid off);[33] she was still paying off the hire-purchase on Ray's Gretsch when the Kinks were making early appearances opening for the Beatles.[34] She also kept ephemera related to their early career.[35] Subsequent discussion of the influence of the Davieses' mother and sisters will be discussed in chapter 5 (on gender and sexuality) and chapter 7 (home and family).

So both Davies brothers grew up surrounded by music, and from quite a young age they actively contributed to the family entertainment. Dave seems to have learned guitar through osmosis and by enthusiastically imitating his heroes. For him, the guitar was an extension of his own volatile emotions; he played the instrument with more energy than finesse.[36] Ray's initial training on the instrument took on a more structured form. His first guitar was a gift from an older sister on his thirteenth birthday when, on a visit home from Canada, she gave Ray a Spanish guitar and taught him a few chords before going out dancing for the evening.[37] This was against doctor's advice, as she had a weak heart, and tragically, she collapsed and died on the dance floor that evening. Her death cost Ray a mentor and a source of inspiration.[38]

Ray received further instruction from another sister's husband, Mike Picker, who also had an influence on both brothers' individual tastes in music. Picker would play records for the boys at the weekends by artists such as Django Reinhardt, Earl Scruggs, Buddy Holly, Eddie Cochran, Little Richard, and Johnny Cash. He also taught Ray how to play Spanish guitar, an accomplishment that intimidated Pete Quaife the first time he heard his classmate play at school. Quaife had demonstrated his neophyte abilities with a rock-and-roll piece and then Ray followed up with a complex classical work.[39] Picker also taught Ray jazz guitar, and he was additionally keen on Hawaiian guitar; the latter interest would inspire Dave to build and play a homemade "Hawaiian" guitar on "Holiday in Waikiki."[40]

LEAVING THE NEST: THE BIG BLACK SMOKE

Blues, rhythm and blues, and rock and roll galvanized British youth, especially boys, as a creative and emotional outlet in the 1950s. The popular music of their parents and sisters' generation had no generational demarcation, so it was normal for children and teens to be as enthused about music-hall and folk music as the rest of their family. Rock and roll, however, was the music of the younger generation. Its immediate progenitors, country-western and blues, were also popular because of the emotional expression found in both their lyrics and the sounds of the music itself. Not only did rhythm and blues and rock and roll become a means of expression of individuality and frustrations, but also active participation on the growing music scene could be a means for young (mostly) men to escape the usual working-class fate of factory work, going down into the mines, or spending a life on the dole queue.

Access to rock and roll in 1950s Britain itself could be a challenge. Enthusiasts struggled by hook or by crook to get the latest rock-and-roll and rhythm-and-blues records from America. If these fifties teens were lucky, they had a friend or a relative who had traveled to America and could be persuaded to bring the goodies back with them. For example, Ray and Dave had their older sister Irene, who brought on visits from Canada precious American rock-and-roll records; George Harrison's sister brought her little brother several records back for him and his proto-Beatle pals to devour. Older youths might go to clubs that sprung up all over England, and not just in the capital. Most, however, made do with listening to the radio, going to the cinema, and, in the later 1950s, watching television to catch the latest hits and to see the artists who performed them.

Radio could thrill as well as frustrate. The relationship between recorded and live music in twentieth-century Britain was defined by a Byzantine collection of laws, rules, and regulations hammered out by various acts of Parliament. Long story short, "needle time" made it difficult for artists to get their records played on those few BBC radio shows dedicated to popular music in both the fifties and into the sixties.

This meant that songs might be speeded up or cut off in order to cram in more music in the allotted time before the show finished. A similar issue affected songs played on Radio Luxembourg—if one was lucky, and the weather conditions right, one could bring in this station across the Channel. Radio Luxembourg played the latest American and British rock and roll, but again, the songs were frequently truncated to squeeze more of them into the programs. From early 1964, the pirate radio station Radio Caroline went on the air, providing yet another way to hear the songs as airplay was critical for the music merchants. Pocket money was tighter for British youth than for their American counterparts, so they wanted some idea what they would be paying for before surrendering money for the record itself.[41]

Film provided access to not only the music but also visuals to go with the sounds and attitudes that defined American music for British youth, especially in the wake of the controversial film *The Blackboard Jungle* in 1955. There was no rock and roll on the picture's soundtrack except for "Rock around the Clock" over the opening credits; the plot of the film itself focused on a classroom full of frustrated young men, rejected by society and warehoused under the eye of disdainful teachers until the students could legally leave school. The association of rock and roll with restlessness and anger against the older generation gave both the film and rock-and-roll music a connection to youth, freedom, and rebellion against authority. Subsequent rock-and-roll films from 1956 onward proved extremely popular in Britain, and American rock-and-roll stars were welcomed by their young fans as heroes on their tours of the UK. Bill Haley, Buddy Holly, Eddie Cochran, Little Richard, and Gene Vincent inspired an entire genre of "Britain's answer to Elvis" (many of these young men created, shaped, and molded by impresario Larry Parnes).[42] A number of these stars influenced the Kinks growing up, and many of them are namechecked on the track "Around the Dial."

Television was a third source of rock music, if one's parents could afford to rent a set, let alone purchase one. One of the earliest shows that featured rock and roll was *The Six-Five Special*, which went on the air in 1957 on the BBC and ran for nearly a hundred one-hour episodes.[43] *Juke Box Jury* was another, and it ran on the BBC from 1959 until 1967; its format was that of records selected from a jukebox and played for a panel of celebrity judges (including, in 1963, all four Beatles) who decided if that selection was a "Hit" or a "Miss." The BBC's rival, the wealthier and splashier (or trashier, depending on the opinion of one's mum) ITV, broadcast shows such as *Oh Boy!* and *Ready, Steady, Go!* ITV was a commercial station and so could afford to actually bring on set the groups that performed both live and lip-synched versions of their latest records, an important factor for budding musicians who wanted to see their heroes' hand movements, attire, and dance styles. ITV also lacked the educational component that was part of the BBC's mission statement. Jack Good, one of the original producers on *The Six-Five Special*, left the program after conflicts with the brass at the BBC, as the latter insisted on interjecting educational interludes in between the music, and Good wanted to show exclusively music to keep the action moving along. The Kinks made their own television debut on *Ready, Steady, Go!* in February 1964 with their first single, a cover of "Long Tall Sally," and there they would debut "You Really Got Me" in August, a few days before the record hit the shops.

IN HER DREAMS SHE IS FAR AWAY IN OKLAHOMA, U.S.A.

Like so many children of their generation, the young Kinks were fascinated by America, experienced through the lens of cinema and popular music, as an exotic land of fantasy and escape from the dreariness of the ordinary. Compared to war-weary Europe, everything associated with America was shiny, new, and larger than life—the United States had the best "music, cars, girls, clothes, gangster, Negroes, cowboys . . . the best of everything, or so we believed."[44] American popular music in all its forms—jazz, rhythm and blues, country-western, and rock and roll—was exciting and liberating; to this, English kids added their own musical and cultural identity.[45] Rock and roll allowed them similar freedom of expression as their counterparts in the States; teenagers could establish through rock and roll and its culture a distinct identity separate from the older generation and their attitudes.

Even after both Davieses established homes in the United States as well as in the UK, their musical expression of American life and exoticism remained and remains firmly anchored on an English base. *Muswell Hillbillies* exemplifies this, as, for example, the title of the LP and its eponymous track are wordplay on their childhood London neighborhood of Muswell Hill; the lyrics and music of the track evoke imagery of country-western and blues music, and America known only through the Hollywood cinema sat side by side with living in a working-class London suburb. "Muswell Hillbillies" bounces along with a country-western beat and is sung, as a number of tracks on the album were, with faux American accents and grammatical affectations; it sees the narrator moving into uniform, dull housing, forced to conform perhaps along the lines of the new model towns put into place in England from the 1970s. Simultaneously, he protests that he won't be trained out of his distinctive Cockney accent. He sings of West Virginia, New Orleans, and Tennessee—hills and hollers he's never seen but that are equally representative of his current life as a London good ol' boy—it is Southern pride and individuality expressed through the rebellious channel of country-western music, adopted by a working-class lad who sees no benefit in the social improvements being thrust upon him. Similarly on the same album, the young woman of "Oklahoma, U.S.A." ignores the industrial grime of urban London to daydream about the wide-open fields of Oklahoma that she knows only through the filter of Rogers and Hammerstein. Many other tributes to America and American rock and roll appear throughout the Kinks' catalog; for example, "Maximum Consumption" is a paean to the junk food excesses of the American menu. "One of the Survivors," from *Preservation*, namechecks a number of 1950s rock-and-roll stars such as Jerry Lee Lewis, Dion and the Belmonts, and Johnny and the Hurricanes. Johnny Thunder, the survivor in question, roams around a dystopian 1970s wasteland, doggedly hanging on to his simpler past, playing "Hound Dog," "Oh Boy!" and "Great Balls of Fire" among other hits—his very survival depends on these tracks. Other songs across the Kinks' catalog reflect the group's fascination with the United States: "Jack the Idiot Dunce" parodies rock-and-roll vocals and beats, and Dave goes all Little Richard on "Bernadette." American-style harmonies can be found on "I Took My Baby Home" and "Around the Dial," and Ray gets a kick out of singing in a Johnny Cash/American voice (for example, on "Welcome to Sleazy Town"). Country-western influence can be found on "Act Nice and Gentle," "It's Too Late," and "See My Friends" (where Ray has claimed he's not attempting a hypnotic vocal so much as trying to imitate Hank Williams, albeit in a voice that's more hay than moonshine fevered) as well throughout *Muswell Hillbillies* and *Schoolboys in Disgrace* (1974). For novelty value, check out "Willesden Green," a track found on the

odd *Percy* album. Sung by John Dalton, it's a country-western mash-up
that replaces the usual American place names with London ones. The
effect is sort of a reverse (and just as disconcerting) Dick-van-Dyke's-
Cockney-accent-in-*Mary Poppins*.

IN A CLUB IN OLD SOHO, WHERE THEY DRINK CHAMPAGNE . . .

A passionate pursuit of American musical forms affected the development of the Davieses' formative musical years and colored the early
sound of the Kinks. Leaving the safety of the hinterlands not only
opened up access to consuming jazz, blues, and rock and roll but also
led Ray and Dave along the path of imitation, emulation, and finally,
creating their own forms of music. Both Davieses subsequently spread
their musical wings in Soho where the foundation for the London pop-
music scene was laid in the postwar period as impresarios and music
promoters, finding themselves in a very different world by the 1950s,
picked up the pieces of the industry after 1945.[46] Like their American
counterparts, these businessmen quickly recognized that popular music
was becoming the domain of the younger generation, and they seized
economic advantage.

The aesthetic divide between "higher"-class artistic music and "lower"-class popular music had been drawn back in the nineteenth century,
if not earlier. While some Victorian legislation opened up various types
of arts and culture to the lower classes (for example, allowing free
admission to many museums), additional nineteenth-century legislation
concerned live music and where it could be performed, and this had an
effect on the type of music that became associated with these venues
and the sort of person who performed or enjoyed it. Family singsongs
might be the carry-over of a father's raucous night at the pub, and
public houses had long been a popular venue for singing and entertainment. Pubs, however, had carefully controlled liquor licenses, and there
were many complex and confusing regulations about who could enter
and who could perform on these premises. As Simon Frith and colleagues comment, "Even the most casual observer is likely to be struck
immediately by the plethora of Acts of Parliament determining what
may and may not be done in which premises at what times and with

which people."[47] Because of the association with alcohol, pub music became associated with the lower classes, drunkenness, and disorder. To avoid this reputation by association, milk and coffee bars began to appear in the 1950s; as they served no alcohol, there was less state control and regulation imposed on them, and it also meant a shift in the demographics among clientele, musicians, and performers from those who appeared in pubs.

Dance halls could be equally perilous depending on the crowd who hung out there; Teddy Boys were no one to cross, and they had little to no tolerance for the "bohemian" music of rhythm-and-blues combos. It is not a coincidence that many early teen British rockers in the mid- to late 1950s cut their teeth more safely at school dances or church picnics (for example, John Lennon met Paul McCartney when Lennon's group the Quarrymen were playing a gig at the Woolton church fete in 1956). Such kids were not only way out of their depth at the harder clubs and pubs but also imperiled of their lives. Part of Kinks lore is the story of how one of their earliest gigs came via the bouncer boyfriend of one of their sisters at a local dance hall. The band was simply three teen guitarists all plugged into the same eight-watt amp, and they were subsequently hounded off the stage by outraged Teddy Boys.[48]

By the early 1960s, Soho was the site of a teeming music scene including many jazz and blues clubs; it was also the home of skiffle and, as Peter Frame notes, the birthplace of British rock and roll at the now-defunct 2i's Coffee Bar.[49] A young man in early 1960s Soho would be spoiled for choice to find a music venue for listening or performing, and the scene became more vibrant after the beat explosion and the success of the Beatles. Many of these coffee bars and music clubs, tiny, cramped, carved out of any free space above or at street level, were gone by 1964; but in the few years before, many of these music venues sprang up all over the West End—partly to accommodate the proliferation of up-and-coming and established groups and partly, of course, to cash in on the sheer numbers of music devotees.[50] The difficulty for clubbers was not only how to choose which of the many scenes to latch onto but also, for some, how to go from being a mere consumer of the scene to an active participant who stood out from the rest. There were a proliferation of styles that seemed to borrow and blend into one another, but jazz connoisseurs sneered at blues and rock and roll as commercial pap; skiffle and rock-and-roll fans looked down on jazz as pretentious noise.[51]

The world of the coffee shop allowed artistic invention, however, even if the art-school crowd of the late fifties and early sixties had very little use for pop or British copies of American rock and roll. For example, Lonnie Donegan was part of the jazz revival, but he also had a significant influence on reshaping the British popular music scene by blending together otherwise segregated musical genres. During intervals of his jazz performances he would play blues tunes with a faster, jazzed-up beat on folk instruments. Thus on the one hand, he was instrumental in creating the "trad jazz" scene among the coffeehouse and art-school hangouts, but on the other, he launched the DIY skiffle craze among their younger siblings. Skiffle, a hybrid of American folk, jug band, and jazz music crossed with British music hall began to thrive in the coffee bars of Soho. Any kid could and did form combos among his friends to play skiffle. Trad jazz itself dominated the arts school scene from 1959 to 1961, but familiarly bred contempt; as trad jazz became more mainstreamed, art-school students moved on to something else.[52]

Jazz lovers may have scorned it, but the next real craze among the art and coffeehouse crowd in London was the blues—bandsmen such as Chris Barber and especially Alexis Korner, the "Father of the British Blues," introduced blues into the jazz scene by adding rhythm and blues to their jazz styles. Additionally, these musicians delivered the real goods: Barber hosted a number of American bluesmen in Britain, including John Lee Hooker and Muddy Waters. The jazz crowd still snubbed the blues as a form of skiffle, but the two forms did begin to blend and catch on. For example, on one of his jazz networking missions in 1963, Ray met with Dave Hunt at the Scene Club to audition for his band, where Ray was mesmerized by the Rolling Stones. His host dismissed them as skiffle rubbish, but as discussed in more depth in chapter 3, Ray was galvanized by their look, sound, and attitude, and the performance motivated him to change from wanting to become a jazz-session man to developing an interest in rhythm and blues.

YOUNG AND INNOCENT DAYS

Although home remained a base and a refuge for him, Dave had also made his way to the center of the London music scene in Soho—at that time practically another planet compared to the outlying neighborhoods. Initially (and briefly) Dave worked in a music shop on the edge of the area—a job that quickly ended as, instead of working with guitars as he'd hoped, he was relegated to the boring task of polishing brass instruments. A fellow teen coworker there was also a keen guitar player, and they hooked up to play out and about with a changing crew of fellow bandsmen. For Dave, the guitar and his incipient band were not only a means of escape from both school and the drudgery of manual labor but also a means to express his anger and pent-up energy. What his shambolic guitar riffs and solos lacked in virtuosity were made up for in energy and emotion, exemplified on the mad, one-string solos found on "You Really Got Me," "All Day and All of the Night," and "I Need You." Dave improved his technique over the years, and there are myriad examples throughout the Kinks' output that demonstrate how his fret-board violence balanced out and complemented his brother's lyrics. The words of "Come Dancing" (1982) evoke the past as the song bounces along on verses supported by music-hall-flavored keyboards, but distorted power chords in the song's middle eight tie the track's sentiments neatly back to the anger and energy of the performers' and listeners' youths.

While Dave was running around town with his band in the early 1960s, Ray, in the meantime, was reenrolled at a local art college. His educational pursuits pleased his mother who saw his art, as with Dave's music, as a way for him to improve his situation and future prospects. In this way he was quite like a number of his soon-to-be musical peers—John Lennon, Keith Richard, and David Bowie were all art-college veterans when they abandoned their courses to devote themselves to music. Ray had temporarily dropped out of art school as a teen originally to spend time away from the remote hinterlands of Fortis Green and to brave the jazz clubs and find musical mentors. He recalls his initial adventure in *X-Ray*, dropped off on the curb in Soho one evening by his sister and brother-in-law who left him alone on the pavement with no little trepidation—whereas Ray thrived on solo walks around the neighborhood after dark, taking it all in.[53] Ray's initial foray into the world of jazz guitar was short lived; he was not only somewhat intimidated by the grizzled veterans on the Soho scene (albeit learning much from them in the process) but also finding it difficult to break into the scene as fully as he would have liked. Ray continued to pursue his musical interests on his art course and initially thrived during his return to school.

In addition to new approaches to art, music, and drama, the art-school lifestyle also encouraged eccentricity, and mind-opening experiences were increasingly fostered in the changing social climate of early 1960s London—although for Ray, the inspiration for his lyrics and Kinks' music came from not imitating the great artists but rather his own epiphany that it was far more satisfying to create his own words and poetry even if he failed miserably in the process.[54] Ray's artistic side and interest in film colored numerous Kinks' tracks; having been introduced to the works of Noel Coward by his middle-class managers, for example, he incorporated the gentle overtones of middle-class music theater in tracks such as "Afternoon Tea" and "Holiday Romance." English literature also influenced various Kinks tracks: Ray's interest in Hogarth paintings inspired some of the imagery in "Dead End Street"; "Big Black Smoke" reminds one, albeit a bit more cheerfully so with its perky rhythm, of Thomas Hardy's more unfortunate waifs; and "Phenomenal Cat" quite easily brings to mind Lewis Carroll or Edward Lear's nonsensical whimsy.

Even after he'd returned to art college, Ray was unable to stay away from the music clubs and, determined to get stuck back into the jazz scene, he was still trying to build his music CV. So Ray returned to Soho. After that fateful meeting with Dave Hunt when he saw the Stones and decided to alter his musical path, Ray also noticed that his brother's band was doing rather well when it came to snagging gigs, playing mostly covers of rhythm-and-blues and rock-and-roll songs, with a handful of music-hall staples thrown in for good measure. Depending on whose autobiography one has to hand, it was at this time that Ray joined forces with Dave's band—or when he took the band away from his brother and put himself in charge. Whichever was the case, by early 1963, three of the original Kinks, the Davies and Pete Quaife (there would be several transitory proto and pre-Kinks on drums until Mick Avory was auditioned into the band officially to fill the fourth plinth), were in place. The blues and rhythm and blues dominate the initial sound of the Kinks and would continue across their entire catalog. Important early highlights include "You Really Got Me," which, as Ray recalls in print and in his *Storyteller* shows, was originally conceived as a slow blues number. Other indicative tracks that show the Kinks' early love of the blues include "I Gotta Move," "Love Me 'til the Sun Shines," and "You're Looking Fine."

Whatever they were called initially, the Kelly Brothers, Boll-Weevils, Ravens, and then Kinks, the band brought together in one package all of the Davieses' musical interests, Quaife's similar musical interests and background (fictionalized in *Veritas*), and Avory's formal instruction in drumming and passion for jazz and big-band percussionists. The Kinks' eponymous first album, thrown together in haste after the commercial success of "You Really Got Me" (see chapter 3), illustrates the band's musical foundations and character at a glance: a bit of a shambles, a reliance on rhythm-and-blues staples, and a dollop of cheeky charm. The album doesn't quite capture the outrage, energy, and violence already extant in their concerts but provides hints of this character and their versatility to come. There are wild, primitively performed covers of staples such as "Beautiful Delilah," "Long Tall Shorty," and "I'm a Lover Not a Fighter"; there are energetic instrumental flair and solos in the tracks "Cadillac," "Revenge," and "Got Love If You Want It." "You Really Got Me," discussed in the next chapter, is the showstopper and selling point of the piece. America colored not only the voice of the Kinks on their first few albums but also their sound. Dave, for example, folded into his sound master classes from touring with James Burton ("Til the End of the Day") and Motown's Earl Van Dyke ("Everybody's Gonna Be Happy"). The Kinks also show their pop side with the tracks "Just Can't Go to Sleep" and "Stop Your Sobbing," later brought to prominence by the Pretenders. This latter track shows early evidence of the Mod ennui that appears in later Kinks tracks such as "Sittin' on My Sofa" and "Tired of Waiting." The Kinks, as one fan who contributed to this project noted, didn't sing many love songs, and "Stop Your Sobbing" serves as a good example of the type of love song they did produce: the track demonstrates irritation with neurosis and dull people as Ray demonstrates no little boredom with the weepy girl of the song.

CONCLUSION: "BEING A FAN OF THE KINKS IS BEING A FAN OF 367 BANDS"

The Kinks have a vast repertoire: in addition to the canon of songs on commercially released records, there are additional "bonus tracks" on CD reissues, there are BBC sessions, and there are surviving live performances and recordings of tracks from 1964 to 1996 uploaded by fans onto the Internet. Certainly all of the influences on and interests of the Kinks appear in the music that spans across this thirty-two-year period, and some of them have been mentioned here, perhaps to inspire discussion (or argument?) among readers. A song-by-song categorization of genre and influence might be well worth a study comparable to Ian MacDonald's exegesis on Beatles tracks in his *Revolution in the Head*.

Many elements combined to create the Kinks in terms of lyrics, sound, and character and performance onstage. There was no one particular direction deliberately taken by any one member of the band in the creation of this sound and performance. The Kinks were equally consumers of and then creators of a band that brought together in one package so many different forms of music. Now that this chapter has laid the general foundation for the band's genesis, the next step is to look at "what happens next." Chapter 3 looks in some detail not only at the beginning of the Kinks as a commercial entity but also at those elements of their character that made them distinctive from the rest of the mob and their experience of being a cog in the music machine of the early 1960s British popular music industry.

3

MARKETING AND THE MONEY-GO-ROUND

You want the singer in close-up. You mean the one with the goofy teeth?[1]

In the early sixties, the British pop industry was run like a machine churning out packaged pop stars along an assembly line. Rock and pop performers glowed like stars wherever there were the bright lights and adoring fans. Frequently, however, the shiny glamor was tin plated, and the life of the rock star was not as exciting as the packaging would suggest. Not only did fans want a piece of the stars (sometimes literally), but also so did managers, promoters, and merchandisers. The glass cage in which the Beatles were kept is as much a part of their legend as is the hysteria of Beatlemania; as George Harrison dryly put it, "[The fans] gave their money and they gave their screams, but the Beatles kind of gave their nervous systems."[2] The demands placed on artists to create the Product were grueling, stressful, and dehumanizing—not to mention frequently poorly rewarded financially.

This chapter looks at the early days of the Kinks in the context of early 1960s English pop manufacturing. It considers the image versus reality, the management and contracts, and the pressures faced by new stars. The Kinks were at the center of a maelstrom, and Ray Davies has noted that he went from being a shy, unconfident singer to a swaggering performer and then back to an artist who craved the anonymity of being another face in the crowd.[3] While many survivors of the sixties have written memoirs about the excitement, disillusionment, and lost innocence at the hands of the music machine, the Kinks turned their experiences into concept albums. *Lola versus Powerman and the Moneygoround, Part One* describes how the pressures of the music business affected the Kinks' image and performance. The Kinks were shaped partly by the image makers and partly by their rebellion against the same. Resistance to this image making, whether it was their look on stage or their sound on the records, early became a defining characteristic of the group: conformity could lead to overnight if not fleeting success, but rebellion, while not lucrative, could make a band more memorable.

1963 AND ALL THAT

Many pop music historians consider 1963, the year before the Kinks turned professional, as the most important year in British rock and roll[4] —even as those in the midst of it weren't always aware of it.[5] The great success of the Beatles meant that there was a surfeit of wannabe pop stars; kids who were inspired to pick up a guitar in the skiffle craze of the fifties now wanted recording contracts, fame, and the screaming girls that the Beatles had, and hopeful musicians aped the Fab Four's facade deliberately.[6] Many groups sprang up across the country until pop music and rock and roll became a bona fide industry. London-based groups in the 1950s had been superseded by provincials DIYing from Liverpool, Manchester, and Newcastle, and numerous London-based groups popped up in competition with the outliers.

The key moment in 1963 for the Beatles was their appearance on *Sunday at the Palladium* that October. It was unprecedented to have pop stars on an otherwise staid, family-orientated show (introduced by Bruce Forsythe), but the Beatles knew how to work their audience. They won them over by not only performing their current hits, including "She Loves You," but also having Paul give a treacly rendition of "Til There Was You" from *The Music Man*, winning over the mums and dads. Rough lad John did as well by admonishing the shrieking teens to "Shurrrup!" at one point lest they drown out Paul's request for the audience to clap their hands. More significant, however, was not the Beatles' cheeky defiance of social convention or even their energetic performance; it was the reaction of the press. The media focused less on the Beatles' show and more on the screaming teens in the audience and the police presence outside of the venue. The press helped to create Beatlemania and its attendant hysteria.[7] In his fictional account of the rise of a Kinks-like blues-rock band in early 1960s London, Kinks bassist Pete Quaife credits erroneously Beatles publicist Brian Sommerville with the tip-off phone call to the police and newspapers, reporting a riot outside the stage doors of the Palladium.[8] Sadly, it's too good to be true: Sommerville did not join the Beatles' team until January 1964, and Beatles contemporary biographer Hunter Davies is otherwise silent on who may or may not have alerted the press that night.[9]

The Beatles' wake of success was populated by young men throughout the country hoping themselves to join the rock-and-roll gravy train—not only the ones with the guitars but also a whole generation of young entrepreneurs who realized there was just as much, if not more, money to be made in managing and producing these new guitar groups.[10] And so the desire to be a part of this mad scene before it fizzled out created a feeding frenzy of not only those who wanted to be rock stars but also those who wanted to prey on rock stars and to squeeze out of the latest pop sensation as much as possible before fickle fan culture moved on to something else.[11] Even the Beatles were aware of this. During an interview on the Fabs' first tour of America in 1964, for example, John Lennon remarked to a *New York Times* reporter, "It won't last."[12] Certainly the Beatles themselves had no illusions about the money to be made. Despite singing how "all you need is love" and "imagine no possessions," the Beatles recognized the business for what it was: allegedly, "Help!" was written after Paul quipped to John, "Okay! Today let's write a swimming pool!"[13] Most money, in fact, was made from music publishing and exploitation of the new groups rather than from being in them.[14] Still the exploitation didn't (initially) deter eager young musicians who wanted a piece of that glamor (and a rare few knew well how to play the game and succeed).[15]

In 1963, the Kinks weren't the Kinks yet, although the various members of the group were keen amateur musicians. Over the course of the year, the band underwent a number of different names (the Ray Davies Quartet, the Ramrods, the Boll-Weevils, and the Ravens) and personnel changes.[16] The brothers and their friends performed on any available stage as early as 1961 at local dances, pubs, and amateur talent contests.

As early as 1962, the Davies brothers were trying to make recordings, at least at home, using a tape recorder borrowed from a brother-in-law.[17] As a fledgling band, the pre-Kinks were no different than the myriad bands up and down the country in doing these things. So throughout 1963, the Boll-Weevils/Ravens/Kinks gigged wherever they could, and they began to cut demo discs to attract a record producer's attention. While Ray continued to work with various blues bands in London, the band got themselves a booking agent (Danny Haggerty) and began to play on American military bases and at private parties.[18] Then, in mid-1963, the Boll-Weevils hooked up with Robert Wace and Grenville Collins.

WELL-RESPECTED MEN: ROBERT WACE AND GRENVILLE COLLINS

The Kinks' earliest management was a family affair as they were driven from gig to gig by various brothers-in-law and chaperoned by an elder sister; a niece ran their fan club, a nephew was their first roadie, and the family played audience to new songs. Despite the familial organization, the Kinks were no cheerful, sunny Osmonds—Ray and Dave have been at odds with one another since Dave's birth, and fights between the brothers and bandmates—on stage and off—have become as much a part of the Kinks legend as the music.[19]

Two middle-class young men, Robert Wace and Grenville Collins, hired the Boll-Weevils originally to back Wace who performed as a lounge singer at society parties. Joe Penhall dramatizes this arrangement in *Sunny Afternoon*, his play about the Kinks' early days: Wace performs a schmaltzy version of "You Still Want Me" (in reality the second record the Kinks released professionally in 1964), surrounded by a swirl of bored society debs and their dates. Suddenly, Dave, as originally played by George Maguire channeling *The Young Ones'* Vyvyan Basterd, shouts, "Fuck this!" and launches into a screaming, dance-floor-thumping rendition of "I Gotta Move." Wace takes the hint and exits stage right as the debs leap up to dance. In real life, Wace and Collins did agree that perhaps they ought to manage the band rather than have Wace front it.[20]

Wace and Collins's middle-class and society background stimulated the creativity if not the outlook of working-class Ray Davies as a songwriter. Wace was from old money, horrifying his parents by going into the music rather than the family business; Collins worked in finances. Neither of them had the experience to manage a rock band comprised of working-class ruffians. A whole new world opened up for the Boll-Weevils—not only a higher class of company but also more money. Dave once remarked that he was "put on this earth" to shag society debs,[21] but one ought to keep in mind this "cultural exchange" was a two-way street. As much as the crude Weevils rampaged across the stage and tore up the speakers with their rough-edged sound, middle-class teens found it trendy to hang out and identify with working-class lads and their birds. This class slumming was a bit ironic, however, as many of these so-called rough lads in bands such as the Beatles, Rolling Stones, and even the Kinks (or a quarter of them) had come from art school if not lower-middle-class backgrounds themselves. London School of Economics student Mick Jagger adopted a "mockney" accent to blend in with the lads; Keith Richards studied music theory at Sidcup College; and John Lennon and even Paul McCartney's accent belied an economic level considerably higher than George and Ringo's (who really *were* from the rougher areas of Liverpool).[22] Still, as Dave has noted, flailing away at an electric guitar gave him (and other working-class kids) a voice by which to express anger and frustration with life and with growing up. Surely the posh kids desired a similar freedom of expression and means to rebel against their own safely structured, predictable lives.

Ray explored these class differences in a number of Kinks songs. While some songs sharply satirize those who aspire to a higher tax bracket and seek to grasp hold of outward signs of material wealth ("Mr. Pleasant," "Most Exclusive Residence for Sale," and "Big Black Smoke"), the ones that twit the *genuine* higher classes have about them a gentle humor, if not a touch of ingenuous envy. For example, "A Well Respected Man" parodies the routine of a conservative, oversheltered, sexually repressed, middle-class city gent who still lives with a set of parents actually more worldly than he (see chapter 4). Other satirical songs took the mick out of the band's own managers' middle-class behavior (they referred to Wace as "Bob the Snob"). Collins was a stockbroker who kept his day job during the band's pre-Kinks year,[23] hence the lines "he plays at stocks and shares." Collins's voice also opens the song "Party Line" with crisp Received Pronunciation ("Hallo, who's that speaking please?") before Dave's descending riff cuts through the plummy tones. Collins's posh voice contrasts with the nasal rasp of the narrator of the song who's trying to get off with the girl on a shared phone line. A third example of affectionate satire directed at the middle class is "David Watts," a song based on a wealthy, flamboyant (a sixties code word for homosexual) friend of Dave's. Fictional David Watts is envied and admired by the singer for his ability to win at all the sports and to win over all of the girls, and the song is peppered with "fa fa fa fa's", a parody of affected middle- and upper-class speech (see also Roger Daltrey's stutter in "My Generation").

Wace and Collins worked hard on behalf of the Weevils, and throughout 1963 they booked them into professional recording studios including Regent Sound Studios in Denmark Street. Here the Weevils recorded covers of American rock and roll, but more significantly, an original beat bopper written by Dave called "I Believed You" to which Ray gives his best John Lennon Liverpudlian vocals. Apparently the band had a number of self-penned songs written by this point, and they desired to record and perform these original songs to differentiate themselves from the other struggling bands. By the end of the year, the managers were determined to get the band under contract. Another impetus for the band to create original material was that music publishers, after the war and especially after the changes the hiatus made on promotion of live music, wanted very much distinct and original artists on their rosters.[24] A recording wasn't as good as a contract, however, and realizing their own limitations, Wace and Collins hoped to propel the Boll-Weevils into professional stardom in the most effective way possible: to get Brian Epstein interested in the group, as he not only had nurtured the Beatles in spectacular fashion but also had a strong stable of other artists under contract, including Gerry and the Pacemakers, Peter and Gordon, and Cilla Black. Epstein, however, declined to represent them after a chaotic audition.[25] Wace and Collins persevered, however, and in December 1963 they presented a selection of the (now) Ravens' demos to Larry Page.[26]

LARRY PAGE, THE TEENAGED RAGE

Coming under the auspices of Larry Page (and subsequently his part-ner-in-publishing, Ed Kassner) was no easy feat for the band—indeed, attracting the favorable attention of a music publisher was a neophyte band's Holy Grail. As the Kinks noted on the *Lola* track "Top of the Pops," it's only *after* a group's record creeps into the Top Ten that they begin to dare to imagine that they might actually make real money being a pop star. The Weevils/Ravens had had their demos rejected numerous times, even after Page took them on. Many groups suffered the same fate, and even the Beatles had been among the try-hards, famously being rejected by every music publisher in Britain. The Kinks' song "Denmark Street," another track from *Lola*, recounts the process of getting the contract. A short little street off the end of Charing Cross Road behind Centre Point and the Tottenham Court Road, Denmark Street is today filled with guitar shops and coffee bars and imperiled by gentrification and Cross Rail construction. In 1963, it was known for its recording studios, publishing offices, and where one went in hopes of becoming the Next Big Thing. It's easy to find Denmark Street, sings Ray in the song—just listen for the sound of the auditioning hopefuls "just around round the corner from old Soho." Ray describes the frus-trations the potential musicians face from the embittered veteran pub-lishers: hopeful bands audition, play their original tunes, and stake their self-confidence on approval and acceptance only to be told—on the track and in real life—that the publisher hates the music and hates the length of the boys' hair, but because he also hates to be wrong, he's going to take a gamble and sign them up. Next step, sings Ray, is to meet the record producer. The vulnerable narrator gives his creation over to another suit, who listens with a cynical ear and tells the singer how much he hates the words and the melody, but he's got a nose for making a buck, and he offers to take the musician on. He'll run the song through the gauntlet of the other hoary businessmen on the street to see "if it makes the grade" and if it has the potential to make it to the "rock-and-roll hit parade." In just a little under two minutes, Ray and the Kinks paint a picture of the nervous, naïve hopeful presenting his piece to cynical businessmen—a song created by an individual and judged for its commercial potential by committee. Ray represents the publishers in the perky tones of a Cockney "spiv" (black-market wheeler and dealer associated especially with the war and the subsequent period of rationing). The song itself bounces along on its music-hall melody, and its jangly piano competes with other cacophonous instruments to capture the feel of the British "Tin Pan Alley." Ray's narration is nearly lost amid the music, perhaps the way a single effort is lost among so many hopefuls. The old-fashioned sound—part of the sing-along nature of so many of the Kinks' mid-1960s successes and a beloved part of their family's musical makeup—here also emphasizes the generation gap between the young musician and the older businessmen who control the product.

Page saw potential in the group and joined forces with Wace and Collins. He secured them another recording session (with Dick Rowe, the man famous for turning down the Beatles), which failed to impress. Undaunted, Page hooked the band up with Shel Talmy, an American record producer working in London.[27] The ins and outs of the Ravens' story becomes complex here, as various parties take credit for subsequent developments in the band's trajectory. Cutting through the Gordian knot of conflicting memories and claims found in the various Kink auto/biographies, one important fact remains: the Ravens secured a three-record contract with Pye Records under the musical direction of the combined irresistible forces of Wace, Collins, Page, and Talmy on the one hand, and the immoveable object of Ray Davies on the other.

Now in the hands of professionals, the Kinks' sound and look would be shaped by a host of variables: Wace and Collins's middle-class mores; Larry Page's streetwise confidence; publisher Ed Kassner's "soulless" eyes; studio engineer Shel Talmy's "American brashness"; publicist Brian Sommerville's spin; and finally the take-no-prisoners approach by image consultant Hal Carter, a veteran of the Larry Parnes's 1950s school of pop marketing. While the band did take on board some of the images and activities foisted upon them by this management group, they also actively rebelled against it once the pressure of producing the goods and parading around in front of the press grew too much for them and, especially, Ray. The Kinks began to chafe under the leash fairly quickly—even before "You Really Got Me" reached number one (in September 1964), and their stubborn rebellion in the recording studio is precisely *why* "You Really Got Me" reached the top of the charts.

Page had to work with a rough set of lads. In *X-Ray*, Ray describes just how rough the Kinks were—not pseudo-Teddy Boys[28] like the Beatles, who were tough partly because of where they came from and partly from honing their skills in their stint in playing clubs in the red-light district in Hamburg. The Kinks were just plain shambolic with no real stage act and a tendency to scrap like cats both on and off the stage. Page saw to refining the Kinks' image: the band were put into matching Edwardian frock coats and ordered to play up their "Englishness" early on. He arranged for many publicity photo shoots that variously involved them uncomfortably perched upon or standing beside elegant horses (the sleeve of the New Zealand issue of *Village Green Preservation Society* is an example) or near famous London landmarks while decked out in their stage clothes.[29] Page also changed the name of the band from the Ravens to the Kinks—partly in response to jeers the band received about their "kinky clothes" and partly in response to their demotion to the bottom of the playbills due to poor behavior. At only five letters, KINKS stretched across the bottom of the bill to fill it out and consequently stood out—it was a provocative word in 1964 and attracted attention. The band claimed they didn't like the name, but on December 31, 1963, the Kinks they became, and none too soon, as on that last day of 1963, Arthur Howes began his tenure as their booking agent.

Page wasn't alone in his attempts to tart up the band's character. Annoyed that their amateur and boorish behavior was jeopardizing their place on their British package tours, Howes hired Hal Carter. Carter was another old-school tour manager, and he was also well familiar with 1950s rock music impresario Larry Parnes, following the same modus operandi as Parnes did when it came to shaping the careers of stars such as Cliff Richard, Adam Faith, and Joe Brown. When Carter met the Kinks, his first instruction to the band was for them to cease washing their hair backstage, and he gamely taught them how to behave properly on stage. They, in turn, showed a distinct lack of respect for their new image consultant, which wound him up.[30] Carter nevertheless took no nonsense off them, and Ray admits that he was dedicated to making something out of them.

Page was only one of the savvy image makers who created a package that would sell. It was vital that the fans cared about that package, so all sorts of nonsense was planted in the press to gain attention—even the

Kinks' reputation for violence at concerts, destruction of and banning from venues across Europe (including exclusion from Scandinavia, period), and police escorts to get in and out of the halls. Reputed violence was an asset as it got them into the papers, following P. T. Barnum's alleged assertion that there is no such thing as bad publicity. Actual facts about pop singers, on the other hand, might be suppressed so that the teenyboppers wouldn't turn away: for example, the Beatles hid from the press for two years John's wife and child. As Ray noted, though, the Kinks' media management wasn't as well organized as the Beatles: "We didn't have a publicity machine that could deal with our idiosyncratic ways."[31] Subsequently, Ray's own impending marriage turned into a three-ringed media circus, with fans outside the church holding up signs saying, "Ray, don't do it!"[32] The Kinks were unhappy with their press coverage almost from the start. For example, the shock of losing the *New Music Express* Best New Band award in 1964 to the Rolling Stones (who had won it in 1963) led to Ray dubbing the paper *The Enemy*.[33] As Dave noted in *Kink*, it was all quite exciting at first: "You could say anything and people would think it interesting or at least newsworthy, and if you couldn't think of anything then you just made it up."[34] Pete Quaife fictionalizes the Kinks' experiences with the newspapers in his novel *Veritas*: thrilled initially to be the cover story of a key music newspaper, the band quickly learns that the paper pursues them only for its circulation numbers and has no interest in actually promoting them. Even now, Ray dismisses oft-repeated tales as folklore: "Stuff appears in the press but we take it with a pinch of salt in private."[35] On vinyl, the Kinks addressed their relationship with the press in the 1969 track "Mr. Reporter," which will be discussed in chapter 5.

Local gigs and press packets were well and good, but the vital step between being amateur players and being professional musicians was the recording contract. The proto-Kinks had made a number of amateur demos; in early 1964, Shel Talmy secured for them that three-record deal with Pye.[36] The first of these three singles was a cover of "Long Tall Sally"—a derivative arrangement sung by Ray with lazy vocals,[37] Beatlesque drumming, and girly "Ooooohs" on the backup vocals. The Kinks had played Little Richard songs in their stage show, but "Long Tall Sally" wasn't part of their usual repertoire—it was, however, a big hit and a showstopper for the Beatles. Pye and Shel Talmy wanted a known commodity for the Kinks' first single. It was common practice for untried groups to record a cover or a professionally penned song for their debut; even the Beatles were originally given a "safe" song to record on their first outing with George Martin.[38]

The Beatles' cover of "Long Tall Sally" captures their roots as a rock-and-roll band and the rough-and-tumble outfit that they were before Epstein cleaned them up. Ray Davies wanted the Kinks' first breakout single to capture in two minutes *their* distinctive personality—their hard-edged, blues-tinged, working-class background; their integrity; and their collective and individual identities as uncompromising youth against the world. Even as the Rolling Stones and the Yardbirds came across as tough bruisers on stage, their initial hits had been more safely pop and commercial rather than showcasing their gritty, dangerous side. Ray was encouraged when the Animals scored a major hit with "House of the Rising Sun," a growly cover of an old blues number; he desired to supersede this achievement with an original song.[39]

But the Kinks had no leverage in early 1964, and in need of a record, they were saddled with "Long Tall Sally" (albeit with a Ray original for the B side). The Kinks' version of "Long Tall Sally" lacks the panache, enthusiasm, and downright insanity given the tune by the Beatles' Paul McCartney, who belted out a dead-on impersonation of his hero Little Richard.[40] Surviving footage shot by Granada Television captures a Kinks' performance of the song at the Cavern Club in February 1964. In the clip, they're seen dressed in an early version of their stage clothes, a combination of black waistcoats and leather. Their presence is menacing and sexy, but even with the video's sound adjusted by a well-meaning modern fan, the vocals seem restrained and hold at bay an underlying sexual and angry tension. The pace drags even as Ray lets loose on a wailing harmonica solo.[41] The B side features "I Took My Baby Home," a beat-driven rhythm-and-blues number. Ray's accent on "Baby" is still colored by a slight Liverpudlian tinge, but the cheerful beat, wailing harmonica, and perky vocals complement the sleazy story of a one-night stand with a girl whose "pile-driving kisses" leave the narrator swooning, his orgasm expressed as a series of drawn out "whoa whoa whoa's." This B side describes the Kinks' character and their effect on their audience far more than does their version of "Long Tall Sally." Nevertheless, the single managed to reach number forty-two on the charts,[42] enough to get the Kinks a place on a package tour of England, mentions in the key trade papers (*Melody Maker* and the *New*

Music Express), and an appearance on the television show *Ready, Steady, Go!* miming to their "hit" in their hunting-green jackets and kinky boots.

If "Long Tall Sally" were the Kinks' union card for domestic tours, "You Really Got Me" would be their passport for the world. On the top of the bill for these early British tours were the already-established Dave Clark 5 (whom the Kinks found prissy) and the Hollies, another, by 1964, venerable act; the latter were friendlier to the lowly ranked and disorganized Kinks than some of their contemporaries. Other early tours included the Kinks sharing the bill with the Beatles—to mixed results, as the not-so-friendly rivalry sometimes ended with sabotaged stage equipment if not performances. Nevertheless, the Kinks were pleased to hold their own against the group from Liverpool and on more than one occasion to steal the screams of their fans for themselves. Early Kinks' shows became notorious for the violence on and off stage. When the group members weren't physically attacking each other with bits of drum kit, then their fans were causing havoc in British and then European venues. Some live performances survive on cine film and are held within British and European television archives; there is also from 1968 *Live at Kelvin Hall*, an example of aural chaos taken from an early 1967 concert in Glasgow.[43] Touring was a necessary evil to get the band out and about into the public's face, but no matter how exhausted it left the band, they still had to head back to the recording studio to fulfill contractual obligations. It's little wonder that Ray collapsed from exhaustion and was replaced on tour temporarily at one point in mid-1965, or that in the year following the success of "You Really Got Me," other shows were cancelled simply due to the band falling ill with exhausted immune systems.[44]

Cleaning up their act was all well and good on tour in the provinces, but it was also vital to get them on television: again the image consultants made their assessments of how to tidy up this group of ugly scruffs. Here after a bit of acquiescence, again, the group rebelled. For example, for an early television performance Ray was forced to wear caps to disguise a gap between his front teeth, and then he barely escaped from the dentist's chair when management decided that the look had to be permanent.[45] Ray describes his orthodontic trauma in his 1996 autobiography, and he makes contemporary reference to it in 1964's "I Gotta Move." Only twenty years old in a group newly famous,

Ray sings in a world-weary monotone as a vicious guitar lick winds up and down the scale around him like a vibrant snake. In the song he notes that he's got to shine his shoes and neaten his hair to make himself presentable, and in a jab against those who would have him submit to the dentist to achieve a bright, white BBC smile, he notes, "gotta fill my gap and comb my hair." The group further tormented television stage hands and directors abroad as well, once ignoring a stage direction to perform a silly, unified dance routine not uncommon with fifties and sixties pop groups,[46] and instead allowed the camera to catch the bandmates dancing cheek to cheek.

British tours, two flop singles, and an appearance on TV would satisfy a flash-in-the-pan group, but the Kinks were still looking for their particular voice from the spring of 1964. In an industry stingy on the clock, time was running out. The second single had also been a flop, so the third and last song on the Pye contract was also their last chance—hope and desperation lent an air of urgency to the startlingly fresh power chords that suddenly farted out of teenybopper transistor radios in August 1964 (UK). Despite their two tepid singles, the Kinks continued to put new songs into their repertoire, as Ray was determined to create a unique sound for the band. "You Really Got Me" proved a hit on the tours, and Ray wanted it for the Kinks' final recording chance. He wanted an original, blues-driven track that would go to number one on the charts and to supersede that foundation for blues on the pop charts laid by the Animals and "House of the Rising Sun." "You Really Got Me" itself was recorded three times before Ray was satisfied with the style of the recording: that the Kinks fought against the release of the single as it was engineered by Shel Talmy shows their independence and their determination to get their *own* product out even at a time when they had no real professional leverage. Talmy's version of the song was too lush and overproduced, too American, for the Kinks' taste; their riffs were buried under Phil Spector–inspired processing. As Thomas Kitts notes, the importance of the riff in "You Really Got Me" and of the song itself cannot be overstated.[47] Ray has noted that the creation of "You Really Got Me" was as if being born: the Kinks at last found a track that captured the band's character.[48] The song started its life in the Davies family front room as Ray messed about on an old piano, working on a slow-moving, hypnotic, jazz-blues lament of a man who desires an unattainable woman, and according to Kinks mythology,

Dave abandoned his tea in the kitchen to find out, as Ray explains in his stage show, "what the fuck was this all about?" Dave added his distorted, growling guitar riffs and increased the tempo of the song, and with a frenzied solo, Dave, as Ray dramatically notes on *Storyteller*, played the band into rock-and-roll history.

"You Really Got Me" reached number one in September 1964 in both the UK and the United States, cheek by jowl on the charts with such songs as "A Hard Day's Night," "I Get Around," and "Have I the Right."[49] It had already become a showstopper in the Kinks' stage act, driving the girls to a frenzy with its blunt sexuality. At the suggestion of Hal Carter, Ray changed the initial address to the subject of the song; originally, he sang simply, "Yeah, you really got me," but Carter urged him to toss in a girl's name, *any* girl's name, to address it personally to the listener. So Ray changed the lyric to "*Girl*, you really got me going"—changing the song from a vague fantasy to one of direct address—but without alienating any girl not called Peggy, Rhonda, or Sue. The song builds to a frenzy over its two minutes and fourteen seconds, changing to higher keys, as the singer gasps out his release and the guitar hammers out a few last chords before panting to a staccato halt—the singer presumably still alone and frustrated but perhaps not for too long (not if the follow-up "All Day and All the Night" is any indication). The excitement, pace, and searing distortion of "You Really Got Me" were unlike anything else on the charts at the time. The tortured guitar and Dave's frenzied solo—its fuzzy, overdriven sound achieved originally by slashing with a razor blade the speaker cones of an eight-watt Elpico amplifier and then driving its screaming howls through a Vox AC30 (at the cost, in earlier experiments, of near electrocution)—put the Kinks on the rock-and-roll map, summing up pent-up teenaged angst in a frenzy of rebellion, anxiety, and unrelieved sexual frustration in its frantic couple of minutes.[50]

This final version of "You Really Got Me" epitomizes the band to this point. After its DIY simplicity, the insecurity in the lyrics reflects that of the band themselves. Its sound represents the rage and frustration of the working classes; its creation encapsulates the homey ordinariness of the band. Musicologists argue that "You Really Got Me" was the origin of heavy metal and the beginnings of punk. It was copied and emulated at once from 1964 by other bands such as the High Numbers (soon to be the Who) in Britain, and then a little later in the United

States, the Doors. Over the next fifty years, the Davies continued to embrace it along with their fans—there is a callback to the riff in the song "Top of the Pops"; Dave teases the listener with its melodic line in "Little Green Amp." Fifty years to the day that "You Really Got Me" reached number one in Britain, Ray Davies celebrated five decades of the song at the Royal Festival Hall in London—but, Ray being Ray, cheerfully undermined any apotheosis of the song. In his promotion of *Americana*, he refers to the tune as "You Really Shot Me," a reference to his attack by a mugger in New Orleans in 2004. The song remains an amazing accomplishment considering that it started over tea at home, later to be recorded by "4 [*sic*] nervous, very quiet guys [who] walked into [IBC] studio."[51]

"SON, YOUR RECORD'S GONE TO NUMBER ONE"

The Kinks certainly didn't rest on the laurels of "You Really Got Me," and the 1971 track "Top of the Pops" off *Lola* captures the pressure on a group to have a hit single and the effects of both riding high on a record's success and the quick nadir into obscurity should it fail. "Top of the Pops" is named after a popular British television show that ran from 1963 to 2006 (and still runs an annual Christmas edition). While some groups thought it was rather silly, it was a key showcase for up-and-coming performers and a part of British culture. The eponymous song itself kicks off with a riff that manages to recall the television show's theme song complemented by see-sawing power chords that also invoke "You Really Got Me" and the harsh sputter of a machine gun. The narrator is overjoyed that his new record has come onto the charts at number twenty-five. Everyone is his friend, and he knows all of his troubles will be over once the song hits number one. He tells his family and his friends of his success, and as the song climbs higher, his confidence soars—and, tellingly, he notes that he might actually be able to make a living as a rock star. Keep in mind that when the Ravens/Kinks were scrambling for gigs in 1963 and early 1964, one was a full-time student, one was a high school dropout, and the others held menial and mundane day jobs (Mick Avory's day job was driving a fuel truck). Many musicians in the era never expected anything to come of their gigging. For example, Bill Wyman notes in 1963 that not only were the Stones paid a pittance initially but also he had trouble scraping together the bus fare needed to get to early gigs—no one was in it for the money but rather the excitement simply of performing,[52] which certainly must have made many groups easy prey for the promoters and publishers.

"Top of the Pops" continues with a musical interlude as voices jabber, representing all of the people who want a piece of the band (including someone shouting, "Shot of a lifetime!");[53] the fictional single continues to climb the charts. The narrator experiences the whirlwind of fame: the big music trade papers, the *New Music Express* and *Melody Maker*, want not only to interview him but also to ask his opinion on important world matters on politics and religion—perhaps a jab at the Beatles' later career as gurus of politics and religion. The singer can't walk down the street without being recognized and women screaming in excitement at the sight of him; he's bemused and amazed that he's suddenly got so many new friends. The song ends rather appropriately with the singer's agent telling him (in song patter rather than a melodic line), "Son, your record's just got to number one." The song ends with a posh voice, followed by heavenly, celestial strains, stating, "And you know what *this* means!" A nasally, faux Liverpudlian voice cuts in to assure the band that now they can earn some *real* money. And of course, as so many bands would come to learn in real life, once one reaches number one, there was nowhere to go but down. As the narrator notes, when a record is high in the charts, everyone wants a piece of the performer, but once it falls, they don't know him for a stranger; then, as Ray, John, Paul, Mick, Keith, and so many others found out, the pressure is put on the songwriter to come up with another hit. And another one. And another. Ray refers to it in his autobiography as "the treadmill of success."[54]

THE MONEY-GO-ROUND: CONTRACTS AND CONFUSION

Now the Kinks had fame; did they have fortune? The Kinks, as other neophyte pop groups found out, had a fairly large chunk of their earnings carved out by a number of other people. Recording and publishing contracts with popular musicians could be Byzantine if not exploitative. The antecedents that determined who was paid what by whom dates back into the nineteenth century. Copyright laws favor songwriting and publishing, as sheet music is a physical thing—writing down lines and arrangements—over the "ephemeral" aspects of the song as sung.[55] And while the songwriter, who in the case of the Kinks, was usually Ray, stood to make more money from the band, there was also a question of who actually *owned* the published song and subsequent publishing rights and who would get a percentage of those record sales and performance rights. Ray was "incorporated" by Page's partner, music publisher Ed Kassner (whose driving personality and hard-bargaining tactics were shaped by his experiences during in War World II in Austria). Ray was persuaded to sign over his music to Kassner for a guaranteed £40 a week for life on the basis of providing security for his family—without understanding that £40 in 1964 would still be £40 in 2016 and so forth.[56] The Kinks themselves naïvely signed a contract that they did not understand (and furthermore might have even been illegal, as Dave was underage) and certainly received no legal advice on how to negotiate, perhaps out of fear of losing their chance at professional music making.

The Kinks' contract with their original publishing company, Boscobel Music (called after the street on which Robert Wace was living at the time) and the tangled network of subsequent management is too complex to delineate here.[57] Much of their income went to other people, and in less than a year, they began to question their income and to rebel against what they felt were increasingly difficult demands on their time—especially Ray, who was being pressured not only to churn out music for the band itself but also for other artists to whom Page would sell the songs (see chapter 8 on covers). The conflict came to a head during a 1965 tour of the United States when the band felt they had been abandoned by Larry Page. They were infuriated over what they perceived as a lack of protection against the American promoters and union officials, and they were upset at discrepancies in their earnings.[58] The result was for the band to pursue litigation against Page and Kassner, which led to their royalties becoming frozen. In the wake of their subsequent four-year ban from working in United States (1965–1969) due to a conflict with the powerful American Federation of Musicians Union, this was a financial disaster.

Ray and the Kinks put into verse the intricacies of their contractual obligations in the song "The Moneygoround," another bitter track from

Lola. "The Moneygoround" is a jaunty little tune reminiscent of the music hall. Poppy and bouncy, it has been staged in Joe Penhall's play *Sunny Afternoon* by having all of the Kinks' administration dance in a circle, bobbing up and down like morris dancers, and clutching pound notes instead of ribbons, which they passed to one another as required by the song's lyrics. Contractual legalese is reduced to a perky children's game; the instructions in the tune complement the absurdity of the staged dance. First, sings Ray, Robert "owes half" to Grenville who then gives half to Larry Page—all told, 40 percent of the Kinks' earnings were immediately skimmed off and handed over to management and publishing. The song explains further financial complexities as Page invests in foreign publication and then splits the return profits to Ray as the original songwriter—but even this soon in the song, Ray's lost track of who owes what to whom and how much the actual profit ought to be. The song realizes his frustration as an artist—the music that he's creating is being bought and sold without even being heard by so many people along the marketing chain. He wonders in despair what it all means. He laments that he goes to see a solicitor who decides to sue everyone involved. The track's cheerful melody here belies the singer's sense of betrayal at the hands of those he thought were friends. The singer is stressed to the point of a breakdown (which did occur in real life for Ray not long after the real money-go-round began) and realizes that while he may be determined to win his case, when he does, he'll be too old to enjoy the profits of his art. The most significant statement in the song is the final line, "I only hope that I'll survive," having described his situation as not unlike being stuck in an inescapable pit. Many of the songs on *Lola* describe the loss of innocence and how easily integrity can be compromised—and how, despite the great toll placed on especially Ray's nerves, the band grew ever more stubborn about fighting against a machine that would ever exploit them. The only positive "loss of innocence" song on the entire album is in fact "Lola," where the naïve narrator's first great love affair comes at the hands of a transvestite, but this one has a happy ending, as she accepts him exactly as he is—and she is the only one on the entire album who does.

CONCLUSION: NOT LIKE EVERYBODY ELSE

Most of the tracks on *Lola* represent some of Ray Davies's most bitter commentary, but they are admittedly not among the best known. The Kinks would cover similar territory with "Working in the Factory" on 1986's *Think Visual*, an indictment of how the music industry reduces art to a business and how marketing and image making supersede integrity. Far better known is 1966's "I'm Not Like Everybody Else," which has become an anthem for Kinks fans to express both their individuality and the exclusive devotion they have as fans of the Kinks. A number of fans who graciously replied to my survey on the group and the group's influence frequently cited the song as one of their favorites, and one that not only resonates with their own personalities but also succinctly defines the Kinks. Released in 1966, the song begins with a descending guitar riff that sounds as if the musical staff has been pushed over and the notes fallen in a jumble onto the floor. Ray wrote the song but handed the vocals to Dave, the Kink who well epitomizes the rebellion of the group against all comers. The singer is candid and honest. He refuses to take second hand; he refuses to compromise. It doesn't matter if it's someone urging him to smile when he would rather frown; it doesn't matter if it's a lover asking him to confide his secrets that he refuses to tell. One complaint that Ray and the Kinks had about fame was the loss of privacy and the feeling of being manipulated. The song's words emphasize their resentment against being told what to do just to push a product. If such behavior makes them feel untrue to themselves, then fame and fortune be damned. Subsequently, the use of the song in advertisements for IBM in Japan featured large groups of middle-aged, white-collar workers singing along with the song. It's been used to sell cars in America—a culture in which "having your own theme song is a thrill," which in fact subverts the actual message of the song. Instead it brings to mind the crowd scenes from *Life of Brian* where the mob agrees, "Yes, we're all individuals."

Nevertheless, while the song has now become as iconic for the band as "Waterloo Sunset," taken within its own context of the Kinks' activities in the first two years of fame and as part of the pop music machine, it becomes even more significant. In but a few moments of musical expression, the Kinks' quarrels; fights with management, publishers, and union authorities; anger; defiance; and rage against the machine are laid bare.

4

HUMOR AND THE KINKS

I'm not very witty at all.[1]

In his memoir of the early 1960s British music industry, Simon Napier-Bell recalls that what distinguished the Kinks from other British bands was "they were funny."[2] Humor runs deeply through the Kinks' character, in their lyrics and their attitude. What especially charms their followers, professional critics and fans alike, is their distinctively English humor. Now what does *that* mean, and how does "English humor" characterize the Kinks in particular?

Iain Ellis has written on the role of humor in early British rock and roll, and how humor provided an outlet for rebellion among Britain's young musicians.[3] Although British rock and roll was derivative of American forms, it lacked a connection to the particular musical traditions and social conditions that shaped rock and roll in the United States. Nevertheless, British rockers expressed similar outrage and youthful solidarity that was found in American rock and roll. British youth used the arts to rebel against postwar austerity and the constraints of rigidly structured, classed society. This cultural revolution was often colored by humor—satire, surrealism, and the just plain silly, accented with self-deprecation.

The humorous context of social commentary is embedded in English culture, and satire as social criticism in English arts goes as far back as Chaucer and his Wife of Bath in the fourteenth century. Key artistic movements in the mid-twentieth century that affected popular culture include the Angry Young Men (AYM) of 1950s British theater, beginning with John Osbourne's *Look Back in Anger* in 1956. Next came the satire movement of the early 1960s led by Peter Cook and Alan Bennett and their revue *Beyond the Fringe*, first on stage, later on television, and then in print (*Private Eye*). Concurrent were those humorists who examined the absurdity of everyday life, for example, Peter Sellers on the radio with *The Goon Show* and David Frost (with writer Nick Sherrin) on television with *This Was the Week That Was* and *The Frost Report*. The latter was instrumental for future Monty Python creators John Cleese and Graham Chapman, who created *At Last the 1948 Show*, and Michael Palin, Terry Jones, and Terry Gilliam, with *Do Not Adjust Your Set*. Humor in theater, film, and television subsequently influenced humor in contemporary popular music.

The Kinks' particular brand of social satire was influenced by not only these programs but also Ray Davies's art and film studies. These elements combined with his skill at social observation and led him to write songs influenced by both satire and music hall. Humor gave mid-twentieth-century working-class youth in Britain an outlet to rebel against the mores of traditional, class-bound society. Ray Davies and the Kinks, and other contemporary singer-songwriters such as John Lennon, Pete Townshend, and Vivian Stanshall, all used humor both to criticize and to contemplate whimsically even the most mundane aspects of English life. And this humorous commentary often takes the mick out of its own pretensions. While the Kinks skewered English characters and behavior, they also acknowledged that such traditions and cultural institutions were an inextricable part of their own makeup. Unlike satirists who use humor savagely as a proactive cry for change, the Kinks used humor to encourage protection of such institutions rather than revolution against them.

This chapter first considers the effects of homegrown entertainment on the Kinks' wit, beginning with case studies on sibling rivalry ("Hatred: A Duet") and on the influence of Ray's sisters when it came to him to write about the lives of ordinary people ("A Well Respected Man"). As Ray noted later in his career, his words were "the only ammunition I had to fight with,"[4] so this chapter will consider briefly the Kinks' satire of authority and social injustice with case studies of "Mr. Reporter" and "Father Christmas." Finally, it will consider the Kinks' Englishness and self-deprecation as a source of their humor by looking at "Holiday in Waikiki."

Despite their humor and their love of particular gimmicks (i.e., their early stage uniform or sing-alongs), the Kinks were no mere comedy act. George Orwell notes in his essay on Charles Dickens that had Dickens "been *merely* a comic writer, the chances are that no one would remember his name."[5] The success of Dickens, including his humor, is that "a joke worth laughing at always has an idea behind it, and usually a subversive idea. Dickens is able to go on being funny because he is in revolt against authority, and authority is always there to be laughed at."[6] The same must be said about the Kinks: they were and are still funny, and they were showmen, but their songs contained a sting in the tale.

NOT ONLY ... SOME CONTEXT FOR HUMOR IN 1960S POP CULTURE ... BUT ALSO SOME RECOMMENDATIONS OF CONTEMPORARY ENGLISH HUMOR

A comprehensive survey of the history of British humor is well beyond the scope of this chapter, let alone this book. Instead, one might start by seeking out general studies of the elusive "English identity" as a discussion of humor is always included in these works. Suggested reading includes Kate Fox's *Watching the English*, in which she pieces together English behavior as a set of conversational and behavioral codes (including a chapter dedicated to humor specifically, 61–72), and Jeremy Paxman's *The English*, which combines themes of humor and family in pursuit of a definition of English identity. Nostalgic memoirs and exploration of "the worst of Britain" that illustrate the English tendency toward self-deprecating humor include Andrew Collins's *Where Did It All Go Right? Growing Up Normal in the '70s* and Tim Moore's *You Are Awful (But I Like You): Travels through Unloved Britain*. Recent genteel television comedies that use humor to reflect on the ordinary include Rob Brydon and Steve Coogan's *The Trip* and Mark Watson's *A Child's Christmases in Wales*.[7] Memoirs of humorists who started out in the early sixties are also useful; for example, Peter Cook wrote an autobiography, and John Cleese and Michael Palin's memoirs are most enlightening, as they are not only contemporaries of the Kinks but also, like the Kinks, consumers of and eventually creators of observational and subversive humor that is rich in English if not universal themes.[8]

Finally, for simple immersion, a goodly amount of material remains from contemporary radio and television (despite the BBC's best efforts to wipe many 1950s and 1960s programs from its archives).

Another medium featuring a mix of comedy, Englishness, and class conflict from the Kinks' own youth is film. The golden age of British cinematic comedy ranges from the postwar period through to the 1950s, particularly the films produced by Ealing Studios.[9] These low-budget films with distinctively English settings competed successfully against splashy Hollywood blockbusters. Plots frequently featured sympathetic everymen simply trying to get by, even if it meant taking advantage of the system during the age of austerity.[10] These films include *The Ladykillers*, *Kind Hearts and Coronets*, and *The Lavender Hill Mob*. The latter depicts a bank robbery, and it may well have lent its name to the Kinks' song "Lavender Hill," which describes wistfully a land of "make believe" where the singer longs to live on "sugar and milk" and "dream[s] of daffodils that sway in the breeze." It's the same sort of peaceful, sunshiny daydream that the drab, ordinary men-turned-criminals of the Lavender Hill Mob hope that their heist will fulfill. Ray revisits the postwar spiv (the black marketer) and the (sometimes disgraced) hustler in a number of Kinks and solo songs: see "Come Dancing" (the video in particular), "Low Budget," "Second-Hand Car Hand Spiv," and "Yours Truly, N10."

Around the time that the Ealing comedies ruled the cinema, another comedic phenomenon was revolutionizing the English stage. In the mid- to late 1950s, a new generation of playwrights called the "Angry Young Men" took back the London stage from lightweight comedies and dramas by writers such as Noel Coward, ending the dominance of particularly middle-class fare from the 1930s and 1940s. These plays were not traditional comedies but rather scathing commentary on middle-class life, and they were meant to raise awareness especially among the younger generation about the social if not political and economic conflict between the working and middle classes. Postwar austerity formed the context for the sudden expression of contempt and satire in midcentury for the Establishment, and what began as the so-called kitchen-sink realism, or dramas, of the late 1950s and early 1960s. The name reflects the plots of these plays, featuring realistic angst, frustration, and desire of the characters to escape the bounds of social convention, evolving into the shattering of class boundaries in real life. These plays preceded the satirical reviews written and performed by university students, first on stage and then on television, and introduced a new generation of actors including Michael Caine and Terence Stamp. These actors represented a more realistic and less "Received Pronunciation" (RP) Britain, and they became part of the new youth social scene in London and popular media in the early 1960s.

Monographs on the new genres of social satire provide context for the movers and shakers of the period and also reveal how class issues became an active part of social media. Start with Robert Sellers who has written on the new generation of actors and pop stars who flourished on the foundations of the social barriers and taboos that were shattered on the 1950s London stage and thenceforth into the cinema of the early 1960s.[11] Follow up with H. Carpenter's surveys first on the rise of the Angry Young Men in the 1950s and then on the history of the satire boom of the early 1960s.[12] Carpenter's book provides a wealth of detail from the key players of the era and discusses at length Peter Cook and Alan Bennett's *Beyond the Fringe* revue and its consequences.[13] Having read Carpenter, take a look at Colin Wilson's study-cum-memoir of the era of the Angry Young Men.[14] Taking exception to Carpenter's discussion of both 1950s theater and the 1960s satirical movement, Wilson's history of the 1950s theater is colored by a lingering resentment of a working-class writer in a middle-class world.[15] In his memoir of the Angry Young Men, he argues that Carpenter looks down on them from the very social perspective they scorned (and claims that as the son of a bishop, Carpenter knew nothing of working-class angst).[16] Wilson honors the satire movement in the early sixties but argues that its mocking of politicians and of social injustice was merely "firing arrows over the parapet then ducking out of sight."[17] Wilson sees the work of the Angry Young Men as truly satirical because these authors were true to working-class solidarity through the proactive calls for social revolution promoted in their art.[18] Collins argues that he saw himself and the others among the Angry Young Men as literary revolutionaries in the mold of Swift or Rousseau, whose satirical writing was a means to raise awareness of social injustice. By Wilson's definition, the working-class Kinks fall into the category of the passive satire of Cook, Bennett, and the others of the university-led satirical boom: observational without being proactive.

In terms of describing the Kinks' social commentary as satire, one might again compare Orwell's comments on Charles Dickens. Orwell notes that Dickens paired his social commentary with his sense of humor:

> [Dickens's] radicalism is of the vaguest kind, and yet one always knows that it is there. That is the difference between being a moralist and a politician. He has no constructive suggestions, not even a clear grasp of the nature of the society he is attacking, only an emotional perception that something is wrong. All he can finally say is, "Behave decently," which . . . is not necessarily so shallow as it sounds.[19]

WHAT'S SOCIAL CLASS GOT TO DO WITH HUMOR IN POP MUSIC?

It's got quite a lot to do with humor in the case of the Kinks, if not in the output of many of their contemporaries. As Jon Savage points out in his biography of the Kinks, the Swinging Sixties could have easily been rebranded the Satirical Sixties, "a time when nothing was sacred."[20] He refers to the youth and pop culture of the early sixties as one of social class "incestuousness and mobility" and says that the satire on television and in print easily crossed over into popular music. Much of the humor in the story of the Kinks' *nachleben*, Joe Penhall's play *Sunny Afternoon*, emphasizes social class differences. In the play, the Kinks' middle-class managers tell the band that they're the latest thing because English society is no longer about class; it's all about *inclusiveness*. It doesn't work both ways, however: when the Kinks balk a bit at Grenville and Robert's enthusiasm for the breakdown of social barriers, the managers chide the band, "Surely, you're middle-class now, yourselves! You're one of us!" Ah, retorts Dave, but do *you* want to be one of *us*? The response from the otherwise upbeat managers is a weak smile and a look of dismay.

As noted in chapter 3, the Kinks' real-life experiences at the dawn of their career saw them immersed in a middle-class world once they began to get gigs. Additionally, as with a number of musicians, artists, and writers in the early 1960s, Ray's art-school experience opened up different worlds and means of expression and culture to these young, working-class men[21] —a number of the vanguard of the satire movement were, like Ray, working-class, scholarship lads. Ray notes in *X-Ray* that art school enabled him to look outside of his smaller world and become aware of the "style revolution," including the likes of John Stevens in Carnaby Street (see chapter 5) and the way that the Angry Young Men and style icons such as David Bailey and Mary Quant were shaking up the youth scene. School and music also allowed working- and middle-class youth to associate easily with one another. According to his memoirs, Ray took it all in stride: the cool thing to do in the early sixties suddenly was to be working class, and Ray didn't have to change a thing about himself—he'd "always been what the silly, confused trendies were trying to be."[22] Social barriers were cast aside as middle-class kids found working-class kids exciting and free, and they wanted inclusion in their world.

Ray's humorous commentaries on middle-class mores were influenced by his observational skills; by his middle-class colleagues, especially Robert Wace and by his a sense of working-class solidarity. This outlook is not unique to the Kinks. As with many of their musical contemporaries who came from a similar economic background, the Kinks did not desert their roots when they gained fame but instead continued to compose songs that celebrated working-class life. This identity can be found in many of Ray's (and Dave's) songs: "Dead End Street," "Autumn Almanac," "Stand Up Comic," "A Well Respected Man," and "Mr. Pleasant." The irony of "Stand-Up Comic," written quite recently by a much older and experienced Ray, is that now wide-boy Jack the Lad[23] notes that all his working-class trappings are quite the fashion, and the middle class ape his appearance, accent, and interests in their quest to be edgy and trendy: "Jack the Lad has become Oscar Wilde." Despite the apparent social equality, however, when the chips were down the Kinks frequently found that their all-inclusive middle-class pals retreated behind the cultural wall of their social status, leaving the working-class Kinks behind to suffer the consequences.

FAMILY LIFE AND GROWING UP: MUSICAL HALL REVELRY AND SIBLING RIVALRY

As we'll see in chapter 7, one important influence on the Kinks' compositions is home and family. Such homely patterns are not unique to the

Davies, and because other working-class lads grew up to be artists and performers, affectionate domestic memories have remained a common meme in British humor.[24] Postwar, homegrown entertainments included singsongs round the piano, and reminiscence might include recalling the front parlor, fishing trips, eel pies, and mum in the kitchen or scolding the lads. Ideal, rosy-colored, working-class nonpretentiousness has been affectionately satirized by comedians from Cleese and Chapman in their 1960s sketch "Four Yorkshire Men" to an episode of Julian Barratt and Noel Fielding's *The Mighty Boosh* in the early twenty-first century.[25] A gentler version of the conflict between working- and middle-class culture also played a role on the long-running television panel show *QI*, which frequently saw its original host, genteel, Cambridge-educated Stephen Fry, pitted against boisterous, "working-class," permanent-guest Alan Davies (no relation), a match made deliberately as a point of entertainment by producer John Lloyd.[26] What all of them have in common is a collective inheritance from nineteenth- and early twentieth-century music hall, with its tendency toward not only innuendo and pratfalls but also sharp reflection on class differences that lay not so hidden behind the jokes.

While contemporary events in the news of the late 1950s and early 1960s had an impact on the Kinks' early style and desirability among the deb set, headlines torn from the press aren't evident in their earliest works Ravens' and early Kinks' songs were covers of music hall and American rock and roll and blues; early original tracks followed blues stylings, simple "moon 'n' June" rhymes in the lyrics, and faux Mersey-beat, that is, the style of beat-group music coming out of Liverpool between 1961 and 1963, for example, Rory Storm and the Hurricanes, Billy Kramer, and most famously the (early) Beatles. As young men may be wont to do, however, the band reacted to the general atmosphere of sex and scandal in the news and played it up to shock both adults and peers. The *Lady Chatterley* trial of 1960, the sensational story of the effects on the government of politicians' lust for teenagers in the 1963 Profumo Scandal, and the increasingly public awareness of homosexuality in the theater and entertainment industry manifested itself in the outrageous campy behavior of the Ravens as they pranced about in leather capes and whips (to the bemusement of their auditioning drummer Mick Avory) and led initially to their own rebranding as "Kinks" (see chapters 3 and 5). Long hair and tight trousers might have outraged the grown-ups, but shrill voices and limp-wristed comedy was common ground for schoolboys. Sex, camp, and silliness had long been part of lower- and working-class entertainment if not in the nudge-nudge-wink-wink found in the cheaply and quickly made *Carry On* films and among pantomime dames and cross-dressing acts found on the music-hall stage. In America, Milton Berle in a dress was a shocking novelty. In Britain, the campy drag act and sexual innuendo were venerable traditions dating back to Shakespeare's clowns in the sixteenth century.

BROTHERS AND SISTERS: A DUET

The Kinks' songs about family add to the band's universal appeal. One particular theme perhaps shared among Kinks fans is sibling rivalry. Siblings can be a source of conflict, and such conflict can be vastly entertaining for those who both observe and sympathize with the situation. Musical siblings proliferate in popular music from the nineteenth-century music-hall and vaudeville stage onward.[27] Often one's first experience as a performer has been singing with siblings, and many sibling stage acts have capitalized on the relationship. *Feuding* siblings tend to fascinate more than the ones who get along perhaps because we identify more readily with quarrels among our siblings than with signing multi-million-dollar recording contracts with them. The Davies brothers' particular raison d'être lends itself to humorous expression of familial conflict. Ray explained that he conceived the song "Hatred: A Duet" as being sung by a "two-headed transplant to sing as a split personality"[28] but then he recast it as a duet shared between himself and Dave. The 1992 track expresses the love-hate relationship extant between the two that is as much part of the Kinks' character as their protopunk attitudes and power chords or their Englishness.

Fans delight in stories of Ray and Dave's fraternal altercations that, over the years, have made Oasis look like the Brady Bunch. The rap sheet includes Dave allowing an inebriated Ray to fall off the stage on occasion; Ray calmly stabbing his younger brother in the leg with a fork when the latter pinched a bit of salad—or was it a chip?—off his plate; or Ray attempting to strangle Dave on the roof of their north London recording studio, and so forth. They still drive each other batty as evidenced, as of this writing in mid-2016, with rumors of a Kinks reunion (each accusing the other of being the obstacle toward a reunion, a hobby of theirs since the 1990s). Numerous artists have jumped at the chance to work with Ray and Dave, and numerous artists have come away with their nervous systems in tatters as a result of the tension between the brothers. Ray has said that he wants to be loved but acknowledges that he's difficult to live with.[29] Adds Dave recently on the subject,

> People forget that in a family you get used to a way of acting around each other . . . you get used to a certain level of abuse. I've seen engineers cower when Ray and I have gone at it in the recording studio, just completely unsure of what to make of it. And then it would pass and we'd carry on—as though nothing had happened—and they'd be completely floored that we could do that.[30]

Ray's recent reaction to Dave describing their relationship as "like Cain and Abel" was, "It's more like Satan and Jesus," but he continued, "Sibling rivalry's such an odd term. There's always rivalry in bands. . . . Dave provides fire, or the fuel to light my fire."[31] It is indeed a complex relationship and, despite the occasion fracas, is also one that has seen genuine support in times of need.

"Hatred: A Duet" effectively summarizes Ray and Dave's wit and their relationship with one another, originally obliquely addressed in 1967's "Two Sisters" (see chapter 7). "Hatred" was recorded in 1992 as part of the sessions for 1993's *Phobia*, the Kinks' last commercially released studio album.[32] "Hatred" is only one of several songs on *Phobia* and the band's previous release, *UK Jive*, that are flavored with humor. Nevertheless, while several songs on the two albums capture the band's Pye-era sound and whimsy, *Phobia* runs some of Ray's favorite themes into the ground, for example, the eponymous song, or the neurotic "Babies" and the narrator's desire to escape back to the safety of the womb. "Hatred," however, is the highlight on *Phobia*, at last addressing the elephant in the family's front room on Denmark Terrace.

The singers trade accusatory verses (Ray) against defensive responses (Dave): how Dave has made Ray's life a misery; how attempts at olive branches are now too little, too late; and how turning the other cheek merely puts the peacemaker in a vulnerable position. Ray compares the feuding siblings' relationship to various global struggles affecting the world at the national level: disagreements on religion and human rights have got nothing on the enmity between the brothers. The common ground between them is the agreement that they hate each other: tied together by blood and separated by their rancor. Never mind if one slanders the other to the press; as Ray warns, "The other has a mouth, too." It's a cheerful and cathartic exchange that acknowledges charmingly the feud that endears them to their fans. The song is arranged in a bright, country-blues style reminiscent of Ray's fondness for Johnny Cash found on *Lola versus Powerman* and *Muswell Hillbillies*.

While there is much humor in the song's lyrics, the visuals of a live performance reveal more of the story. For example, Ray and Dave performed the song (backed by the Branford Marsalis Band) on *The Jay Leno Show* on May 25, 1993.[33] In the clip, the pair exchanges cheeky smiles as they sing at separate mikes. They point at one another as they share lines on the verses; American commentators on the various You-Tube mirrors of the performance take especial glee that the pair point with their second fingers, claiming that they're "flipping one another off."[34] Both perform their parts in their own idiosyncratic fashion. Dave, off to Ray's left, attacks his guitar solos with enthusiasm while Ray plays the consummate vaudevillian, dancing about, throwing out jazz hands, and encouraging the audience to sing along. Nevertheless, Ray's flashy showmanship visibly irritates his younger brother, and as Ray attempts to razzle-dazzle the audience, Dave shoots him a look of undisguised exasperation. *That* is the essence of the feuding siblings; that unconscious glance surely brings a smile to the observer's face and enhances the song's humor—for us, if not for them.

An equally important familial influence on the humor in the music of the Kinks comes from the Davieses' sisters.[35] For example, the tragic circumstances of one of his sisters, crippled in a car accident before he was born, made Ray realize that he could write songs about ordinary people. In addition to overcoming her injuries, this sister had a child not only born out of wedlock but also fathered by a man from French West Africa[36] —in 1950s conservative white north London, this made life hard for the little niece,[37] and Ray and Dave followed their mother's example of being protective of the girl against racist comments. As a consequence, and in admiration of the strength of character seen in the protective solidarity of his family, especially his mother and sister, the story of his sister and niece's experience showed Ray that "songs could draw attention to the trials and tribulations of ordinary people," a revelation that set him very much on his poetic path.[38] Such songs would inspire other storytelling songsters (such as Pete Townshend) and help to create an "English mystic" that distinguished the Kinks from other groups in the 1960s.[39] "A Well Respected Man" was also composed right around the time when the Kinks were hobbled by the American Federation of Musicians' ban on performing in the United States (see chapter 3). Ray began to move away from teenybopper lyrics and focus on these storytelling compositions, and the band thus reinvented itself over the next couple of years, drawing on their Englishness to create character-driven songs.

One of the first of these is "A Well Respected Man," which was the result of a holiday that Ray and his wife took in July 1965 as a break away from the relentless pressure on him to produce more hits. Their holiday at the Imperial Hotel in Torquay, Devon, "the English Riviera," was cut short because Ray felt awkward and out of place as he not only was recognized by staff and clientele but also felt snubbed and even mocked for attempting to "pass" as one of the wealthy visitors and to rise above his station in life—another theme that Ray would explore in song (for example, "Mr. Pleasant"). He took as an insult an invitation to a round of golf with several middle-class guests, especially as Ray felt they had invited him only so they could say they had "played golf with a pop star,"[40] and he packed up the family belongings and went home to London.[41]

In creating the "A Well Respected Man," Ray fulfilled his desire to start "using words well"; as Hinman points out, this was also the point in which he ceased to envy American musicians and to embrace his own Britishness.[42] While the Kinks continued to tour around the world in the mid-1960s (save for the United States), they still horrified critics with their overt sexiness and violence on stage and the audience's destruction of the venues. Ray insisted that the band continue their raw, amateur persona on stage as he felt any polish would be selling out. Conversely, however, Ray spoke to interviewers about his homesickness for his wife and child, and how he was concentrating more and more about writing songs about people.[43] The song certainly wasn't their first ballad, as "Tired of Waiting" revealed the Kinks' capacity for producing thoughtful, introspective songs, but social commentary on "A Well Respected Man" was a departure from the Kinks usual blues-driven or angsty-teen output.[44]

The Kinks became so strongly associated with creating social portraits that by the eighties and nineties, Ray appeared to be making light of his own "search for new neurotic themes."[45] It must be stressed, however, that "A Well Respected Man" was not only new territory for the Kinks but also a fresh development in pop music in general, preceding, for example, satire of the Beatles' tracks "Nowhere Man" and "Taxman," the Who's "I'm a Boy," or the Small Faces' "Lazy Sunday Afternoon" by nearly a year. In his recent memoir, *So Anyway . . .*, John Cleese corroborates the freshness of such social satire in pop culture. He explains how twenty-first-century parody sketches of news broadcasts follow a well-trodden path, but in the early sixties such comedy was fresh and unusual, especially so for young people to mock staid institutions such as the BBC. Cleese notes that such programs were popular then because much of British comedy had become rather stale and predictable by the end of the 1950s, catering to the audience rather than challenging them, comedy writers fell back simply on tired catchphrases, puns, and stock characters.[46] We ourselves don't realize how exciting this comedy was as we hear and see it now out of context: similarly, after decades of sanitized "classic rock" "best of" lists and blanket programming in the form of *I Love the . . .* the actual *context* of innovation is sometimes neglected.

Musically, "A Well Respected Man" belies the satire and anger in its lyrics. It opens with a gentle, acoustic, twelve-string riff that prepares the audience for a story. Then the song gambols along with a lively, Cockney rhythm section; its jaunty two-beat invites a clap-along from the listener while the chorus invites a call-and-response. Ray sings each verse with more urgency—despite the cheerful music, the vocabulary and accents mock the man's station in life (going to the *regatta*, waiting for his *pater* to die, and so forth). By 1965, Ray had abandoned his faux-American rock-and-roll vocalization, and this song is wholeheartedly English, in tone, content, and class; and the vocals are sung in a mock-RP accent, returning to Davies's everyday north London twang in the choruses. The chorus is for the observers who may have praise for this upright, seemingly responsible young man, but the verses are Ray on his own, expressing his anger for what he sees as ignorant reward for laziness and lack of ambition.

The lyrics of "A Well Respected Man" also belie the complimentary title—the man may be well respected, but he is, in reality, an unambitious man-child, held hostage by precise routine, and is passively dependent on the actions of his family to succeed. The man and his parents are shown as living dull, desperate lives behind the scenes of their affluent, middle-class facade. In verse one, the man's routine is revealed—rising at the same time every day and taking the same train into work. He's safe in his sheltered world because he relies on following the orders of others. Lateness and spontaneity are not a part of his psyche. His own father only pretends to work—it's Mother who actually goes to work every day, flirting with all the young men while Father stays at home and cheats with the maid. The young man's occupations are safe and passive—he "plays at" stocks and shares; he goes to the boat races—his work and play are indistinguishable. The cycle of bourgeois comfort will continue, as this young man made lazy by class will inherit his father's "loot" and gain a wealthy wife through his mother's machinations—not the girl next door, whom he pines over but won't approach, but the one whom his mother chooses. He'll be rewarded for doing absolutely nothing. To add insult to injury, he's also quite the snob, preferring the smell of his own sweat—ironic, of course, because he seems to expend no effort over the course of the day on anything that would cause him to perspire.

Despite his chances for social opportunity, he remains boring, predictable, and childlike. Nevertheless, he's "good" and "fine" and is well respected by those around town who see him coming and going. They know nothing about him, but they respect the facade as they observe him dutifully commuting—one is reminded of the factory workers in Paul Simon's vicious "Richard Cory" (itself based on a poem by E. A. Robinson). Does Ray respect "the man" of the song? Does he want us to? Absolutely not. Compare the apathetic drudge of "A Well Respected Man" to the hero of 1966's "Sunny Afternoon": a descending bass line introduces both the song and the narrator's declining fortunes. He's escaped from the horrors of "Dead End Street," and he's made good initially: he's got a stately home, loads of money, and a yacht. We know all of this because he tells us that his wife's abandoned him, and she's taken it all with her. The money is gone, taken by the taxman. His reputation is shot because the wife has run back to her parents complaining of his drunkenness and cruel behavior. The house will surely be repossessed next. He's got nothing left—or has he?

The hero of "Sunny Afternoon" would shrug, resigned to his fate. There's an implication that he's come from nothing and he'll go back to nothing, but he's not at a total loss. He celebrates the good weather, his idleness, and an "ice-cool beer" while waiting, presumably, for the bailiffs to come and collect the rest. The rousing chorus invites the audience to sing along with him and to celebrate the sunshine on his face and a complete lack of obligations, a very English attitude.[47] "These things happen"—possibly the most aggravating words to hear in the face of a disaster, but at the same time, they are surely one of the most unarguable ones. Well-respected men are miserable in their lockstep existence; "Mr. Pleasant" has everything he wants and nothing he needs. The Sunny Afternoon fellow accepts his loss with a Micawberian attitude that suggests he will probably rise from the ashes as "something will come up."

REMEMBER THE KIDS WHO GOT NOTHING: SATIRE AND SOCIAL ISSUES

The Kinks' humor targets the posing middle class (or social climbers), the Mods, and the nostalgia seekers. Occasionally, some satirical observations are angrier than others, especially when they are directed at authority, the press, or seasonal hypocrites. Dave, for example, especially had little time for authority figures, a dislike dating back to his school days. His frustration with those in charge appears in some of his early compositions ranging from issues with his lost romance as a teenager ("Funny Face," for example) through to vented spleen aimed at politicians and the press in later Kinks and then his own solo work. Those songs include, for example, the main theme of Dave's solo album *Glamour* (1982) and in the Kinks' 1988 track "Dear Margaret," a vicious, yet cheeky, address to the then-Tory prime minister. The press also came under fire by Ray in the somewhat obscure and Dylanesque track "Mr. Reporter," featuring vocals by Dave (Ray tended to have Dave in mind when he wrote a number of his Bolshie songs such as this) and, more familiarly, "I'm Not Like Everybody Else."

The Kinks' relationship with the press had soured early on, particularly when the *New Music Express* announced the Rolling Stones as the winners of its 1964 Best New Band award—the same award they'd won in 1963 when they *had* actually been a new band.[48] The snub kicked off a decades-long distrust and dislike of journalists and perhaps explains why so often the Davies have convoluted their own mythology during interviews, if not walking out when the questioning becomes too personal or trite. "Mr. Reporter" from 1969 itself takes shots at the fourth estate. The track's narrator complains that the reporter pries into his personal life and that he twists singer's words around. The press forge lies when there's no actual news to report. Dave sings vocals with a lazy, nasal snarl, accompanied initially by a simple folk-guitar rhythm section. Musically, the song builds up in intensity with a brass section that almost ends up completely overwhelming the vocals. The lyrics are quite shocking. The narrator is so fed up that he's willing to kill the journalist for his libel,[49] and he taunts the reporter for continuing the cycle of abuse created by the man's own ignorance and childhood trauma—and he suggests that the reporter holds his job only because he's too stupid to do any other work. Ray demonstrated further annoyance with the press's interference in the personal lives of the band in the 1980s. During his relationship with Chrissie Hynde, he was appalled at how they dogged her when she was in labor with their child (part of the inspiration for the song "Heart of Gold").[50] A few years later he delivered a diatribe onstage against the press at a Kinks concert at the Albert Hall in 1993 in response to recent articles that repeated how the band's own record label had dismissed them as an "oldies band" and "rock-and-roll dinosaurs." He ordered any reporters in the room *not* to review the concert; most of them reported on Ray's rants instead.[51]

Outsiders weren't the only targets for the band's lyrical wrath. The Kinks both amused and scolded their own fans and listeners over seasonal hypocrisy with 1977's "Father Christmas." The track kicks off innocently enough with a tinkly keyboard motif that's quickly punched to one side by a barrage of power chords as it throttles the traditional British Christmas track that all bands must release by law and that, with luck, will become a lucrative holiday staple and a ringtone. "Father Christmas" turns the typical holiday sappy and cliché-ridden tune on its ear and makes a point about injustice without becoming maudlin (see "Christmas Shoes"). As with any good Christmas single from the working-class set, it's got a catchy, sing-along chorus (see Slade's "Merry Christmas, Everybody," Wizzard's "I Wish It Could Be Christmas Everyday," and Shakin' Stevens' "Merry Christmas, Everyone"). However, rather than encouraging granny to get up and dance with the kids, "Father Christmas" describes working-class kids who mug the narrator as he plays Santa in his grotto. They don't want the latest toys (dolls for their sister or a Steve Austin suit for their brother) as these baubles are useless. They want money for themselves and a job for their dad—and a machine gun if Santa's got one, so they can shoot all the other kids on the street (a sentiment accompanied by Dave's vicious guitar riffs). While a shocking statement to modern listeners, in 1977 the anarchy of punk was the order of the day, unemployment was at an all-time high, and there was violence in the streets of England's major cities as a result of anger over unemployment and immigration issues. Ray's hue and cry for public awareness is more effective in the Kinks' Christmas ditty than any of the *Preservation* trilogy's heavy-handed cynicism and neuroses about the dangers of the nanny state (chapter 6). There is of course the joy of fantasy of being a kid with wads of cash in hand if not guns to fire with abandon, but the singer, Ray, pauses the chaotic fantasy to sing a capella and to remind those listeners who are enjoying their holiday wine and cheer to "remember the kids who got nothing."

JUST AN ENGLISH BOY ON HOLIDAY: SELF-DEPRECATING HUMOR

The Kinks' characteristic humor is a theme that runs throughout the chapters of this book from their reaction to fame and becoming cogs in the machine of the music industry (chapters 3 and 8); issues of sexuality and gender (chapter 5); political commentary (chapter 6); home life, childhood, and nostalgia (chapter 7); and their legacy and popular image (chapter 8). So far this chapter has considered the cultural context for humor in their music—childhood influences, family inspiration, and social revolutions of which the band was part and parcel between the fifties and eighties. Another theme of this book is the Kinks' identity as *English*. It is appropriate then to finish this chapter with a look at how the Kinks combined their sudden rise to fame with characteristic English self-deprecation—the fish out of water on the one hand and on the other the realization of the English "tall poppy syndrome," that is, the English predilection to cut down anyone who attempts to speak up for him- or herself for "making a fuss." Americans are taught from the womb to blow their own trumpet and that the self-made man is part of the American dream. The English remain embarrassed when it comes to demonstrating talent publicly or rising above one's station through commercial success[52]—Thomas Wolsey (1473–1530) remained the "butcher's boy" his entire life, and Margaret Thatcher, the grocer's daughter from Grantham. As John Cleese's character remarks in *A Fish Called Wanda*, "Wanda, do you have any idea what it's like being English? Being so correct all the time, being so stifled by this dread of, of doing the wrong thing . . . you see, Wanda, we'll all terrified of embarrassment."[53]

While a number of Kinks tracks focus on everyday life or become infused with Ray's neurological cynicism, 1966's "Holiday in Waikiki" sparkles with the novelty of the innocent abroad. The track summarizes with humorous chagrin how an English boy's distant admiration of the glamor of American culture is smashed once he actually gets there and is faced with the reality of slick commercialism. "Holiday" was written during the Kinks' last tour of America before their ban but before they reached Hawaii itself. Ray assumed that the place would be spoiled by gimmicks for the tourists, and he was delighted to find beautiful beaches and quiet places.[54]

The lively beat of "Holiday" gallops along, opening with the sounds of the surf (rags in a bucket), syncopated bongo-style percussion, and Hawaiian guitar—the latter one of the first artifices of the song, as Beach Boys fan Dave had to jerry-rig up a "Hawaiian" guitar, lacking an authentic steel one. The reverberating result underscores the melody like an exotic bird that punctuates every line. Nothing is as it seems for the narrator, who, when faced with the cultural shock, repeatedly reminds us that he's just "an English boy on holiday in Waikiki." He's there only because he won a competition rather than on the strength of his own wallet. Disappointment abounds: Coca-Cola takes the place of exotic drinks; the grass skirts on the local hula girls are made of PVC. Even the "Hawaiian island dolls" extolled by Brian Wilson and the Beach Boys in *California Girls* are a sham—as one young lady tells the English boy, her father is Italian, her mum's a Greek, and she's from New York City (undoubtedly sporting a juicy borough accent to boot).

Everything comes with a price tag: he can't swim unless he pays a fee, and the *gen-u-wine* Hawaiian ukulele costs thirty *guineas* not pounds— a comment outing him as not only a tourist but also one out of his social league. Guineas have not been minted since 1814, and they were currency of the wealthy. They are used today only in British shops of bespoke goods where the price tag isn't on display.[55]

Innocence was lost, and worldliness arrived with fame, but it too was met with self-deprecating humor if not embarrassment. In 1972's "Sitting in My Hotel," Ray laments how, as a now-famous star, his friends would laugh to see him—his posh clothes and fancy coiffed hair, "prancing round the room like some outrageous poof." John Dagliesh, who originally played Ray in *Sunny Afternoon*, sings "Sitting in My Hotel Room" with a knowing melancholy, but not without humor, acknowledging with a raised eyebrow the audience's chuckle at the line about prancing about. This self-deprecation doesn't suggest that the Kinks were pessimistic or gloomy about their own fortunes—far from it. The Kinks instead remembered their roots, and while they were admired by fans for being "ordinary guys," they missed *being* ordinary guys. The track exemplifies that aspect of Englishness that adds resignation to one's situation, mixes in humor, and draws together the group and audience in solidarity.

We've seen in this chapter how the music of the Kinks connects various aspects of English culture through humor: music hall meets angry young men meets satire meets the underdog who's making do and muddling through. Their humor could be affectionate or absurd ("Apeman" and "Plastic Man" spring to mind); it and nods and winks at its English audience. At the same time, it simmered with rebellious undertones. Humor was a weapon against authority and created class solidarity that not only goes back to the Kinks' childhood[56] but also has been a part of English expression of working-class antiauthority for at least two centuries. *Sunny Afternoon*'s Wace and Collins exclaim that class boundaries were on the way out, and cultural historians certainly have written about the Kinks' generation as the first to experience freedom from class boundaries that had an unsettling, rather than liberating, effect (see chapter 7). Ray and the Kinks were in the middle of this cultural revolution as observers rather than proactive radicals. Their response, to mock rather than to react, is itself very English. As Kate Fox notes, were they presented with an 1984-type revolution, the English would probably react with "Oh, come off it!" and an eyebrow raised in disbelief that someone thought so highly of himself to initiate a change in society.[57] Self-deprecation, frequently rendered through understatement or irony, resonates strongly with the English, who since industrialization may go on strike and "not-my-job" it to bring things to a halt (working class) and write strongly worded letters (middle class) rather than actually participate in fisticuffs to introduce egalitarianism. That would be, after all, too French.

Thus the Kinks were both the products of and the consumers of English humor, and the band's humor affected their identity as well as created solidarity among their fans. Their increasing Englishness did concern their management, especially after the band deliberately focused on their homeland in their lyrics and sound after their 1965 American ban—even if the early marketing played up the band's eccentricity as a selling point. Were the Kinks actually ever in danger of becoming *too* English to be popular off British shores? Some whimsy traveled fine across the Atlantic, especially after America became enamored of all things Albion when the Beatles showed up in 1964, and the slapstick of Benny Hill and Mr. Bean play well in foreign markets. Surreal humor and satire is slightly more exclusive. For example, Monty Python did all right as a cultish phenomenon originally in the United States, but it wasn't everyone's cup of tea with its surreal blackouts and sketches—even if they deliberately avoided topical scenarios that would either date or make the humor "too British." Similarly, the Kinks' management and record labels had some concerns over certain Kinks songs becoming too "English" to travel well outside of Great Britain, but that Englishness has turned out to be exactly what non-British and especially American fans wanted, and humor plays a part in that. English humor is turned inward and it is exclusive, an us-versus-them, all-class war that subverts social niceties. Contextual footnotes may be needed for the outsider, but even that creates a bond of inclusive solidarity among Anglophile fans. Native fans are equally bound by the Kinks' working-class humor, and they find common ground with their gripes and complaints, if not themselves accustomed to reacting in the same dry manner to life's indignities. The Kinks may well not have satisfied Colin Wilson on the proper use of satire as a weapon of the working class, but their rebellion against authority, dressed in cynical if not self-deprecating humor and performed with catchy choruses, strengthened their fans' devotion, if not identification with the band's defiant individuality.

5

I KNOW WHAT I AM, AND I'M GLAD I'M A MAN

Sexuality and Gender in the Music, Performance, and Image of the Kinks

Sexual intercourse began
In nineteen sixty-three
(which was rather late for me)—
Between the end of the "Chatterley" ban
And the Beatles' first LP.
—Philip Larkin, "Annus Mirabilis," 1967

Sex and rock and roll are familiar bedfellows. Sexual tension, sexual anxiety, and sexual release are implied or frankly stated in rock music, inherited from the open, blunt, and frequently humorous references to sex in rock's musical parents, country-western and rhythm and blues. The expression "rock and roll" itself started life in rhythm and blues as a euphemism for sex, for example, "My Daddy Rocks Me with One Steady Roll" (1922), "Rock It for Me" (1938), and "Rock and Rolling Mama" (1939). DJ Alan Freed rebranded the term to mean dancing and to signify a good time, but adults feared that rock-and-roll music would change their children into lazy, degenerate animals interested in not only sex but also possibly the *wrong kind* of sex; deviation from the social norms, it was feared, would lead to the breakdown of order and traditional institutions of Western society.[1] Authorities since the 1920s have made the effort to protect the nation's youth from lascivious music by enacting bans on particular records if not performers.[2] Performers, too, have gone out of their way to shock the older generation with their actions onstage and off, and to sneak into their music as much sexual euphemism as possible. Many studies of rock music address its sexual character (especially in terms of aggressive masculinity and misogyny, issues of moral depravity, and "shock rock" tactics). More recently, popular music scholarship has examined other sexualities expressed in rock music and by rock artists—feminism in rock, for example, or queerness within rock and roll, especially aspects of sexual ambiguity and expression found in seventies glam and nineties queer rock. In the 1960s, the Mods and the British Invasion also raised questions about sexuality especially in regard to the masculine image. The ambiguous sexuality found in the Mod scene complements similar sexual ambiguity of the Kinks' music and performance. The Kinks not only explored sexual confusion but also validated it with a dash of humor. As Dave Davies ponders the person hogging up the phone in "Party Line," he muses whether she is tall or thin—and "if she's a she at all."

This chapter will first discuss 1963's "sexual revolution" in Great Britain, focusing particularly on its expression in pop music and how the Mod culture of the early sixties reshaped and subverted acceptable gender roles in the late 1950s and early 1960s for men. It will also consider how rock groups straddled a blurry line of distinction that separated masculine from feminine attributes and "camp" from "straight" behavior. Throughout this chapter, where the Kinks fit into this sexual revolution will be considered: as consumers of and influences on Mod culture, their reaction to Mod pursuits, and most especially how they expressed their own thoughts about and experimentation with their own sexual desires through stage performance and in their music.

THE SEXUAL REVOLUTION OF 1963: FEELING RESTRICTED IN CONVENTIONAL CLOTHES

The sexual revolution of the early 1960s was a reaction to the sexual repression that had long boiled under the surface of British society. Youthful trends in music, art, and the celebrity life in general unveiled "the festering mess of sexual ignorance, prejudice, and repression only slightly ameliorated since the nineteenth century."[3] Larkin's pithy poem touches succinctly on several events that toppled the stony walls of British moral conservatism and allowed the start of the "Swinging Sixties." One was the *Lady Chatterley's Lover* obscenity trial in 1960. Originally banned in the UK, the book was widely published and distributed when Penguin Books was cleared of obscenity charges.[4] Another was the development and sale of the Pill (1961), which had a profound impact on the lives of young, unmarried women who were no longer fearful of pregnancy and scandal and gained freedom of their bodies; they could have an education, a career, or simply enjoy life. A third event was the 1963 Profumo scandal wherein a pair of teenagers testified in court about their affairs with various British cabinet officials, raising questions about secrets leaked to the Soviets. Member of Parliament John Profumo resigned, the Conservative government collapsed, and questions were raised about corruption and immorality within the upper classes of British society.[5] Finally, the success and ubiquity of the Beatles on the national scene in Britain in 1963 helped to paved the way for and legitimize other outrageous pop acts that openly challenged social norms.

At least in the media, youth was at the epicenter of this upheaval of social convention in the early 1960s. Shawn Levy describes the changes wrought on theater and film, art, photography, and fashion by such (usually) London-based movers and shakers as actors Terence Stamp, Michael Caine, and Julie Christie; photographer David Bailey; and fashion gurus Mary Quant and Vidal Sassoon.[6] It seemed as if overnight there appeared a "classless" generation of youth in Britain, one with money to spend and parents to shock. Music and youth culture was still controlled and marketed by businessmen who were "middle-aged [and] . . . ran very cautious businesses,"[7] but they saw these changes as a chance to tap into the pockets of these new young consumers.

While it looks revolutionary in retrospect, sexual liberation and youth-driven social outrageousness took a long time to trickle down to the general British public. While the Chatterley trial and the Profumo affair scandalized, changes did not occur overnight as indicated by a contemporary study by Charles Hamblett and Jane Deverson. They published in 1964 *Generation X*, a collection of interviews with young people aged between sixteen and twenty-four from all over Britain.[8]

Extremely popular at the time, the book gives voice to young men who were worried about getting a decent job and finding a place to live, and to young women who were preoccupied with marriage, children, and the domestic arts. Very few actually comment on the current rock-and-roll scene; the ones who do dismiss it as silliness compared to the realities of making a living and supporting a family. Among the celebrated trendsetters and rock stars, too, was found a similar mundane reality: Bill Wyman was an "old man" of twenty-six in 1963 with a wife and children to provide for,[9] but even his younger contemporaries were fairly conservative. Paul McCartney and George Harrison, for example, were not at all happy that their London actress girlfriends did not retire from the business to raise fabulous babies; Ray Davies himself was married with a child when "You Really Got Me" was a top hit in the charts (September 1964). Thus the craziness of the music scene of the early 1960s must be seen against the realities of ordinary life—the sort of ordinary life that Ray Davies longed for in his music and wrote about in his songs: "Suburbia was and would always be a major influence in my writing."[10]

Nevertheless, rock and pop music did provide the means for new youthful expression, especially among the Mods: Mod culture was where music, fashion, art, and theater intersected. The Mods were style conscious, and their musical heroes gave young men the freedom to become absorbed in their own appearance. As Nik Cohn put it, the early sixties became a time for male teens to "dress like a rainbow, grow your hair down your back, make noise, act most any way you felt like, and you didn't automatically get your face pushed in."[11]

THE CARNABETIAN ARMY MARCHES ON

The Mods' interest in style changed completely how men shopped in the UK.[12] It wasn't simply outlandish clothing that distinguished them but rather their meticulous attention to detail; much of what they wore was inspired by European fashions and fostered by an interest in grooming and fashion as a means of masculine self-expression.[13] Prior to the Mods, a boy who paid close attention to his appearance might be mocked as a cissy—code speak for homosexual at a time when homosexuality was illegal in Britain.[14] Young Mods also gave careful attention to their posture, their stance, and how they walked, gestured, and danced.

Mods skated the line between masculine and feminine appearance, but they were absolutely masculine. Again Cohn notes, "Mod was strictly a male world . . . their girls trailing forgotten behind them, and they'd dance all by themselves, sunk deep in their narcissistic world . . . if there was ever a mirror in the club, there'd be a frantic rush to get in front of it and everyone would pose, pout, ponce about, and they'd get high on themselves."[15] Mod was an expression of *decadence*, not *deviance*, and they accomplished this by competing with their peers and shocking adults by crossing the sexual line in public through dress and behavior—whether it was camp, aggressive masculinity, or some flavor of a (usually European fashion) kink in the shape of zips, rubber, or PVC plastic. Once the initial shock was past, familiarity rendered the taboo breaker as harmless if such things were not made mainstream.

Teenaged Mod boys became well versed in "matters of the cloth"—cut, tailoring, and drape—and would turn their noses up at cheaply made clothes and style knock-offs; their disposable income went into their wardrobe and into the records and music that was associated with their scene.[16] And even with the risks of thumping from peers and disapproval from parents, being a Mod turned out actually to be a *safe* way for a teenaged boy to rebel. In his colorful memoir of growing up in sixties Britain, middle-class Alan Clayson wholeheartedly embraced the Mod scene, wearing taunts about his hair and clothes as a hard-earned badge of honor as Mod style filtered out of London. He argues that the long hair was controversial, but parents might actually chip in for the Vespa as long as one didn't fight with leather-clad boys or take amphetamines called, at the time, "Purple Hearts"—even the local vicar might praise a young man for looking smart and well turned out. So despite a "dress sense in constant flux," even as early as 1962 the Mods were associated with "clean pseudo-suavity."[17]

Shopkeepers noticed this trend and took advantage of it. One key figure was former salesclerk-turned-boutique entrepreneur John Stephenson.[18] Stephenson opened up a little shop in then-unfashionable Carnaby Street and turned the man's shopping experience into an "event" with elaborate shop window displays and current music. He called all of his clientele "sir" and made them feel special about buying clothes and decking themselves out.[19] Cohn credits Stephenson with changing how male London shopped.[20] Initially, Stephenson's clientele were the theater crowd, but when Cliff Richard started to buy from his shop in the late 1950s, other pop stars followed. The real breakthrough in terms of fulfilling Stephenson's goal of catering to "masculine men" came in 1962 when then-current heavyweight champion Billy Walker not only started buying from Stephenson but also posed in drag for shop-window displays. There was no looking back once the 1962 Pierre Cardin–besuited Beatles hove into view. Says Cohn, "The teenage boom [was] a cult that turned Carnaby Street from a backwater into a massive worldwide madness."[21]

Homosexuality was still illegal in the UK in 1963, but the Mods and these musical pop stars aided the transition from camp to cool fashions for men because of the crossroads between the pop music and film world, the bohemians and the Mod lifestyle, and the gay subculture in London. Nevertheless, a man with long hair and stylish (if not women's) clothing challenged the code of behavior acceptable for heterosexual men in conservative British society.[22] Pop-star culture didn't make it suddenly safe to declare alternate and gender-bending sexualities publically. Many of the music impresarios of this era were gay (e.g., Larry Parnes and Brian Epstein), but even their protégés, who benefitted from their image-making prowess, might turn on them. It was dangerous to be outed as homosexual—electronic music genius Joe Meeks found his reputation destroyed. He was persecuted when he was outed, and he ended up committing suicide. The Kinks addressed this fear and the extremes to which some men might go in 1978's "Out of the Wardrobe." The hero, Dick, is a burly, hairy, strapping six-footer, anyone's idea of a manly man. But, according to the verse, in 1965, Dick marries Betty Lou because back then "you had to be butch to survive."

WERE THE KINKS MODS?

Popular and scholarly histories of the period usually include the Kinks when describing the Mod scene. Musically, the Kinks' early bluesy sound and "lazy vocals" gave them Mod cred, both found, for example, on 1964's "I Gotta Move" (where the guitar's frenetic riff fails to energize the lazy vocals) and "Sittin' on My Sofa." The latter track especially exemplifies Modish ennui—the Kinks can't even summon the energy to go to the club and pose like the rest of their peers; they're prone on the couch, barely able to sip at their sodas. Another example is the hypnotic "Tired of Waiting for You" (1965). Ray sings that he's won the girl he so desired, but now that she's keeping him waiting, he can't be bothered. As a typical Mod ("directionless" as J. E. Perone notes[23]), Ray shrugs off the situation: "It's your life, and you can do what you want." He asks her in his almost-expressionless, even-toned vocal, "What can I do?" He doesn't sound particularly put out about her absence, but instead he's annoyed that she's interfering with his schedule as he begs her not to keep him waiting. Only then do the vocals grow insistent, underscored by urgent drum rolls and Bo Diddley-esque percussive guitar riffs, before trailing off into a disinterested moan as the song ends.

As far as their appearance went, the very name of the Kinks evoked shocking sexuality. The name was appropriate, as the *Oxford English Dictionary* defines a "kink" in the early 1960s not necessarily as a sexual deviant but as someone obsessed over his clothes. But unlike the Mods who looked toward Europe for their fashion trends, the Kinks' look was decidedly English initially, in their original stage uniform of matching hunting jackets, frilly shirts, and riding boots.[24] Once they shed the Edwardian look, Dave Davies especially indulged in both theatrical and women's clothes, makeup, and lacquered coifs; he had a large gay following in the band's early days and enjoyed dressing as a woman in public to shock and to gain attention.[25]

While the Kinks may have looked and sounded the part, their *attitude* toward the Mod obsession with appearance and fashion was another story. Many of the Mods were art-school alumni too, but Ray was never particularly fashion conscious or interested in standing around posing. According to the story, his inspiration for 1966's "Dedicated Follower of Fashion" resulted when a hipster mocked Ray's plain clothes at a party. Ray responded by throwing a punch and writing a number-one single with a catchy chorus. Ray's Dedicated Follower shows very little interest in girls and cares only about going to all of the right shops and being seen in all of the right places—Regent and Carnaby streets, and Leicester Square. He changes his clothes as frequently as he pulls the pages off the calendar, one week in polka dots and the next week in stripes. Contrary to what the scholars and memoirs might say about a Mod's masculinity, Ray casts some doubts on it—his Follower isn't happy unless he's pulled his "frilly nylon panties *right up tight.*" Ray's voice rises and tightens with the vocal line to suggest the Follower is packing himself into garments meant for a smaller, if not female, frame. Perhaps the clincher, as it were, is Ray's parting shot that the Follower is "as fickle as can be" sung in a camp falsetto before jumping back down to his carnival-barker pitch as the final chords bring the song to a crashing halt.[26]

The song is less of a mockery of the Follower's sexual orientation than it is of Ray's criticism of the Follower's empty-headed slavishness to fashion and the pursuit of the superficial. Mocking the desire for material gratification is a common theme in a number of Kinks songs, whether to do with the trappings of material wealth ("Mr. Pleasant" or "Most Unusual Residence for Sale") or pathetically notching up the bedposts as does the subject of 1966's "Dandy."[27] "Dandy" conjures up another Mod clotheshorse. Instead of his wardrobe, however, the track focuses on the dandy's sexual conquests: he embodies the type of Mod whom Cohn claims views girls only as additional accessories to his outfit. Stan Hawkins's interpretation of the song focuses in part on Ray's "vocal straining" and increasing emotional tension as he repeats "You're all right!" higher and higher toward the end of the song—less an affirmation of camaraderie and more increasingly sarcastic commentary.[28] Hawkins notes also the vocal tone taken by Ray reflects a more lower-class image than the pseudo-social climbing affected by the Mods—and here Ray invokes a centuries-old British tradition of social snobbery that can be found as far as Chaucer and Shakespeare's comedies. In addition, as Mods were démodé by 1966, the "Dandy" is additionally mocked for clinging to his youth and being out of touch with the very "fads and trends" followed so religiously in "Dedicated."[29] Indeed, it's the materialism and not the choice of fashion mocked by the Kinks: again, in "Out of the Wardrobe," Dick likes to dress in women's clothes because he feels like a princess and less restricted than he would in conventional togs. He's *not* a dandy, emphasizes Ray, nor a "common-place closet queen"; Dick is living out a fantasy and has no regrets once the secret's out. Freedom of expression is celebrated; pursuit of selfish gain is not.

WELL, I'M NOT THE WORLD'S MOST MASCULINE MAN: SEXUAL AMBIGUITY AND THE KINKS

So the Kinks mocked the Mods' vacuity and questioned their sexuality, but what of the Kinks' own sexual imagery? They had the longest hair of all the current bands; on landing at the John F. Kennedy Airport in New York in 1965, Ray was asked, "Are you a Beatle, or a girl?" His recalled response varies in the sources from, "I'm a girl, and so's my brother" and, "No, I'm a queer." Whichever it was, it landed the band in a holding cell for a few hours, nearly deported from America before even clearing customs.[30] It was no easier back home: long hair was the most obvious indicator of rebellion against gender norms and could label the wearer as being homosexual; as Clayson puts it, "Long hair [was] a red rag to adults."[31] He adds that *long* hair wasn't the problem necessarily but rather the painstakingly coiffured hairstyles of Mod and beat boys was objectionable because it marked them as "bardic beatles [*sic*] who believe that masses of woolly, straggly hair are a sign of intellectualism."[32] It was especially perilous in the provinces; a touring band relaxing over darts in a pub might hear, "Get a load of that cissy heading for the gents—wrong one, mate!"[33] Clayson adds that boys in the 1960s had to fight every literal inch of the way; he describes boys who had their hair shorn by irate teachers and how a local bruiser defended himself in court after beating up a man he saw in the street by stating, "Well, he had long hair, didn't he?"[34]

It wasn't only the Kinks' appearance that distinguished them. As Gildart notes, the Kinks in particular were set apart from contemporary bands by their "nuanced reading of gender" in their music,[35] unlike the more simplistic and misogynistic viewpoints adopted by their peers such as the Rolling Stones—or even the Beatles ("You Can't Do That" and "Run for Your Life").[36] What gave the Kinks their distinctive sexual ambiguity was that they were all over the map with the signals they gave off. On the one hand, they *were* aggressively sexy on stage at the behest of their image consultant, Hal Carter. Dave took to this readily, flinging himself onto his knees to slide toward the edge of the stage, legs splayed hoping that the seams of his trousers would split, a similar stunt practiced by P. J. Proby.[37] Even Ray took to riling up the Kinks' screaming teenaged fans with saucy smiles and suggestive pouts and gestures. Footage of early Kinks performances found on YouTube show him wrapped suggestively around the microphone stand when not pursing his lips or arching a come-hither eyebrow at the teenyboppers.

Conversely, the Kinks were also well known early on for their "obsession with homosexuality" and camp; both Davieses recall how they teased auditioning drummer Mick Avory, speaking to him in girlish voices, cuddling one another, and acting with limp wrists. Avory, dressed neatly in his Boy Scout uniform, with a fresh haircut to impress, noted he wasn't sure if he wanted to join a "group of queers."[38] On stage, Ray would shake a limp wrist and strike poses at his shrieking female audience. While commonly associated with homosexuality,[39] campy behavior could actually underscore aggressive masculine sexuality. "Camp" was "flamboyant" or "eccentric" and a safe means to be gay without being prosecuted or vilified for being homosexual across the social classes. Similarly, exaggerated, feminine gestures and attention to attire was associated with the genteel class of theater actors and with "delicate" behavior associated with the middle class,[40] such as Kinks managers Robert Wace and Grenville Collins. The Kinks certainly camped it up on stage amid the sexual aggression of their early days, and they found campy behavior a satisfying way to aggravate those in authority, especially in conservative America.[41] For example, the band infuriated a television director who had wanted an unwell Ray to perform a dance step during his performance—instead the camera swung around to greet Ray and Mick Avory dancing cheek to cheek.[42] When in Seattle, Ray and his wife were threatened by a restaurant owner for holding hands, so the rest of the band showed their solidarity by offering full-on, male-on-male deep kissing.[43] Such behavior continues as a part of the Kinks' image; a highlight of *Sunny Afternoon* sees a fictional scruffy Dave wearing men's boots and a woman's sparkly pink dress, swinging across the stage from a chandelier (and he remarks later that the girl he'd been with (and lost track of) was last seen wearing his underpants). Thus a considerable number of antics perpetrated by the Kinks were meant for laughs or to shock adults as well as their peers—typical teenaged behavior expressed by performers who themselves were barely out of their teens. Such antics were understood and appreciated by their teenaged fans, themselves struggling with their own hormones and who could identify with the sexual confusion and experimentation acted out by their more famous peers.

Even the more aggressively masculine bands displayed feminine characteristics in their looks if not behavior without jeopardizing their masculinity. Displays of feminine and queer characteristics were pleasing to fans of both sexes as well, especially if such behavior underscored the performer's masculinity. For example, P. J. Proby sent his female audience into a swooning frenzy every night performing his act as a cross between Elvis and "some impossible drag-queen."[44] His preferred costume was a blue velvet suit, hair tied in a bow, and buckled shoes, and he would flutter his eyelashes and mince about with one hand on his hip—but he got away with it because of his strong, masculine voice and absolute self-confidence as a performer. Proby himself claimed that he got all of his moves by studying the various girls in his audience.[45] Another example is the Rolling Stones. Andrew Loog Oldham, their manager, wore fashionable clothes and makeup. Brian Jones was the most Mod of the group, where Mick Jagger was aggressively masculine and overtly sexual on stage to the point of pantomime (which simultaneously made him popular with both the girls who wanted a "bad boy" and with homosexual fans).[46] Cohn stresses that Jones was not gay but that he "did the whole feminine thing . . . rush to the front of the stage and make to jump off, flouncing and flitting like a gymslip schoolgirl."[47] Similarly, the Who's clothing and attitude fit the Mod bill, and Pete Townshend's lyrics addressed issues on confusion in gender identity: "I'm a Boy" is the lament of a young boy who wants to be as rough and tumble as his playmates, playing cricket on the green, riding his bike, and getting bumps and bruises, but his mother dresses him up as a girl, makes him wear makeup and curls, and even takes his male name away from him.

Finally, there are the Beatles—people in 2016 seem to forget how feminine the Beatles appeared when they came onto the scene in 1962.[48] Their earlier years on stage were as tough, leather-clad, smoking-and-drinking Teddy Boys,[49] but part of their success after Brian Epstein's repackaging of them was their Cardin suits, high-heeled Cuban boots, and their long, grease-free hair. While they were marketed as the perfect boyfriends, they also appealed to the girls by *singing* like girls—shaking their hair to emphasize its length and jumping octaves suddenly to falsettos in songs such as "She Loves You" and "I Want to Hold Your Hand" to the frenzied response of their female audience. The Beatles' peers on tour laughed at them the first time they heard

"She Loves You,"[50] but the Fabs subsequently had the last laugh as the female audience would go crazy in response to the chorus. They were also kept strangely innocent of sexual attraction to girls in their films; plenty of gay banter abounds (especially in *A Hard Day's Night*),[51] but despite chasing after school- and showgirls over the course of that film (without actually catching any of them), they remain aloof from the girls who want a piece of them. They remain actually unattached for their fans' fantasies—an elaborate subplot featuring Paul McCartney's budding romance with a young woman was excised from *A Hard Day's Night*,[52] and the boys remain puzzled by the attentions of Ahme in the film *Help!*

The Kinks' feminine aspects take a different tack than those found in these other bands. Rather than external accoutrements, the Kinks tended to internalize certain feminine characteristics, expressed as a need for nurturing and security. For example, Dave worked through any feelings of confusion with his sexuality through hands-on experimentation, and he has been open about his relationships with both men and women. Ray, on the other hand, expressed the complexities of his feelings more cerebrally through his music. One example of an expression of insecurity in terms of masculine roles can be found in 1967's "David Watts." The song's narrator is a schoolboy who compares himself to the school champion. David Watts can do no wrong academically or athletically: he scores top marks on all of his exams; he wins all of the prizes at sport. The narrator desperately wishes he could have all the things that his hero has got, especially as Watts's achievements result in all the girls wanting him. The hell of it is, of course, that despite the female attention, Watts isn't interested "for he is a pure and noble breed." Up until this line, the song has been building in a desperate frenzy of envy as the narrator monotonously chants Watts's accomplishments and accolades until the scene shifts to the narrator lying awake at night. Here the vocals and melodic line rise and grow more desperate. At the mention that Watts refuses the attention of all of the girls, however, the instrumentation drops back to a simple, pulsing, two-note bass line as the vocal line repeats, "Wish I could *be* like," underscored by a chorus of "wishes, wishes, wishes."

David Watts was a real person, and stories of his relationship with the Kinks are well known to fans.[53] The masculine public school hero of the song was in real life an ostensibly upright, respectable, upper-middle-class music promoter who counted among his friends a number of authority figures. Ray comments that Watts was a retired military man who had a deep and masculine voice and wore conservative clothing. It was drummer Mick Avory who pointed out, perhaps tongue in cheek, that Watts was wearing white socks, sartorial code for being homosexual.[54] In his memoir, Dave notes subversion of authority figures at Watts's house—fears that the police were raiding the premises turned out to be unfounded, as the policemen knocking at the door were friends of Watts who in turn joined in the romping and camp at the party.[55] Indeed, behind closed doors, Watts transformed from a stiff and proper British gentleman to someone who was a "delightfully funny, witty, flagrantly eccentric and flamboyant homosexual."[56] Dave wondered if perhaps Watts was so enamored of him (and the Kinks) because of the "[queer] signals he heard in our music,"[57] as Ray "tended to write lyrics that suggested at the very minimum some interest in the exploration of male-male couplings."[58] Dave himself was pursued by Watts, but despite his own sexual versatility, even he became intimidated by Watts's ardor.[59]

The real David Watts apparently had no interest in women but rather loved and admired the beauty and youth of boys and saw his own former youth and good looks embodied in young men. This aspect of Watts's personality appealed to Ray; he noted that just because someone prefers the company of men, it doesn't mean he is a homosexual.[60] The friendship established between Watts and the Kinks was based on strictly emotional ground relieved of rigid male social expectations. Surely this must have been refreshing to Ray considering the feelings he expressed in 1965's controversial "See My Friends."

The hypnotic instrumentation of this musically innovative track was influenced by the Kinks' tour in India, when Ray heard the early morning chants of people at work down by the edges of the river. He found the droning melodies peaceful and meditative, and he attempted to re-create the same sound in the studio on this track. The harmonics and overtones were fed back through the amplifier to become the first Eastern-influenced rock music in the West.[61] The lyrics were no less alien than the strange accompaniment. The track was called originally "See My Friend," but this was revised to "Friends" at the insistence of the record company. "Friend" was apparently an implicit code word for "homosexual," and much to Ray's annoyance, the record company feared that the combination of the title and the lyrics would prove too controversial for radio play. Ray alternates between the word "friend" and "friends" throughout the song, perhaps on purpose—and the track's meaning, as with many other Kinks songs, is fraught with ambiguity.[62]

Certainly the song is about loneliness and the pain of rejection; as such, it could be interpreted as another song of teen angst. The melodic line starts off calmly as Ray sings of his friends: they are introduced in the opening verse as "playing across the river." He then relates the departure of "she"—she is gone, and he's been left alone. As he sings of his loss, his voice rises in pain and anguish. Calm returns as he again points out that there's no one left except his friends across the river. "She," we learn, has not only left him but also gone *across the river*, and he wishes he'd gone across with her. The vocals soar as the lament grows: Ray mourns because of the separation, if not isolation, and that there is no one else left for him to love *except*—and here the guitar here changes to a positive, heavy riff—those same friends across the river. With this declaration, the song settles into its peaceful drone again as the verse describing the friends playing across the river is repeated, and the song fades out on a wandering, Eastern-flavored melodic line.

Interpretation of this song ranges the gamut from Ray's confession of homosexual longings to simply a longing for love—of any kind, from any one, as fulfillment of a basic, human need. The expression of the latter by a man in mid-1960s British culture, however, would be perceived as something certainly bent: no real man is going to confess up to such a feminine need as to be loved. When the Kinks sang "I Need You" in 1965, for example, it was to the accompaniment of power chords; testosterone demanded that the woman in the song satisfy his very masculine sexual needs. Ray initially added fuel to the fire regarding "See My Friends," first claiming the song was about homosexuality in contemporary interviews but even then remained deliberately ambiguous.[63] Initial reviews of the song mentioned nothing about homosexual connotations, which allegedly annoyed him. In subsequent interviews at the song's release Ray deliberately discussed homosexuality, sexual confusion, and how the song could be "about anybody" who was searching for love and comfort. Years later, he commented in *X-Ray* that the song isn't *necessarily* about "sounding gay" or a gay relationship—his plaintive, nasally vocals, he claims, were an attempt to sound like Hank Williams,[64] and he has complained that too many people have been searching for meaning and subtext that simply aren't there.

Despite Ray's calculated and deliberate attempts to cast a sexually ambiguous net over the meaning of the song, he has admitted that the track does reflect his own feelings as "a youth who is not sure of his sexuality."[65] In 1965 he was laying bait in the press about the song's "gay overtones"; but writing in 1996, he reflected, "I just believe that when you need comfort, when you are in despair, any arms are welcome. It doesn't matter what sex they belong to. People place so much emphasis on gender. Love is love."[66] The song would have struck a chord in 1965 familiar to an anxious teen struggling with his or her own sense of identity—sexual or not. It's humanly universal to feel alone and lost at times, unable, due to peer pressure, to express one's feelings. Such anxiety is going to be further amplified by social and cultural indicators in consumer goods and popular media aimed at teenagers, especially in an era where sexual signposts were constantly changing and the means to rebel and shock one's parents were, more than ever, expressed through sexual behavior. The Kinks themselves were not only exposed to the same pop culture as these teens but also caught up amid its creation. Everything they did as pop stars would be put under a microscope; their lives and antics were fair game for the very trade papers that they were consuming. Whereas other teens could keep a diary about their innermost feelings and sense of confusion, Ray's reflection and inner turmoil ended up on vinyl records. "See My Friends" could certainly be (and certainly was) interpreted by listeners as a song about sexual identity, but it is very easily a song about being an outsider, feeling alone and unloved, and being stuck on the other side of some uncrossable boundary (i.e., the metaphorical river in the song). It is not a far cry from the anguished teen who exclaims, "No one understands me!" or "I'm not like everybody else!" M. Geldart notes too that the use of Indian rhythms and cadence in the song complements the sense of "outsider" and sense of "otherness,"[67] which are, in fact, universal anxieties of teenagers.

Ray has since argued that the song could be about anybody who's ever felt an outsider or has suffered the pain of loneliness, but it is noteworthy that he casts himself here in a submissive, feminine role, desiring domesticity, protection, and comfort. In that respect "Lola" is *the* significant song about the feminine need for affection and behavior to appear in the Kinks' repertoire. It was, Ray noted, simply a love song, and it represents all of his own sexual ambiguities as a "humorous shaggy-dog story."[68] "Lola" was released in 1972, a few years after the laws against homosexuality in Britain had been repealed and when glam, known for its androgyny, was taking off in the country. Jon Savage argues that Ray presented in "Lola" the themes that David Bowie and others would make a career out of subsequently in the 1970s.[69]

Kinks fans are well familiar with "Lola," and it's become enough a part of general popular consciousness to be a common clue in American crossword puzzles.[70] Most people know "Lola" on its own partly because it put the Kinks into the top ten and partly because it's a popular sing-along at Kinks and Ray shows (not to mention Al Yankovic's "Yoda" parody, a favorite of *Star Wars* fan Dave). The song's context within its concept album *Lola versus Powerman and the Moneygoround, Part One*, however, is often overlooked; as seen in chapter 3, *Lola* was Ray's response to the stress of the early days of the band, contracts and litigation, and the pressures of fame. At about the time *Lola* itself was made, Ray was having personal troubles that were stressing him out as well as the band's struggles, and he was experiencing anew the problems of fame and a desire for privacy and anonymity.

The story behind Lola is complicated enough to be the subject of "a glossy paperback,"[71] and her real-life identity is as mysterious as the meaning of the song itself—deliberately so. Johnny Rogan quotes Ray as saying the real Lola was a close friend and that he refused to divulge Lola's identity or actual sex.[72] Kinks lore muses on Lola's identity— perhaps she was Candy Darling, whom Ray once dated,[73] or the transvestite whom Robert Wace once pulled in a Soho bar, and so forth. More important is what her character represents in the song and on the album. Most tracks on *Lola* are about being ripped off, exploited, and betrayed by men—men that are unfeeling, unemotional, and only interested in the quick buck that the band can provide as pop stars. The album's eponymous track, on the other hand, describes the least judgmental and most comforting person whom Ray encountered on his journey through the music industry.

As discussed in chapter 3, "Top of the Pops" describes the push-me-pull-you effects of a young pop star by the image makers, promoters, and producers who want to create a sellable product. "The Moneygoround" illustrates the complexities of the contracts and the pressures put on the group to produce. Ray recalls in his 2014 memoir, *Americana*, how he was changed from "just an ordinary bloke" who had had his "innocence overwhelmed by corrupt power, money, greed, [and] loss of identity,"[74] and this bitterness is well expressed throughout the *Lola* project itself—with the exception of the eponymous track. The narrator loses his sexual innocence to Lola, but this loss is a positive metamorphosis, as Lola changes him from a boy to a man.

The track comes very much to terms with the possibility *and* acceptance of possessing masculine and feminine qualities within one person. The song's famous line—"I know what I am, and I'm glad I'm a man, and so is Lola"—is ambiguous, and its meaning is the subject of heated debate among Kinks fans. Nonjudgmental and affectionate, "Lola" is an example of the narrator's desire for nurturing and comfort. Lola is gentle, kind, and sympathetic—she knows what she is, she is confident, and she knows the narrator is an uncertain, naïve boy, but she's going to lead him on his way to manhood. The narrator meets Lola in "Old Soho," giddy with excitement to be in this sleazy, scary, and exciting world for the first time, and there he finds this person who takes him as he is and awakens him sexually. In fact, after the climax of the song, when the music itself swells to great intensity and intense revelation of his joy and comfort, as the singer comes back to down to himself, the music is calmer. The vocals reflect his contentment—he also knows the truth now and has been made a man, but the specifics of how, why, and by whom are irrelevant. Lola has gently and kindly made a man out of him, and he thinks of her fondly, not with resentment or embarrassment. She has given him the affection he needs, she's reaffirmed his masculinity, and she has done so in a way that requires no pressure on him to perform. She may be mysterious, but her true persona is a private matter, and the lesson learned by the narrator in the song is that there still exists nonjudgmental love and acceptance in a "crazy, mixed up shook up world." The upshot of the song too is that the character gives the narrator confidence, and so did the single to the Kinks: Ray remarked that it was a "lifesaving" track for the group and propelled them back into the top ten on the singles charts.[75]

CONCLUSION

There are a number of provocative aspects within the music of the Kinks, especially as shaped by Ray Davies's songwriting as he explored themes of "the ambiguities of how one arrives at one's self-identity."[76] The Kinks, not as popular or scrutinized as the Beatles or the Rolling Stones when it comes to shock rock, cultural innovation, or subverting conventional mores (and morality) between the generations, were still a part of the Mod scene and subsequent challenges in youth-led entertainment.

It is a strange juxtaposition to look at these songs and then to read *X-Ray*—where Ray can speak quite cruelly of women and can be vulgar in places about sex and promiscuity in the rock star's life. There is, arguably, a sense of detachment from the author and these descriptions—he makes it clear in the book that he says many of these cruel things to get a reaction from another character (who is, due to the complexities of narration in *X-Ray*, a younger version of himself). There persists throughout, however, an underlying desire and need for affection, nurturing, and comfort. If Ray or the Kinks are simply out to shock, perhaps such strange musings could be designed to get a reaction—from himself, fans, and interviewers. Ray's own intelligence belies that he's playing games, and he wants people to know that he's playing games. As Rogan noted with the success of "Lola," the commercial turnaround restored Ray's confidence in that people were listening to his work, even if they were bewildered by what it meant.[77]

The Kinks certainly reflected social challenges to accepted norms of sexuality in their clothing, appearance, and performance from their early days of whips and leather to their pink hunting jackets (and Dave Davies's mid-1960s briefly lived modeling career) and lazy vocals; but they lacked the same attitude toward appearance and consumer consumption pursued by the Mods. In Ray's lyrics, one finds a mockery of the external feminine trapping of the masculine Mod scene, as he pokes fun at the "Carnabetian Army" in "Dedicated Follower of Fashion." Instead, the sexual themes of the music are internalized and feminine— emotions, feelings, and desires outside the norms expected of 1960s British heterosexual men, and certainly ones not expressed without fear of reprisal. By casting his lyrics with deliberately obscure and ambiguous language, Ray slyly expresses his need for feminine security and longing for domestic comfort. A complex personality, Ray seems to have sought such comfort from childhood onward in whatever form—from female relatives to girls at school and groupies of all flavors—anyone who is gentle and maternal. Thus he casts his narrators in submissive, female roles, seeking comfort and protection while remaining clearly masculine.

6

HERE COMES MR. FLASH

Anti-Utopia, Politics, and Social Consciousness

If you must send a message, send a telegram.[1]

In September 2014, there was a conference panel in Cork, Ireland, that looked at the Kinks' political commentary (specifically in regard to the band's image of "English character" at home and abroad) in the 1960s, 1970s, and 1980s. One conclusion reached among the participants was that the Kinks were less reactionaries than they were observers on the human political condition. Ray Davies has been ambiguous politically from one end of his professional career to the other:

> 1966: "I hope England doesn't change," [Ray Davies] told [Bob Dawbarn]. . . . "I hope we don't get swallowed up by America and Europe. I'm really proud of being British. . . . I don't care if a bloke votes Labour or Conservative as long as he appreciates what we've got here. . . . I want to keep writing very English songs."[2]
>
> 2012: "Davies's politics were always difficult to pin down. 'Sunny Afternoon' can be read as an ungracious moan about the progressive fiscal policies of the Wilson government, but it's executed with more charm and ironic distance than The Beatles' whining 'Taxman.' Sometimes, on '20th Century Man' for example, he sounds like a free-market libertarian . . . but the sublimely mournful 'Dead End Street' is, if anything, a song of the left."[3]

He quietly supports others without committing himself: for example, Ray's daughter Natalie remains a force of nature in the ongoing fracking controversy in Great Britain.[4] It's understood that Ray supports her and that he's against the destruction of the environment, but he remains enigmatic from committing one way or another to engaging in any sort of activism. Such coy behavior frustrates Kinks and Ray fans who *know*—or *think* they know—their hero's mind.

During the discussion session that followed that conference panel, one audience member insisted that the Kinks *did* have a political agenda and that there was *no way* that Ray is now *not* a member of the UK Independence Party (UKIP), whose stance on traditional English values and whose harsh, anti-immigration policy make most Tories look like Ken Kesey's Merry Pranksters. His reasoning? Ray has spent his entire musical career singing the praises of the English way of life, of empire, and of preserving "the old ways, for me and for you/what more can we do?" Surely someone with this back catalog must be xenophobically conservative.

The Kinks do sing about Englishness, about empire, and about preserving the old ways, and Ray did appear in Danny Boyle's set piece "A Day in the Life of Britain" at the closing of the 2012 London Olympics. The Kinks may have become identified with preserving "English ways" with so many of their works, but Ray also introduces "Waterloo Sunset" as a song for all of Britain, and he's made it clear over the years that that includes *all* who come to her, and wish to identify with her. Both Ray and Dave Davies have shown lifelong solidarity to their half–West African niece (as Dave notes, the first black kid on their street), and *Come Dancing*'s plot includes a strong theme of antiracism in sister Julie's choice of Jamaican beau. This is hardly the stuff of a UKIPer's dreams.

This chapter focuses on the Kinks and their political commentary during the 1970s. First discussed generally is the political, social, and economic context of 1970s Britain (and the response of pop culture), followed by the Kinks' *Preservation* albums as a case study. Finally, the chapter compares the Kinks' political works and the role of the punks in late seventies Britain. Rather than having an influence as political activists in the way that artists such as the Clash, U2, or Sting would ultimately have, the Kinks' political commentary remained instead observational and effected a strong response on themes of identity—that of the individual and defiance of authority on the one hand ("I'm Not Like Everybody Else") and a sense of a collective British, or English, identity on the other.

WERE THE KINKS A "POLITICAL BAND"?

Ray Davies and the Kinks had a sharp sense of humor and diminished those in authority and those with pretensions of social climbing. Issues related to class relations and economic woes appear across the body of their work; 1966's "Dead End Street," for example, looks at the frustration of being locked into an inescapable cycle of poverty, so deeply in debt that even the £10 Pommie scheme is unobtainable.[5] But even in despair the track reveals that there was hope and awareness: the traditional Sunday roast is replaced by bread and honey, but this British ritual is still practiced. The shouted "Dead end!" chorus as Ray recites a litany of poverty, anonymity, and the vicissitudes of dead-end life sounds almost like a football chant; there's solidarity even in poverty. Ray has remarked that the song's cheerful Dixieland brass sound and its themes of hard times and financial depression reflect that, despite the so-called social revolution and classless society, change hadn't really happened for the working class. He notes, "I think [the track] exemplified a period in England where people were thinking, hang on a minute, what's really happening here?"[6] Dave felt that "Dead End Street" was the inspiration for the Clash's "London Calling" and noted that the song "was the epitome of what the Kinks were all about . . . character, pathos, yet containing an underlying sense of hope."[7]

Most of the Kinks' overt political criticism, however, is concentrated in their seventies and early eighties output. During this time, they produced several dark tracks. For example, "Acute Schizophrenia Paranoia Blues" off *Muswell Hillbillies*, the *Preservation* trilogy, and Dave's vicious "Dear Margaret" off 1988's *UK Jive*, works that reflect the grimness and pessimism that infused a part of British culture in the seventies and early eighties. Nineteen seventies Britain itself is a complicated decade to define.[8] Memory plays havoc with the facts. Depending on the source, Britain in the seventies was an economic and political disaster headed toward a complete and utter breakdown of the social order by anarchic skinheads and a military coup not unlike Pinochet's Chile in

1973, or it was a warm and magical time of the best of *Doctor Who*, space hoppers, and glam and disco on *Top of the Pops*.[9]

Britain in the 1970s endured inept politics (although recently the subject of reevaluation in academic writing, the Heath government is considered by popular historians to be one of the worst in Britain's history),[10] endless strikes, and a genuine fear that England would suffer if not a complete breakdown in order but collapse to become a third-world military dictatorship. A vocal minority of talking heads predicted the end of democracy and the beginning of a totalitarian state in Britain before the end of the decade. As the 1970s made the general public more aware of Britain's decline culturally, people eagerly looked backward—"heritage escapism" thrived in the form of museum collections (e.g., one of the most successful exhibitions in the mid-1970s was the Victoria & Albert Museum's 1974 exhibition "Destruction of a Country House").[11] Also popular were "old-fashioned" sitcoms and drama on television such as *The Good Life*, *Dad's Army*, and *All Creatures Great and Small*; bright, perky pop music filled the charts and offered relief from the gloomy headlines, politics, and power cuts.[12]

THIS IS MY STREET: HISTORICAL CONTEXT FOR PESSIMISM AND *PRESERVATION*

In the seventies and eighties, some members of Parliament (MPs) claimed that Britain was actually a wealthy nation even if it was poorly managed and a tremendous gap existed between rich and poor. Several of these same MPs had absolutely no idea what true poverty meant as they were themselves isolated from the other strata of society.[13] There had been a rise in prosperity—very slowly—from the fifties, but this was also a time of social blindness with a glossing over of widespread poverty and hard times. Britain's economy suffered in the seventies due to poor investments, the oil crisis, and endless strikes and work stoppages. The years from 1967 through to Margaret Thatcher's tenure as prime minister (1979–1990) saw Britain in perpetual economic crisis with a decline in fortune and quality of life—in the mid-1970s the inflation rate in Britain was over 20 percent.[14] The crisis in society affected only some strata of the society; to many, the ages of closures, redundancies, and bankruptcies was an age that also brought new sources of wealth. The media showed, in the papers and on television, the desperate poverty and hopelessness among Britons, but such images only served to create a sense of detachment. Political or economic crises had no real meaning to those Britons outside the danger zone, and televised poverty or strife depersonalized it for many. Indeed, for a number of current writers who were children in the 1970s, the strikes were adventurous, make-do times or simply inconvenient in a way quite similar to the memories of those who'd lived during the war as children. According to these nostalgic memoirs of the 1970s, a blackout might only mean no *Doctor Who* or *Top of the Pops* that week. This is not to dismiss or belittle the true hardships that were indeed felt in certain areas and communities of Britain—race riots, IRA terror bombings, and poverty on the estates. But that shabbiness of Britain—"everything was brown" as my spouse recalls, or as seen in the grittiness of the 1970s British television drama *The Sweeney*—combined with the nation's persistent heritage nostalgia to create a different picture of 1970s Britain that sits on the shelves side by side with academic studies that analyze objectively this period.

Recent scholarship looks to reconcile the dichotomy one finds when considering the 1970s along cultural issues and attitudes. Popular social historians of this era include Dominic Sandbrook and Andy Beckett who complement traditional economists and Marxist historians such as Eric Hobsbawm.[15] Colored by the struggles of political and economic strife, this era wrestles too with an identity crisis—not just for itself but also for its survivors, that is, the fear of loss of British or self-identity not only in the face of government actions and reform but also ahead of waves of migration and consequent racial turmoil.[16] George Orwell's essays on Englishness during the war and in the postwar period are worth a look as he ponders over the definition of "Englishness"; how the English defined themselves (and how they were and are defined by outsiders) has remained in flux from the end of the Second World War.[17] Such ideological attitudes, with their attendant baggage from the imperial and war eras, were initially challenged by the social and cultural changes in Britain in the early 1960s. Then, by the 1970s, these attitudes were challenged anew by the large influx of Commonwealth immigrants and subsequent racial tension in the seventies and early eighties—the latter issues still being tackled into the twenty-first century with European Union (EU) policies on immigration.[18] The paradigm of "British identity" is still relevant to twenty-first-century politicians and government officials such as then–Home Secretary Theresa May, who has several times tweaked the "Life in the UK" test aimed at immigrants and refugees from Eastern European, Middle Eastern, and African countries who seek asylum, if not residency and citizenship, in the United Kingdom.[19]

PESSIMISM, POLITICS, AND POPULAR MUSIC

Mainstream popular music genres throughout the 1970s tended to be fun and escapist. Glam and glitter, led by such artists as Marc Bolan, Slade, or Suzi Quatro, were colored by infectious, anthem-like choruses and otherworldly costumes, characters, and camera angles, and followed by the sparkle of disco. Popular culture among the "intellectual artists," however, took a turn for the serious;[20] if artists (Rolling Stones, Rod Stewart, etc.) weren't fleeing the country to avoid the horrendous taxes that their success cost them, then they were creating pessimistic works on the state of their beloved England. The Kinks' seventies oeuvre that predicted a gloomy future and satirized the helplessness of the individual against government corruption was complemented by commentary by other artists on the shambles of political authority, public education, and social welfare: Pink Floyd and David Bowie each set Orwellian themes to music (*Animals* and *Diamond Dogs* respectively).[21]

So while the Kinks can't really be classified specifically as political *activists*, the music that they produced in the 1970s and early eighties were influenced by their impressions of politics and economic changes that affected them personally. They carried their own baggage against authority with them into the decade, especially considering difficulties the band had experienced professionally right from the start. By 1969 the Kinks were just coming off the four-year interdict from not only touring the United States but also even having film performances broadcast there. This ban had lost them income in addition to fans who had lost touch with the band and the musical direction that the group was taking in the late 1960s. The Kinks had suffered other professional setbacks as the result of the lawsuit that they initiated in 1965 as a means to wrangle back for themselves a fortune in lost royalties and to extract the band from the draconian contract that they had originally signed with Kassner Music.[22] The Kinks, and especially Ray, felt the court case—which he described in X-Ray as "a battle of the classes: West End versus the City"[23] —went against them simply because they were working class, despite the so-called classless-society myth perpetuated by English pop culture from the early 1960s.[24] On leaving the court in 1966, Ray reflected that "the idea of the working man and the upper-class man joining arms after the Second World War for the great battle ahead was total nonsense,"[25] even as he was working on what would become "Waterloo Sunset" and wondering if his brother-in-law's move to Australia had been the right decision. He added, "I had become classless because of my success, but litigation put me straight back on that cold suburban street surrounded by greyness,"[26] and "I was drawn back into a world where rules from another age applied . . . where a person's accent and background were considered before you were judged and given your 'rightful' place in society."[27] The process of the trial made him feel alienated even from the Kinks' two managers, Robert Wace and Grenville Collins, because he "realised that they felt secure among their own kind, the so-called professional classes . . . at times I wondered whether or not they were actually on my side."[28]

PEOPLE DRESSED IN GREY: "20TH CENTURY MAN"

Pye Records dropped the Kinks from the label after the release of Lola, despite the success of the eponymous single, because of the lack of US tours in the 1960s and the poor sales of albums such as Village Green and Arthur. They were, however, picked up by the bigger and wealthier, American-based label RCA, who gave the group artistic carte blanche. The first RCA album, Muswell Hillbillies, saw the Kinks reinventing themselves—new label, new decade, and new chance—and creating a work that acknowledged their American influences.[29] The album also introduced an added layer of neurotic pessimism to the satire, humor, and cynicism that had characterized their late sixties work, especially in regard to authority and personal identity.

These themes, begun on Muswell Hillbillies and seen especially in the tracks "20th Century Man" and "Acute Schizophrenia Paranoia Blues," come to fruition on Preservation Act 1 and Act 2, albums and stage shows of 1973 and 1974 respectively. Increasingly across these works appear Ray-created characters that reflect his own fears about the state of British society on the one hand and the own personal and professional difficulties he was facing on the other. The Kinks, who'd celebrated traditional English institutions and despaired of having the chance to have pride in empire the way their grandparents did, demonstrate on these tracks the turning tide of popular opinion against empire,[30] as well as the intrusive if not frightening changes in society itself. The abrupt change from the mid-1960s idealization in popular music, literature, and other arts of happy suburban life and the green pastures of mythical village greens (a theme not unique to the Kinks in the mid-1960s) to fear, anger, and pessimism on both sides of the Atlantic can be attributed to the brutal events of 1968: political assassination, the escalation of war in Vietnam, strife in the Eastern Bloc countries (in particular, Czechoslovakia), and the increasing conflict between political authorities of the older generation against the younger.[31] The Summer of Love in 1967 and the optimism of the younger generation was replaced with anger, disillusion, and violence as the preservation of one's own self and individual character became at stake.

Muswell Hillbillies kicks off with "20th Century Man," a track that describes an "age of machinery" and sarcastically celebrates the fruits of technology: napalm, bombs, and biological warfare. According to the song, the twentieth century has become an "age of insanity," and "the green pleasant fields of Jerusalem" are lost; all are trapped in an unpredictable society consuming disposable goods. The 20th Century Man longs for the past. He rejects not only the societal changes of the present day but also the artistic reaction: he wants to return to Shakespeare and Gainsborough, complementing a comment Ray made years later about art school: "Did Davies, product of a secondary modern, find [art school and the idea of working-class, kitchen-sink modern] liberating? No, he did not. 'I wanted everything to be as it was,' he says, with a kind of yelp. 'I liked the Old Masters. Russian icons. That's how I wanted to paint.'"[32] The new society described in "20th Century Man" and later in *Preservation* is impersonal, all by-design, and mass produced; it is driven by an array of consumer goods from frozen peas to TV dinners. These consumer goods provided a smokescreen to hide the government's intent on erasing the individual's freedom of identity and of choice;[33] the song's narrator mourns his birth into the welfare state because he's lost his privacy and liberty to the civil servants and the "people dressed in grey."

In "20th Century Man," Ray declared, "I'm a paranoid schizoid product of the twentieth century," and the follow-up track, "Acute Schizophrenia Paranoia Blues," continues the discourse. The narrator fears to go outside because there are demonstrations in the street, and this might be a prelude to World War III. He no longer trusts the denizens who populate the former sanctuary of the village—the milk-man, the grocer, and the lady next door. They could be spies, they follow him home, and they invade his privacy; he withdraws and re-treats indoors. This fear of loss of identity and loss of self persists strongly into the Kinks' subsequent work. For example, there is *Star-maker* (1974), a Ray solo project made for Granada TV, later realized as the Kinks' album *The Kinks Present a Soap Opera*. Here Ray portrays a rock star who becomes so obsessed with portraying an ordinary man that he loses his own identity to his subject; they switch places, and the star ends up as an anonymous "face in the crowd." Ray's paranoia of this loss of identity lasted beyond the Kinks; his Orwellian autobiography, *X-Ray*, begins, "My name is of no importance." Ray's fears are not out of line with the counterculture's general distrust of any authority that allegedly acts for the good of society. Compare ITV's 1969 program *The Prisoner*, in which Patrick McGoohan's character was held captive in a superficially idyllic "village" that was in fact a secret government pris-on—no one has any names but everyone is instead assigned identity numbers, and those in charge use torture and drugs to try to extract from "Number Six" the reasons he suddenly quits his government-sup-ported, secret agent job. "Number Six" does actually tell them—he just wanted to go on holiday—but it is dismissed as his captors devise ever-more-arcane means to get the truth out of him.

HERE COMES MR. FLASH: *PRESERVATION*

The most indicative of the Kinks' politically dystopian works from this era is one of their most overlooked. *Preservation Act 1* and *Act 2* are more or less part of a trilogy (*Schoolboys in Disgrace* being the third) in which Ray created characters that combine his own fears, insecurity, and paranoia about not only the state of British society but also his concurrent personal issues.[34] Rather than plod through the tracks of each album in order, it is more useful to examine their overarching themes. Preservation is the main theme: throughout *Village Green* and 1969's *Arthur*, the old values and traditions were still attainable and can be maintained, even if the narrator was grown up or moved away from home. With their themes of paranoia and fear of future change, however, the two *Preservations* focus on irretrievable loss and despair of any hope.

The works remain advisory and observational: no call to arms is raised; no suggestions for restoration are made. In fact, as the world of *Preservation* begins, the Tramp, who acts as Ray's mouthpiece, tells us of the conflict between the corrupt Mr. Flash and the rich and evil Mr. Black; "Introduction to the Solution" describes the lies and deceit of the authorities and the fighting and the panic on the streets. The Tramp mourns that he can only stand and watch passively and wishes he could "just disappear." Observation and manipulation are key weapons for Mr. Black. In the track "When a Solution Comes," Mr. Black gleefully watches the world go to hell in a hand-basket, "biding his time and waiting on the sidelines" as he too watches everything go wrong; with a little manipulation of the people, he chuckles, he will build a new society.

Ray's loss of identity, his paranoia, and his fear of the invasion of privacy permeate these complicated albums. The plot spools out not unlike that of a Greek tragedy in which the greedy and corrupt manipulate the easily led, all hurtling toward destruction, accompanied by a chorus of floozies and do-gooders. On the albums, Ray ceases to exist as his narrators become the principle characters of Mr. Flash (a character he alternates with Dave), Mr. Black (among others), and the Tramp (the character who seems closest to home), who is bewildered, afraid, and unable to understand why the conflict continues in the action of the album as well as in the real world. As he observes the politicians, the unions, and the working classes, the Tramp complains that while society spirals out of control, no one will actually *listen* to anyone else. His answer to the question "Why [don't they] negotiate and try to be civilized?" is that no one cares, "nobody listens and no one will understand." Performed during strike-ridden 1973, with a reference to the great union strikes in Britain of 1926,[35] "Nobody Gives" observes that nothing has changed; the strong will always abuse the weak. It is bleak; it is pessimistic. The Tramp himself is reminiscent of the fifth-century BC Athenian orator Demosthenes, the only one who saw through Philip of Macedonia's facade of comradery and in vain, through his *Philippics*, warned the Athenians to beware of Philip's agenda.

Preservation Act 1 is self-contained with only three main characters: Mr. Black, Mr. Flash, and the Tramp. *Preservation Act 2* is far more complex; contains a greater number of characters; and, as with David Bowie's 1974 *Diamond Dogs*, is inspired by Orwellian themes reminiscent of *1984*. For example, linking the songs and advancing the story line are "announcements," exposition for the increasingly alarming and oppressive plot. According to the story, a new People's Army has been created; it's led by Commander Black, and his goal is to overthrow the current government led by the flamboyant, hedonistic Mr. Flash. Mr. Flash represents the politicians whose smokescreen of consumer goods hides the truth from the citizens. Perhaps it is a reflection of how, in the real world, popular entertainment was preferable to the harder-edged, thoughtful musical works of the so-called intellectual artists (including progressive rock) that failed to sell as well as Marc Bolan, Slade, or the Bay City Rollers—the Tartan Army didn't care any more about Mary Whitehouse's crusade against violence and immorality in the media and entertainment industry than does Mr. Flash for Mr. Black's promises to "free" and to restore society from all pleasurable and any immoral influences.[36]

Mr. Black and the People's Army, meanwhile, score a victory, having been in battle, according to an announcement, in a "small village with mass casualties." Mr. Flash is imprisoned and awaits a treason trial, and the world of *Preservation* is placed under martial law with strict rationing of food, fuel, electricity, gas, and water. Entertainment and TV are shut down; radio is restricted to the official channel. So much for the passive joy of "Wonderboy" or the sanctuary of the village green. As the Tramp, Ray muses over the same loss, as he asks in "Oh Where Oh Where Is Love?" where romance has gone and what has happened to the love of ordinary things and fairy tales that entranced people in years before. The idyllic life, if it ever existed, he sings, has been replaced by homicide, suicide, and rape, by hatefulness and bitterness. Perhaps it is no surprise that the only survivor from *Village Green* is the criminal Johnny Thunder, who, in *Preservation Act 1* has become "One of the Survivors," a rogue wandering the countryside on his motorcycle, doggedly holding on to the past and determined to ignore the present. He is a dangerous relic out of time in his leathers and his devotion to fifties rock and roll, but he is the only one equipped with the skills to survive in a world deprived of sincerity and love. Is it any wonder that Kinks musicologist Johnny Rogan once pointed out not only that the subject matter of these two albums is complicated, but also that he doubts anyone ever just sits down to enjoy a random selection or two off (especially) *Preservation Act 2*.[37]

As the announcements subsequently inform us, Mr. Black turns out to be no better than what has come before (cf. the Who: "Meet the old boss, same as the new boss") and in fact swings in the opposite direction. He has no intentions of keeping any of his promises; Mr. Black intends to play the corrupt off each other. Despite these threats, Flash and his cronies continue to live their lavish lifestyles at the expense of the poor and see Black as no threat. Throughout, Ray, speaking through the Tramp, has only observed and elucidated. He offers no solution himself, mourns only loss, and retreats; his is an urgent but passive reaction to the loss of identity. Rather than fight as a rebel, he prefers a complete disappearance from society to that of a drab, faceless existence.

In *Preservation Act 2*, the captured Flash, doomed to have his brain cleansed and mind conditioned, denies his fate and complains that he wishes to stay as he is: "I don't want to live and die in an artificial world." Mr. Black, who represents all of the evils of seventies society, exults in the idea of filling the world with eugenically engineered, artificial people: everything clean, no disease, and everyone beautiful and designer made. The idea of a push-button future was indeed stressed in the advertising of the late 1960s and early 1970s—and while many did embrace the idea of ready meals and disposable white goods, Britain's DIY and "make-do" attitude continued to coexist strongly with if not supersede the idea of "throwaway" society, especially by the end of the century. During the Depression, then World War II and the years after, and into the early sixties—Ray's formative years—it had been all about making do and pulling together, the Great British resolve he so admired from his parents and grandparents' generation. The world he mourned and wished to preserve was theirs, not his. His was the first real consumer generation in the UK. Certainly British teens in the late fifties and early sixties didn't have the same amount of pocket money as their US counterparts, but retail jobs and employment was there for teens to buy clothes, records, cheap drugs, and fun—and to break a number of social and class barriers as they found music and movies and entertainment in common. Instead, they found themselves floundering and conflicted, lapping up consumer goods but with no real sense of fulfillment ("Can't Buy Me Love") or sense of cohesive identity, other than dissatisfaction around which to rally in the face of social upheaval as their parents and grandparents had faced in the 1930s and 1940s. They sought to preserve empire and respectability. What did Ray's generation have to save? Consider, for example, the track "Money and Corruption" on *Preservation Act 1* that examines the plight of the hardworking working classes—the one time when Ray sings collectively of "we"—the hard-laboring classes slave all day to keep the wealthy fat. "Money and corruption [now ruin] the land," the chorus runs. Crooked politicians treat their constituents like sheep—hence Mr. Black's rise to power as the people plead for a savior. He promises them new gadgets, home luxuries, and a five-year plan that will see everyone with the modern comforts and appliances; he promises to look after the workers and the "union men." It is complicated stuff as a foray into political commentary. The Kinks wouldn't be quite as blatant about the failure and self-ishness of society again until 1977's "Father Christmas" (see chapter 4).

From the mid-1970s and early eighties, it would be other youths, outsiders from America and working- and middle-class kids from Britain, who picked up the mantle from Ray and the Kinks to rebel against mass-produced pop music on the one hand and to embrace their Englishness on the other—flogging natural dialects and accents in the face of bland BBC Received Pronunciation and celebrating in their kitchen-sink dramas their families, childhoods, and home. Ray's escapism might be seen as cowardly by some, but the Kinks' and his fight had been a long one up to this point. Continued real-life defiance of authority may have affected their fame and fortune, but it won them respect from fans and critics who saw them as "authentic" in their rebellion, sticking to their convictions at the cost of mainstream success.

Meanwhile in the mid-1970s, however, the other Kinks became be-wildered by these increasingly distraught and arcane works.[38] Ray had indeed isolated himself from the world in some respects at this point as he was ensconced in his own recording studio up in north London, free to indulge at length in his new projects without the money-go-round pressuring him. Nevertheless, the band grew weary of the stage shows; Dave walked out stating that he felt like a "hired hand" in his own band.[39]

PRESERVATION OF THE PAST AND THE PUNKS

At about the same time that the Kinks were touring and performing the stage shows for *Preservation*, punk rock was kicking off in the UK, coming into full swing by 1976 and 1977. Whether one argues that punk was an accurate reflection of Britain's angry young men or whether the epitome of Britain's punk bands, the Sex Pistols, were manufactured simply to create controversy and line Malcolm McClaren's pockets,[40] their *fans* certainly reacted to the music and calls to anarchy and destruction as an outlet for their own frustrations. This may indeed have had a knock-on effect to changes in British society in the 1970s, although the impact and influence of this aspect of their character varies. In the 1970s, and early 1980s, for example, the punk scene flourished as a social movement and channel for the anger of, in particular, young men. UK unemployment figures for young men between the ages of eighteen and twenty-five are in double digits. Depression from unemployment was also the leading cause of suicide in this demographic during this time.[41]

Punk rock and its social repercussions themselves are documented in a vast and divisive scholarship if not general history.[42] Punk was never a huge commercial success in the 1970s as, on the one hand, pop, disco, and other mainstream music far outsold it. On the other, punk fans and critics themselves undermined sales—punk is the only 1970s genre that maintains any respect from critics for its authenticity, integrity, and anger; even contemporary critics praised it for these qualities. Unfortunately, praise lent it an air of respectability, which of course a true fan would have rejected. Isolation and rejection of fame was one of the hallmarks of punk and its fans, and the solidarity in finding solace in rejection undermines the original purpose. The bands themselves were in conflict. The Pistols, for example, dropped Glenn Matlock allegedly for being too talented, adding the musically useless but satisfyingly rude Sid Vicious to the band's lineup (supposedly making certain that his bass was unplugged at all times). Other bands, such as Blondie, found themselves with the choice of starving to death as authentic unknowns bucking the system or of smoothing off their rough edges, gaining a recording contract, and making a decent living.[43] The real nail in the coffin for any group was an appearance on *Top of the Pops*, where David Bowie once horrified grannies across the nation by draping his arm across Mick Ronson's shoulders—a program seen as corny by some acts but ultimately a desirable goal even as snarling punk rockers appeared cheek by jowl with the Wombles, Chaz and Dave, the Brotherhood of Man, or the Nolan Sisters.[44] The Stranglers may have taken the piss with their performance on the show in 1977, but it doesn't change the fact that they made the appearance in the first place.

Leaving aside Malcolm McClaren's motivation for forming the Sex Pistols, the punk scene in Britain was a reaction against the poverty and hopelessness of the seventies—antifashion, harsh music, and jarring looks. It was also, as Nick Rombes noted, deeply rooted in nostalgia,[45] and not, in some ways, unlike the outlook that the Kinks took toward the past. Despite its disdain of the establishment, punk and its relationship with nostalgia is one of the main themes that tie together Rombes's study of punk as a cultural phenomenon. Punk is not simply the music: it is an attitude of defiance, independence, self-sufficiency, and DIY— "doing it yourself." So by this broader definition, "punks" *could* include Herman's Hermits,[46] the Captain and Tennille,[47] Jimmy Carter,[48] or an episode of TV's *CPO Sharkey*.[49] The Ramones, in whom Rombes holds most stock (he has elsewhere written on them),[50] exemplify punk's nostalgic character. They took their image from the fifties punk, the hoodlum in a leather jacket and pegged jeans, and their attitude from memories of growing up listening to sixties girl bands and watching sitcoms on television. They have as much in common with the nostalgia for the fifties as anyone else did in the early seventies for that not-so-innocent time.[51] Punk arose from working-class fatalism and desperation, not teen boredom as some later rosy-colored filters would have it. In many respects, punk was a continuation simply of the tribalism found among teenagers from the 1950s with the rockers and Teddy Boys, followed on by the Mods, and becoming the various seventies and eighties subcultures of skinheads and rudeboys (i.e., 1960s Jamaican term appropriated to describe the subculture of ska and ska punk fans from the late 1970s onward), among others. Punk rockers screamed their disillusionment with British society—and like the 1960s pastoral Kinks and the

1970s paranoid Kinks, punk never sold well, no matter how much rock critics admired it for its unabashed anger and rawness.

But rather than leading the vanguard of the punk movement and bringing about the end of modern society, the Kinks, being of another generation, faced the sources of their anger and bitterness with humor and satire. The Kinks had retreated from the world of politics by the mid-1970s; stripped away the musical-hall extravaganzas, brass bands, and backup dancers; and, by 1979, snapped out of their navel-gazing, elaborate social-criticism phase and briefly hit the top of the charts again. Their music was commercial, accessible, and reminiscent of the old days in both sound and fury, beginning with *Low Budget*. The late seventies saw a return to the Kinks' rock-and-roll roots and renewed commercial success in the United States. Ray's humor and the band's increasingly radio-friendly songs enlivened their first two albums of the eighties, *Give the People What They Want* and *State of Confusion*. The latter contained the song "Come Dancing" that, because of its commercial success, overshadows some of the raw, angry emotion and social cynicism expressed in the other tracks on that album.

"Come Dancing" introduced both the period when the Kinks came back on a high note commercially (albeit briefly) and a period in which they were reinforced and remained as group who represented British identity, fashionable alongside the kitchen-sink dramedy of Madness, the Stray Cats, and other new wave and ska revival bands in the late seventies and eighties. Ray himself had one last paranoid dystopian fling with *X-Ray*, but when he went on tour to promote the book in 1996, the dark, Orwellian sci-fi framework of the story was abandoned, and instead he focused on being the Storyteller or the 20th Century Man who reminisces about his school days to an enrapt audience (these days on stage he refers to his father as the 20th Century Man).

CONCLUSION

The influence of the Kinks' political satire is negligible: Dave's early eighties, heavy-metal-handed, politically critical solo albums were met with mixed reviews, and Ray's penchant for paranoia has earned him comments such as "wallowing in his own weirdness"[52] or "strangely soulless"[53] —both comments from fiercely respectful Kinks historians.

The Kinks' real legacy with their politics were the use of their guitars to express anger against the authority of all comers and how Ray's hobby-horse of identity and preservation became well respected itself and folded into the works of the succeeding musical generations. The 1970s groups such as the Jam looked back on the piss 'n' vinegar rebellion of the 1960s Kinks against authority as they rebelled against the mold of contemporary forms of popular music, that is, of glam, disco, or progressive rock. The 1990s Britpop groups influenced by the Kinks and other Mod groups embraced the idea of promoting their Englishness through lyric, accent, and sound. These latter musicians came of age during the social upheavals and racial tension of the 1980s on the one hand, and they desired to flex their musical muscle to break free of the dominance of American grunge on the radio, on the other. In the early twenty-first century the Kinks, and especially Ray, have come sometimes to represent idyllic Britain and a sense of idealized unity of identity in an era controversially affected by calls for national referenda and Brexit (i.e., the controversial vote whether or not Britain should remain in the EU) and superficially colored by royal jubilees (Golden and Diamond in 2002 and 2012 respectively), not to mention Britain (by way of London) displaying its culture and identity to the world in Danny Boyle's 2012 Summer Olympic set pieces. In the latter, the Kinks, represented by Ray, were included as a signpost that defines "English culture" to the rest of the world.[54] Boyle chose a number of working-class and pastoral themes to represent British history, identity, and among the musical highlights, he included the music of, or reference to, several of the 1970s "intellectual artists" mentioned in this chapter. For example, Bowie's "Heroes" became the theme of the British athletes. Ray performed a live version of "Waterloo Sunset" in front of a display of newspaper taxis. Pink Floyd was represented visually in a short video piece, also produced by Boyle, that featured swooping visuals as a camera over Boyle's vision of England throughout the years. One of the memorable cultural landmarks featured in the film was the pink pig flying over Battersea Power Station: a tribute to the sleeve of Pink Floyd's *Animals*. The legacy of this album is not, however, its vicious satire on the British state and the counterresponse to the anger of the punks; rather, it's that the damned pig broke loose and floated away, much to the irritation of the farmer in Kent on whose pasture it landed. British identity has become—and perhaps always has been—less the hardships, and more getting past them and becoming more, as Ray said about the Kinks, a collection of political disasters turned into cultural triumph.

7

I MISS THE VILLAGE GREEN

The Past as Refuge

North London was my village green, my version of the countryside.[1]

Because of economic prosperity in Britain between 1955 and about 1968, working- and middle-class youth found themselves to be a "classless" generation and benefitted from social mobility unavailable to their parents or grandparents. From the mid- to late 1960s, popular music reflected the optimism of what Eric Hobsbawm called a new Golden Age for Britain, whether it was the counterculture's artistic and experimental sounds or mainstream perkiness inherent in pop.[2] Even the simple things in life were appreciated by even the coolest of the trendsetters: in the mid-1960s, there was plenty of cheerful rock and pop celebrating childhood and the joys of suburbia, especially in 1967. The Beatles sang warmly of their past on tracks such as "Strawberry Fields" and "Penny Lane" with its "blue suburban skies." They kicked off the "Summer of Love" by throwing off the trappings of being a relentlessly touring pop band and reinvented themselves as the psychedelic pseudo-Victorian *Sgt. Pepper's Lonely Hearts Club Band*. That same year other groups, including the Kinks, similarly elegized the ordinary; the Kinks found paradise in the lives of the commuters "swarming like flies" around the railway station in "Waterloo Sunset," and all the Small Faces wanted to do was get on with their neighbors in "Lazy Sunday Afternoon." British rock reached back to the music halls and bandstands for its inspiration in songs such as "Winchester Cathedral," a 1920s-style novelty hit, which won the 1967 Grammy for Best Contemporary Recording.

The Kinks slotted right into this optimistic, homey pop appreciation of English family life, especially from 1965's "A Well Respected Man" onward. As the Kinks turned inward to focus on English life and themes, they combined a number of these social elements into their music. Part of it was Ray Davies's increasing interest in character-driven songs and writing songs about ordinary people. Another part was an increasing focus on English themes and English-flavored songs as the American work ban against the Kinks kept them not only out of the States but also away from changes in the music scene such as psychedelia and sonic experimentation. A third factor was the strong influence of family and childhood experiences that drove the sound and words of much of the Kinks' work overall. While the Kinks are well regarded in this respect these days for this familial character, it cost them in the late 1960s commercially, not that Ray was ever interested in being a trendsetter when it came to music (or fashion). The Kinks scored a number one hit in late 1967 with "Autumn Almanac"—a paean to the English gardener and his allotment. The song completely strips the chorus to the starkest simplicity, "Yes, yes, yes, it's my autumn almanac!" with one chorus simply repeating "yes" eight times. ("They don't write 'em like they used to," Ray usually cackles during concerts at this point.) By late in the year, however, the trend for cozy nostalgia was wearing thin; despite the success of the single, the Kinks became viewed by fans and critics as a novelty singles band in Britain. Even those arbiters of cool, the Beatles, scored a dud by presenting on Boxing Day what amounted to a home movie: the Magical Mystery tour captured the Beatles heading off on a mystery coach tour complete with aunties, saucy pub entertainers, and ballroom dancing.

By 1968, music-hall-inspired and homey songs were regarded generally as a tired gimmick. The optimism of the counterculture changed on both sides of the Atlantic from a "Golden Age" to one of crisis (see chapter 6) as the younger generation loudly rejected the notion of material prosperity as vain and superficial, and the value system of the establishment was rejected as selfish, greedy, and socially destructive. Against these trends, the Kinks' music seemed to move backward and to side with the older generation. Rather than tuning in, turning on, and dropping out, the Kinks embraced the customs and institutions of the past, including wearing as a badge of honor accusations that they were spokesmen for Victorian sensibilities and the positive attributes of attaining respectability.[3] As D. Simonelli points out, the Kinks may have retreated from the psychedelic experimentation of the later sixties and turned inward, but Ray's knowingly cynical expression against the exploitation of British youth culture (especially in the media and in pop culture), his inner anger, his willingness to work hard, and his appreciation of deference ultimately gave the Kinks "an authentic voice" with which both to criticize and to admire tradition and respectability.[4]

This chapter then looks at the theme of family and sanctuary in the works of the Kinks. For context, there is a brief discussion of the "heritage escapism" phenomenon that appeared in Victorian and Edwardian working-class society as a reaction against industrialization and crowded urban conditions.[5] The Kinks' odes to the village green and idealized home life is part of a revival of a trend that reappeared in English popular culture after the war, and especially in the late sixties and early seventies in folk rock. Next addressed is the question of whether the Kinks were *nostalgic*, that is, longing for the past of an "England that never was" or if the Kinks are better described as seeking *nostos*—the search for home and the re-creation of past emotion to improve one's current and future state. Discussion includes the influence of Ray and Dave Davies's family and their experiences in childhood on the universal themes that appear in the Kinks' music and the complexities of both supporting life at home and the need to grow and change, as illustrated in tracks such as "Rosy, Won't You Please Come Home" and "Big Black Smoke." A case study of the track "Come Dancing," the band's first top-ten hit in a decade, wraps up the chapter as the song represents not only the reversal of the Kinks' commercial fortunes but also the particular appeal of the group's celebration of family life and the stability of a happy past.

THANK YOU FOR THE DAYS

The creation of *nostalgia*, that is, longing to return to an ideal past, is a Victorian invention. Some lay it at the feet of Charles Dickens and his rosy-colored memories of Christmases with gentle snow falling over sooty London; fat, roasted geese on the table; japes, games, and firelit stories. As part of the cultural consciousness, however, nostalgia for the never-was, especially visions of an idyllic, green, pastoral England, has its roots in the rise of the industrial age of the eighteenth and nineteenth centuries. Factories and cities were supposed to be an improvement over the harsh reality of country life, but urban industrialism was brutal for the lower classes; innovation was supposed to improve the quality of life, yet it brought crowding, poverty, slums, and dirty air. One reaction in popular culture was a proliferation of idealized country songs and folk music in the eighteenth and nineteenth centuries. The later Victorians turned nostalgia into an industry, cranking out ephemera festooned with golden-haired children to disguise the realities of crowded, smoke-filled factories, high infant mortality, and other harsher realities of industrialization. So effective were they at creating this idealized, cherub-festooned image of their past that the surviving artifacts still color their era for us in the twenty-first century. Similarly, rapid changes in postwar Britain led popular artists to create pastoral works at a time when the old traditions and institutions seemed to be under threat.

Dominic Sandbrook notes that what probably initiated the most recent trend in heritage nostalgia was the death of Winston Churchill in 1965—partly because Churchill was the last of the old age of British heroes and partly because the definition of what made for a hero changed so rapidly as the 1950s became the 1960s. C. Bray concurs and views both Churchill and T. S. Eliot's deaths as significant markers of the end of "old Britain." He notes that Churchill and his generation saw the battles of World War II as a means to preserving the institutions of the British Empire rather than as a way of protecting the next generation. He wonders, did Churchill's funeral signify the end of Britain's "romantic visions about the country itself?"[6] This is an interesting thought, especially given the exchange between the bright, young Beatles and the older city gent in 1964's *Hard Day's Night*. The gent objects to the boys' music, appearance, and very presence in his first-class train carriage, claiming, "I fought the war for your sort!" Indeed he may have, but Ringo retorts, "Bet you're sorry you won!"[7]

As noted in chapter 6, the British general public was assured by the end of the sixties that they were moving forward into a push-button, disposable age. All thoughts of rationing and making do from old and worn-out things, a legacy of the Depression and the war, were off the table. But the shiny and new proved disillusioning by the end of the decade; the bright future promised both by the government and by the counterculture of the late sixties wasn't coming to fruition. Looking back to the past and the good old days appealed; it became cultural escapism as collectively people could reminisce about the old days— and how even if they weren't necessarily *good* old days, people had hung together, coped with the crises, and above all maintained a sense of dignity if not gentle humor about hardship. This is the attitude that prevails in the Kinks' work: they've not necessarily advocated escaping to the past; on the contrary, they urge the listener to draw on the joys of the past to make for a happier future. For example, in 1989's "Down All the Days (Til 1992)," the listener is reminded at once that while the past is close, the future awaits. It's a bright and optimistic track that express- es hope for future generations as well as the simple joys awaiting ordi- nary people with each new sunrise.

The Kinks, then, are not about longing for the past that never was.[8] Ray certainly dismisses the idea: it's really only trotted out in online paeans to *Village Green* or in brief newspaper and magazine coverage about Ray's latest projects (where another favorite is to quip that Mus- well Hill has no village green). Indeed, while drawing strength or admi- ration from the actions of his parents and their generation, the Kinks show disdain for those who would bury themselves in the ways or insti- tutions of the past. A close listen to many songs quickly reveals that for every gentle word said about the past, there's a cynical line or a rude voice expressing that sentiment. For example, 1969's *Arthur* kicks off with "Victoria," which describes the accident of being born into a glori- ous empire that covers the globe, a land to die for wherein there is freedom even in poverty. Victoria loves them all, from the rich to the poor and from the east to the west. Still, the first verse describes sexual repression of the old days, as well as the meanness of the rich in their estates—the village greens described here are the domain of the wealthy; the poor get to fight and die for the land that they love. In addition, the early verses are sung in mocking tones; Ray reverts to his real voice when speaking of his love for the land of hope and glory and "my Victoria." On the same album, the antiwar song "Yes Sir, No Sir" recalls the good old days of obedience and willingness to die for one's home, the days when boundaries were well understood and customs involved a well-made cup of tea, not going through a full-body scanner. Again, however, the *lyrics* are one thing on paper, but the *vocals* are another. Ray sings the tune in such a mocking tone that the soldier's obedience becomes less heroic and more foolish. A final example is "Village Green" from 1968's *Village Green Preservation Society*. Here the narrator wistfully revisits the village of his childhood, the place he left for better opportunities in the city. He misses its simplicity, but he also notes wryly that the provincial house that he escaped is now a "rare antiquity" to be photographed by clueless American tourists. If the message is lost on the casual listener here, certainly Edgar Wright and Simon Pegg understood the cynicism in the song's imagery as they chose it to set the stage for the superficially charming village depicted in the 2007 film *Hot Fuzz*—a village so award-winningly perfect that its residents murder anyone who threatens the pretty scene.

Even as the Kinks poke fun at the conventions of the past, however, they don't vilify them. Not only did they promote the customs and values of their parents and grandparent's generation, but also they targeted what they saw as contradictions in the aspirations of the youth movement in Great Britain to ascend from working to middle class—all the while desperate to maintain working-class integrity. Unlike the Beatles or the Rolling Stones, who as early as 1965 were part of the mainstream establishment, the Kinks' cynical, yet affectionate, commentary was admired by their contemporaries as the "authentic" voice of the working class.[9] The Kinks are sharply knowing in their criticism of rebellion against older customs. They remarked on the hypocrisy and despair that resulted when the younger generation did rebel against the older, and when that brave new world turned out to be a hostile, unforgiving, cold environment. As B. Martin notes, "Most young people want the semblance and symbol of revolt without its reality, they want to threaten without cracking known social molds, while the world around remains familiar and therefore safe."[10] Christopher Partridge concurs: transgression against social norms is transitory, and such rebellion provides fresh ideas and new perspectives that are then folded into the mainstream way of thinking as the rebellious generation ages.[11]

ROSY, WON'T YOU PLEASE COME HOME

The Homeric concept of *nostos*, which has become our modern word *nostalgia*, reflects a desire of and longing for a return to the comfort and safety of the home (rather than "homesickness" or the longing for an idealized past). A classic example of *nostos* in literature is the journey of Odysseus. Odysseus, on his twenty-year voyage back to his kingdom of Ithaca, sought a symbolic rebirth for himself as well as a search for models for his kingdom while wandering across the seas. Similarly, many Kinks songs express *nostos* as a means to embrace home as an idealized concept of simplicity, respectability, and other values of the older generation and England's past. Home and family life established the foundation of Ray's musical interests, and it frequently represents in Kinks lyrics sanctuary and stability in the face of change, upheaval, and uncertainty. A key characteristic of the Kinks' *nostos* is that their music is simultaneously introspective and inclusive: the audience becomes part of an extended family not just by joining in the sing-along choruses but also because they identify with similar circumstances in their own experience. The songs reflect universal, personal themes that go beyond simple teen angst and sexual frustration found in many rock-and-roll and pop songs without becoming so artistically obscure as to alienate the listener. Finally, as Odysseus traveled onward to restore himself as the rightful heir to his throne, he had to assume numerous guises along the way to remain undetected among the dangerous pretenders who threatened both his home and his kingship. In many ways too, the music and in-song characters created by the Kinks reflects this particular integrity. The Kinks became spokesmen for the idea of respectability—old fashioned on the one hand but radical on the other as they point out the hypocrisy of those who attempted to distance themselves from the mores and lifestyle of the older generation.

Within the oeuvre of the Kinks' music, Ray was singing of home as a sanctuary as early as 1965's "Where Have All the Good Times Gone?" Here Ray expresses a deep longing for the happiness of earlier times before the pressures of fame. The verses of the song alternate between verses that describe the simplicity of life before the fast track that success has brought and choruses that repeat like a weary plea, "Won't you tell me, where have all the good times gone?" As Ray noted in a 2015 public talk in Southampton, he never set out to be some spokesman of

England's grand past or to be a political satirist.[12] Instead, as he reminded the audience, he had been a young, inexperienced kid when he
wrote "You Really Got Me" and his early songs were about "you and her
and I and she" because he wrote about what he felt at that moment—
getting a girl and getting her *now*. When pressed by the moderator
about how his songs invoked longing for the past and asked if he deliberately set out to shape his listeners' feelings with his music, Ray argued
that he wrote about whatever inspired him at the time. As he said wryly,
as much as he would have liked to wander in the woods looking for
fairies and gaining inspiration, he was pressured by tours, contracts,
deadlines, and wages. His songs subsequently took on a life of their own
depending on the listener's interpretation, something with which he has
no problem.[13] The subsequent discussion among the two guests and
moderator at that talk helped to shape this chapter, that is, how others
interpret and "use" the Kinks' character to shape their own—whether
as the misfit individual finding himself a voice, the canny advertiser
appealing to a particular sector of his viewing audience, or a journalist
perpetuating the idea that the Kinks' greatest characteristic is their
obscurity.

When Ray started to write more socially aware lyrics, it was because
he felt compelled to study and observe people, not only his peers but
also the most immediate people around him, his family and relatives,
watching them going about their daily business and observing what
made them happy. He told the audience that his own inner feelings as a
child and young man were too unhappy to serve as inspiration, so he
turned to those who were more positive and cheerful even in the face of
adversity. Hence, he composed songs that reflected his parents' and
grandparents' reflections on times past and not necessarily times past
itself. They had lived through the hard times of Depression and World
War II, and they described to him those years as "the good old days."
Ray was impressed by this as a child, and he longed for the same
camaraderie that united them happily in the face of adversity, happiness
that was expressed through their music. As Ray remarked, "My sisters
[were amazing]—they enjoyed their life. They lived through the Second
World War. They remember the blackouts and the bombs and having
to hide in shelters in the back garden—going in the subway when there
were bombing raids in London. And—but yeah. They loved it. They
wouldn't have exchanged that time—amazingly—wouldn't have ex-

changed that for any other reason."[14] So while he drew on the past, he wasn't wishing to *return* to the past but rather hoping to take it as inspiration for a happy present, and, with luck, a happier future.

Themes of identity with or love of an idyllic thus did not come from Ray or Dave reading up on a Marxist manifesto as a child. They wrote about subjects of interest to them, drawn from their personal lives and what moved them to tears or laughter. They were not writing consciously with an eye toward their music becoming part of a history, anthropology, or sociology textbook—Dave in particular has always been outspoken against the empty exercise of academic analysis while Ray advocates songwriting as a key means of communication.[15] A look at the inspiration of family on Kinks music helps to set the context here for understanding the universal themes of home, safety, and the comfort of family in their output. While the songs may be personally inspired, the themes within include their audience and draw them into a familial relationship with the group itself.

HAVE A CUPPA TEA: HOME IS WHERE THE SUPPORT IS

The true authority in the Davies home was their mother Annie, a well-admired woman who ran a chaotic but welcoming household. She was strong willed and defensive and caring of her children. For example, worried that the younger boys weren't getting as much attention as they needed, she sent them to live with their sisters' families where they could thrive. Another striking example was when she noticed Ray's emotional difficulties as a child and sought specialized care and schooling for him, something almost unheard of in 1950s working-class Britain. She was admired by everyone—not just family but also universally by outsiders who were interviewed by Ray's biographer and others.[16] Dave notes that it was his mother who made the decision to move from Huntington Avenue (where the family were regarded as noisy interlopers) to Denmark Terrace.[17] She competently ran the very tiny home with people constantly coming in and out on a next-to-nothing budget;[18] again, Dave remarks that the children lacked for nothing despite the hard economic times: she "owned very little in her life, just a few ornaments and treasured photos that sat on her mantle shelf. But she was a very rich woman in her heart."[19]

Her sense of integrity was important to Ray and is reflected especially in the songs where he speaks cynically of those who believe they can buy the respectability that is lacking in their inherent character. Much of that may come from the money-stricken situation the family found themselves in when they moved from the King's Cross area to Fortis Green during the war; Mrs. Davies kept her daughters at home rather than evacuating them, and the street wasn't too thrilled by these noisy new neighbors. Ray and Dave suggest that this is where the family developed a strong solidarity as a group against outsiders; perhaps this influenced Ray's unease and distrust of all of the people who suddenly wanted a piece of him once he was famous.

In addition to the Davieses' mother, Ray and Dave's many sisters were extremely important to the character and influences on their younger brothers' choices in music, instruments, and musical instruction (see chapter 2). The sisters also provided inspiration for the direction for the Kinks' character songs, as Ray often shaped songs around family members to express his joy about his family and personal relationships and to cope with his inner turmoil and anxiety. For example, "I Go to Sleep," later covered by the Pretenders, was composed as he anxiously awaited the birth of his first child. "Wonderboy" was written to express the joy he felt at the arrival of his second. "Art Lover," erroneously viewed by some creepy fanboys as a weird song about incest,[20] in fact deals with his emotions during a difficult custody battle for his own children. "Two Sisters," from 1967, explores Ray's jealousy of and bitterness toward his younger brother's single freedom while he himself was tied down to a family and the personal and professional responsibilities and obligations that went with it. This track is told from the point of view of the elder sister, Priscilla/Ray, a married woman with a house and children, and envious of her carefree, younger sister Sybilla/Dave. Priscilla is chained to her washing machine and the cooker while her younger sister runs about with "her liberty and her smart young friends." It is only when Priscilla regards her small children that she decides "she was better off than the wayward lass that her sister had been" and reconciles herself more happily to her domestic life of comfortable routine. Ultimately, the track is a reflection on the positive stability of home, the rewards of respectable family life, and the affection of children compared to a life of aimless inhibition, uncertainty, and hedonism, certainly an unusual position for a rock star to take in the midst of the flower-power generation in 1967.[21]

Not only was home an influence on the Kinks' work, but also home and family served as symbols of stability and security in the face of uncertain change. "Waterloo Sunset" is a song of the comfort of a familiar place, one that might be unglamorous, dirty, and simply functional, passed by without a second glance by "millions of people, swarming like flies" around it, but full of meaning and significance in a private way when observed by an individual. With such private memories and associations, such an ordinary place becomes a "paradise." "Autumn Almanac" describes the beauty and happiness found in the humble chores of suburban living (and the subsequent backache), weekend rituals of football and Sunday roasts, and the proud description of an nondescript street—but an important one nonetheless because, as the narrator affirms, "This is *my* street," one he swears he will never leave even if he lives to be nearly one hundred years old. As he sings, Ray reminds one of a child making a vow, as his voice rises higher as he sings, the same way we as children spoke of a loved thing with earnest conviction; meanwhile, the background vocals sigh, "Come on home, come on home." Ray's delight in making a paradise out of the ordinary may have been out of step among the movers and shakers of the experimental scene, but it reinforced the Kinks' "authenticity" among fans who *are* ordinary. In 1966, during an interview, Ray commented, "People should realize that things like food and tea are important," and Peter Quaife concurred that the best thing ever is to go to the movies and have a pint and a smoke; all of the Kinks argued that Sunday dinner was "the greatest realization of heaven."[22] More to the point, the lyrics suggest that despite social climbing or the new "classless" society, the street metaphorically represents one's particular identity, shaped by childhood experience, regardless of the social or economical changes in his life; as the narrator insists in "Autumn Almanac," "It's a part of me."

NOW HER MOTHER PINES HER HEART AWAY: REJECTION OF HOME AND ITS CONSEQUENCES

Rebellion against one's elders, mainstream authority, or social class is nothing new in working-class genres of popular music, of which rock and roll is a part. Martin points out in a sociological study of rock music that rebellion is part of a natural "rite of passage" for teens especially as they act out against particular symbols of order or of the older generation.[23] There is a distinctive ritual to these acts of rebellion and not simply sloppy improvisation.[24] Rebelling against home and family life would be the most immediate outlet for a frustrated teenager; the counterculture of the mid- to late sixties amplified and gave an outlet to encourage this behavior,[25] exemplified perhaps in growing out one's hair, listening to parentally objectionable music, or even more dramatically, running away from home. Martin notes that after this expected rite of rebellious passage, the rebels settle into very similar routines held by their parents, and the innovative becomes the norm.[26] Celebrating homeliness could be reckoned as an ironic sort of rebellion in 1967 (i.e., establishing communes and societies free from those norms that traditionally defined the nuclear family structure), but the direction of the Kinks' hominess was different to the Small Faces ("Lazy Sunday Afternoon"). The Kinks' embrace of home and family was more immediate than the media's counterculture darlings, the Beatles, who, like even the Rolling Stones, were actually part of the cultural establishment by 1965.[27]

The old ways weren't completely rejected by the younger generation. According to Paul McCartney, one can muse on the past if it's couched as a time yet to come; in "When I'm 64," those who scrimp and save and buy a cottage in the Isle of Wight do so in their comfortable old age—"many years from now," after the fun and the good times. Music-hall tunes and sentiment are left to the older generation. It's hip to get up and dance to the type of music "Your Mother Should Know," but it's not the style to be permanently adopted. When it comes to the old folks and their children in the here and now, the Beatles' "She's Leaving Home" is indicative of the direction that the counterculture was headed in terms of increasing dissatisfaction with the traditional values represented by family and home. Groaning under the weight of soap-opera-inspired violins and Paul and John's earnest vocals, "She's Leaving Home" is told from both a third-person point of view and the point of view of the parents. The girl described in the verses sneaks out in the middle of the night, frustrated by her oblivious elders to her needs. The bewildered adults wonder, what had they done wrong? They'd worked so hard for her; they'd bought her everything money could buy—except fun (complementing the Beatles' previous complaint only three years earlier that money couldn't buy love). The impact of the song is further strengthened in that Paul based the tale of the unhappy girl on a newspaper article about real-life runaway Melanie Coe.[28]

By way of contrast is the Kinks' "Rosy Won't You Please Come Home," Ray's 1966 plea for his sister Rose to return to England. Here the narrator isn't the parents or a third-person narrator sympathetic to the peripatetic girl but rather the same guy who moaned, "Oh get 'em off!" in reference to a young lady's knickers a couple years earlier in "All Day and All of the Night." Both the lyrics and the vocals of "Rosy" are plaintive; they reflect the hopeful bribe of a child who tells his sister, "I'll bake a cake if you tell me you are on the first plane back home" and that Christmas—and life in general—has just not been the same without her. Ray's voice alternates between the strong tones of an adult ("Oh, my Rosy, how I miss you, you are all the world to me") and the quavering of a small boy's every time he sings the title question, rising up on the high notes, as if he is about to break down in tears (unromantically, he was probably suffering from a raging case of hay fever, as was the case on the recording session for "Sunny Afternoon," "See My Friends," and other tracks). He recalled in *X-Ray* that he did collapse, weeping, several years later in reaction to his sister's departure, having stoically withheld an emotional response to the separation from quite some time.[29] The song fades out on the narrator's pleas, having offered to Rosy the knowledge that her room is clean, waiting for her, and that no one else has taken up residence in it.

"Rosy" offers hope—the girl can return to her home at any time and be warmly welcomed. Rosy has left home to join the "upper classes" and doesn't know her family anymore, and the family mourns this loss. Elsewhere, the girls in Ray's scenarios who leave home are rarely rewarded with positive experiences. For example, in "Big Black Smoke," the girl runs away from home "sick and tired of simple country life" and a secure future with the boy next door. She ends up in the misery and despair of the big black Smoke (i.e., London); the smooth-talking boy who lured away this frail and pure girl steals all of her money, leaving her to pop pills and to sleep rough in doorways. As ever, however, the Kinks can be ambiguous about the fate of one leaving home and familial innocence as found in "Village Green." Here the narrator himself is the one who has left home for better things, despite having met a girl called Daisy and innocently enjoying kissing her "by the old oak tree." Returning to his old home away from "all the noise and soot of the city," he finds himself missing the little shops, dewy mornings, and his sweetheart. He returns to find the village has continued without him and his girl Daisy, married to Tom the grocer and happily running the shop. But even as he's missing an idealized version of the village as a place remaining innocent and safely out of time (similar themes of escape and innocence are found in "Animal Farm"), he watches with some bemusement from an outsider's perspective that the only people truly entranced with the village are not the locals but rather the transient tourists and visitors such as himself.

Such songs about home, rejecting home, and returning home mirror how youthful rebellion rarely falls into a black or white divide,[30] and the Kinks musical thoughts on the subject embodied ambiguity. Striking out on one's own was one thing that might bring a change in fortune, if one remembered one's roots and visited occasionally, but outright rejection of home and family (and by extension social class) could lead to misery and home- or classlessness. Bray notes a similar issue in 1965's *Stand Up, Nigel Burton*, a pair of dramatic plays aired on BBC One, in which Nigel, as written by Dennis Potter, realizes that he no longer identifies with his coal-miner father after receiving an Oxford education.[31] Much of his angst comes from wanting to be at home but feeling out of place when he is there. As with "Rosy," the girl in "Big Black Smoke," or the narrator in "Village Green," Nigel represents some of the problems faced by the younger "classless" society in Britain as a result new social mobility: they might become alienated from their working-class parents or home life even as they benefit from the opportunities provided by their parents and that home life. The simultaneous need for and rejection of home and family found in many songs of the Kinks represent confusion and an identity crisis perhaps understood by many of their fans.

The Kinks might have earned disdainful sniffs from the hipsters for their sharp witticisms and knowing lyrics as they sang about home and hearth, but they gained respect for the same from their musical peers: Paul McCartney and Pete Townshend, among others, spoke of Ray Davies's lyrics with high praise. At the time, however, fickle fans and marketing tastes moved on, and the Kinks no longer fit into the character of late sixties pop culture; psychedelic fans wanted musical experimentation that blew their minds and raised their consciousness, not lively music-hall tunes. Their younger siblings wanted bright bubble-gum pop records from the Monkees and Gary Lewis and the Playboys. British fans, too, lost an interest in the band that had been well regarded in 1964 and 1965 as a hard-edged, sexy, protopunk singles band who could hold their own against the Beatles and Rolling Stones. *The Kinks Are the Village Green Preservation Society* in contemporary context saw the Kinks not addressing social and emotional angst but rather suggesting that one's parents might have something of interest or importance to say.[32]

COME DANCING

Village Green and the years following it represent a low ebb in the Kinks' fortunes; much of the seventies saw them deeply involved in theatrical stage shows such as *Preservation* as discussed in chapter 6. When the Kinks returned to the cultural (and commercial) landscape in the late seventies it was in America, not Britain, as bands such as Van Halen helped to revive the Kinks' commercial success in the United States. Similarly, the Pretenders scored an early hit with a cover of "I Go to Sleep," and Ray entered into a relationship with the Pretenders frontwoman and famous fan Chrissie Hynde. Hynde may well have influenced the writing of "Come Dancing": Ray apparently took great pleasure in showing her around his childhood haunts in London, and despite the rather tumultuous relationship they shared, she did seem to inspire the creation of this lively reflection on his sisters and family. The song's story line and the image of 1950s British working-class childhood and entertainment were reinforced in America by its appearance on the newly minted MTV. While the British had been creating short music films for decades to support hit songs, music videos as a ubiquitous commercial venture in the United States were a new marketing ploy. MTV found that there was a shortage of videos from American acts when it went on the air in 1981, and consequently, British artists, including the Kinks, were placed into heavy rotation. The "Come Dancing" video thus helped to reinforce the Kinks' image of representing Englishness and English life, especially in the States. The track completed what Pye Records had started in 1966 and 1967 with the ersatz whimsy of the liner notes on *Face to Face* and *Something Else by the Kinks* ("Welcome to Daviesland . . ." and other heavy-handed exhortation of ersatz English eccentricity), and Reprise Records continued in 1969 as the newly unbanned Kinks returned to the States for the first time in nearly four years, a tour that advanced under the banner "God Save the Kinks."

"Come Dancing" gave the group a number one single for the first time in almost a decade, and it was part of a cycle of British kitchen-sink rock-and-roll dramas prevalent on radio and as videos at that time. Not only does the song's chirpy, infectious music-hall beat and nostalgic lyrics point to happy memories from Ray Davies's childhood, but also the song stands out as an upbeat and positive song for the Kinks after a number of years of moody concept albums and rock operas in the 1970s. It reflects the general happiness of the Kinks' revived commercial success that they enjoyed in the late 1970s and early 1980s as their music was rediscovered by a new audience following a number of vibrant covers from new, young musicians who had themselves grown up as Kinks fans; as Ray struggled to come to terms with his own growing pains and sense of alienation, he had been shaping the childhood and youth of the next. Finally, as with the songs off *Village Green*, the personal reminiscence of "Come Dancing" had universally appealing themes of family, childhood, and memory on both side of the Atlantic.

The "Come Dancing" track is complemented by Julien Temple's accompanying music video, which these days can be found in varying states of quality on YouTube. The song opens with a gentle hit-hat drum-beat introduction, bursting into life with a rolling synthesizer arpeggio that pulls the listener into a scene of dreamy nostalgia; underscoring the bouncing big band horns is a thumping oompah beat. The narrator related happy memories of watching his sister, a dance-hall enthusiast, prepare for an evening out with a suitor—ultimately thwarting her date into spending all of his weekly wages to show her a good time and gaining nothing from it but "a cuddle and a peck on the cheek." The suitor patiently waits for the sister to make her grand entrance; later in the song, the mother of the family waits equally impatiently for the daughter to return. Mum interrupts the lingering goodbyes outside by the garden gate and drags the sister/daughter back inside. So powerful is the narrator's memory of his mother and sister in the song that the listener hears Mum's scolding voice faintly down the years too, demanding to know if the sister is "going to stay out here all night." The song mixes the past with the present: there is some chagrin in the first verse as the "danse palais" (dance hall) of these happy memories no longer exists; the place of escapism has been knocked down and replaced by the mundane not once or twice but three times—first with a bowling alley, then with a supermarket, and finally with nothing but a car park. *Sic transit mundi* (thus passes the world).

Despite the disappearance of the dance hall and the material remains of a happy youth, the song remains characteristically uplifting: the little boy has himself grown up to front a rock band (played by the Kinks, of course), and who blast their power-chord-driven sounds across the song's middle eight. A gentle rhythm guitar ends the instrumental section and returns the song to the story of the sister. She's grown up herself, but the song ends on a joyful note, as the narrator tells us that his sister sends off her own daughter to go out dancing and get away with all of the fun that she never could. He thinks that he, too, might ask his sister to step out dancing for old times' sake—and the song draws to a triumphant conclusion with a flourish of brass.

The video's visuals fill in gaps for the listener and draw even more connections between the past and the present. As the video and song begin, the little boy who represents our narrator as a child is seen peeking around the doors of the dance hall and sees an orchestra that is a mix of bandsmen as well as members of the Kinks in period clothes. We see the little boy throughout the film, cheerfully watching his sister and ignoring the fist-shaking scorn directed at him by the suitor, played by Ray, who later appears as the grown-up boy now a man leading the rock band. The sister also links the past and appears again in period clothes during the modern sequence when the narrator continues the story as a member of his own rock group. She stands in front of his own dancing fans at the foot of the stage, twisting in her hands the black-market silk stockings offered to her in the past by her black-marketeer suitor. She catches the eye of the rock-and-roll band with a knowing smile. The suitor himself also links the past and the present. As the video opens, the camera drifts past the big band musicians, swirls around the dancers, and zooms in on the suitor, who, dressed as a 1950s spiv, acts as the initial narrator. He reappears in the final, modern-day rock-and-roll sequence, as the camera also spins around grown-up narrator and rock-band leader Ray, turns into the audience, and pans across them up toward the balcony to pick out the spiv, standing perfectly still and emotionless, still in his old-fashioned clothes and oblivious to the happy modern fans around him. The spiv finally ends the video when the music finishes; we see him standing outside the present-day rock-concert venue, angrily looking at the Kinks' concert poster. Suddenly, he tears the poster down with a snarl of disdain. This is a typical Kinks touch and a happy memory for those looking back, but for the spiv, stuck in the past and thwarted of even the "cuddle and a peck on the cheek," less so.

So the song is a family affair, with memories of sisters and a tribute to an uncle: Ray deliberately based his spiv character's look in the "Come Dancing" video on his Uncle Frank's appearance. Dave notes that in his makeup, Ray looked exactly like the man, a real-life "Jack the Lad," described elsewhere by as "lively, funny and rude, yet sentimental and caring."[33] More amusingly, for those with very sharp eyes, is that the mum in the video appears to be played by younger brother Dave.

"Come Dancing" put the Kinks back into the top twenty for the first time since "Lola" (1972) and in the top ten for the first time since "Tired of Waiting." Its infectious, commercial sound ensured much airplay and made the Kinks more accessible to new fans than the complex concept albums of the previous years. While the Kinks themselves never reached such commercial heights again (and ceased performing as a group in 1996), Ray Davies has continued to revisit his past as exemplified in his 1990s *Storyteller* and 2000s *Americana* tours, among others. Critics of the *Storyteller* show initially made comments about Ray's rumpled appearance and mad hair, and his awkward initial poise and lack of acting skills, but he charmed even the snarkiest critics who have gone on to remark that the show is one of comfortable reminiscence. *Storyteller*, like its source *X-Ray*, mixed fact and myth; one might argue that Ray has at last merged with "the character" he created to express his bitterness and disconnect with gentle memories in the present day. The bitter character of Mr. Flash of *Preservation* and *Schoolboys in Disgrace* and "RD" of *X-Ray* has given way to the Storyteller; as Ray commented on "Down All the Days (Til 1992)," "I'm losing my bitterness."[34]

CONCLUSION

The collection of social memories (home, family, and personal past) found in Kinks music from the late sixties through to the early eighties reinforces a sense of familial identity and represents a means of stability in otherwise troubled or uncertain times. Both Ray and Dave in their individual work repeatedly refer to the family front room of their childhood as a sanctuary, with its womb-like comfort and as a place to which they could retreat even as adults. Family and social life centered on the front room as noted by Ray, with the parties and the sisters courting their boyfriends there.[35] Many Kinks songs would be composed, rehearsed, and evaluated by the family there, including "You Really Got Me."[36] Ray wrote later, "It's hard to describe that old front room. It had a magical quality. I felt in some strange way God was always there, judging and giving guidance where necessary."[37] Dave also speaks fondly of the front room, where he once nearly electrocuted himself while searching for what would become the Kinks' and his signature sound.[38] Later, as a young married man, he went back to his mother's house, feeling burdened and stressed out by fame and reputation, and composed his own signature track, "Death of a Clown."[39]

The conviction of these songs of home and family are believable to the listener, the majority of the fans being people of modest means (certainly in comparison to a successful rock star), as it is not some celebrity waxing about his childhood home from the safety of a Beverley Hills mansion. Even as adults, Ray and Dave have not strayed from their roots: Ray's studio, Konk, is in north London near to the family environs; both Ray and Dave currently maintain homes in London; and Ray remains an active contributor to the community in and around Hornsey and Hampstead. The realism, and the sense of identity, ring true and enhances the shared experience of the homey subjects of many Kinks songs—quite a contrast to, for example, wealthy rock and rap stars still singing about the streets and the 'hood they have long since abandoned.

Ray has said in his recent (2014–2016) *Americana* promotion that he hasn't got a home anymore, a consequence of fifty years of touring and travel, but north London remains a beacon that lures him back to England. Ray has been frequently spotted (as of summer 2014) hanging about in nearby Highgate Hill, sitting on a bench, playing a guitar, and serenading passersby. He supports the local Muswell Hill area. He's loaned Kinks memorabilia to Bruce Castle for an exhibition, promotes local artists in exhibitions in Konk, supports children's music programs at his old school, and has performed in charity shows to help raise money to preserve the Hornsey Town Hall. Not surprisingly, after he serenaded Great Britain and the world with "Waterloo Sunset" at the 2012 Olympics closing ceremonies, he got into a taxi, left the venue, and went to his local pub to watch the rest of the show from there—as privately as did any of us around the country, yet sharing in the entire experience. So much of the performance, music, and lyrics of the Kinks' output is especially inclusive of the audience with which they identify through the characters of and in the songs, and the Kinks recognize similar circumstances in their own experience. This invites the listener to participate—not just in the sing-alongs but in the shared memories as well. While many of Ray's songs are part of a "fictional universe,"[40] the characters and scenes in them are familiar to the listener's own experiences. Of course the music of the Kinks works well to illustrate a sense of national identity and solidarity of class consciousness, and they are not unique as a band whose output can be attached to contemporary social conditions. Therein lies one of the strengths of the Davieses' work, this inclusion by association, and one that shapes the impression they make on their fans, as will be discussed further in the next chapter.

8

THIS STRANGE EFFECT

The Kinks as Others See Them

[It's] quite simple really, but ever since those early days there have been many songs which Ray appears to have written with me in mind, and yet we have never had a conversation—so how could they be?[1]

On April 24, 2015, Ray Davies appeared at the Fulcrum Festival at the University of Southampton to participate in a discussion panel on music and memory. The idea was to bring together an artist (Ray) and a scientist (Dr. Tim Wildschut) to discuss how music shapes particular memories and how the desire to re-create the emotional circumstances of past feelings provides inspiration for future actions. The professor's research focused on nostalgia, defined by him as a longing to re-create somehow past feelings through social connections centered around a particular phenomenon (as opposed to defining nostalgia as necessarily a restoration of general cultural or social norms through artificial constructs). He has studied music in particular and how it unites groups of otherwise unrelated people in their search for a time when they were happy. As Ray and the panel agreed, the connection between music and feelings doesn't necessarily have anything to do with the lyrics of particular songs. Music that necessarily strikes the listener as the most poignant may be driven less by the words and more by the context of memories and emotions the song evokes.

Ray was invited along to the festival because of the Kinks' catalog of songs about the past—family, growing up, and traditional cultural institutions—as well as the Kinks' storytelling songs about everyday, ordinary life. At once at the start of the talk, however, the "n-word"—nostalgia—was declared *verboten*. Instead, the focus was on *reflection* and how particular aspects of music gives otherwise diverse people a collective and cultural identity. Throughout this book, various aspects of the Kinks' character and music have been, so far, considered from the inside out, and it's been examined how their output was shaped by elements from Ray and Dave Davies's individual lives and experiences. Looking from the "outside in," audience reflection on and reception of the Kinks' music has brought about particular expectation and shaping of the Kinks' image. This image has become from the first power chords of "You Really Got Me" a focal point for both those seeking a similar identity, commercially or individually, and their heroes. Ray's own search for comfort and happiness in music in the face of isolation and loneliness itself mirrors how music fans find similar comfort in the same music. The desire to recover those feelings leads to seeking out like-minded others, a social phenomenon currently under investigation in fan studies across genre and media.[2]

To that end, this chapter will look at what seems at first to be odds and ends, but it will, with luck, demonstrate if not ultimately parse the means by which the Kinks as a musical group unify their fans and admirers, and how their own identity—as rebels, as misfits, and as Englishmen—have had such a profound impact on their rather intense, loyal fan base over the past fifty years. First is a consideration of various covers of the band's music and how, initially, impersonal commercialism shaped the choice of these covers between 1964 and the 1990s. The discussion then looks at the differences in selection and distribution of covers wrought by the Internet as recording, uploading, and dissemination of Kinks covers is now easily done by amateurs who are subject to instant feedback from anyone with access to the Web. The second part of the chapter considers the fan culture surrounding the band, supported by comments and responses supplied by fans for this project via a survey conducted online in 2014. Finally, the chapter will consider the Kinks' own reaction to fame and fandom—having been fans themselves of other musicians—to explore the contradictory nature of a band that has always been inclusive of its fans while at the same time decrying the

stress of touring and baggage that comes along with celebrity and objectification. In other words, this chapter is a look at an overarching but as
yet unaddressed theme of this book, "What have the Kinks ever done
for us?"

COVERS: ALVIN AND THE CHIPMUNKS SING "YOU REALLY GOT ME"[3]

The immediate impact of the Kinks is the music. There would be no
fans—from casual to super—without the music, nothing for the adver-
tisers or movie merchants to work with and nothing for the labels to
sell. Original releases are one thing, but tracks take on a life of their
own when they are covered by others, both professional musicians and
amateurs. So what of the Kinks' catalog has been covered? And does it
make a difference if it's the hits or the obscure stuff? Compiling all of
the extant covers of Kinks songs is a daunting task; fortunately, the
Internet rides to the rescue with Dave Emlen's "Unofficial Kinks Web
Site" KindaKinks.net, which includes a spreadsheet of Kinks covers that
can be filtered by song title, artist, or country and year.[4] A quick check
can easily turn into an afternoon of sifting and tweaking the filter pref-
erences, and hours disappear while chasing up French versions of "A
Well Respected Man" on YouTube. As of this writing (May 9, 2016), the
covers page ranges from 1964 through to 2014.

For the purposes of the discussion here, the filters were set to rum-
mage through the covers by year of release. Straightway a fun fact leaps
out at the viewer: about half of the songs listed here were released after
2000, and many of *those* songs fall into categories of deep cuts, B sides,
and amateur releases—if not fan covers, then fan-made video and audio
files made of live performances. The Internet and its attendant social
media have had a noticeable, if not strange, effect on Kinks material
and the approach toward it. Before the Internet, however, was the
analog sixties with, and throughout that decade, top ten hits. *Billboard*
charts, record sales, and radio airplay drove the cover choices in those
days, since both established artists and up-and-coming bands needed
tracks to fill out their albums, and covers were and are a quick-and-dirty
way to do so. Topping the list of covered hits, from a handful beginning
in 1964, "You Really Got Me" remains the popular track for artists to

cover into the twenty-first century—although the numbers here may be somewhat skewed by Van Halen's fifty-plus live versions (and of course because of the popularity of VH's original cover, many believed at the time that they were the original artists).[5]

Setting the filter on Emlen's site to release date, one can trace the general shape of the Kinks' Pye chart-busters from 1964 through to 1970. Large blocks of "You Really Got Me" are followed by "All Day and All of the Night" starting from 1964,[6] and both resurge at intervals through the subsequent decades. "Tired of Waiting" has a strong showing from 1965; "A Well Respected Man" proliferates in 1966. "Lola" has the next significantly big block in 1970, and in between the "big songs" of the 1960s appear smaller runs of other successful singles, including "See My Friends," "Sunny Afternoon," "Til the End of the Day," and "Death of a Clown." Many of the covers should come as no surprise: anything commercially produced that comes in bunches are going to be the hits and, not unusually, tracks that appear on the myriad compilation of Kinks songs that have been appearing since the 1965 American release *The Kinks Greatest Hits* through to the most recent compilations and anthologies. These covers include the most iconic tracks of the Pye years, the anthems that define the Kinks' sound and character as rebel rockers or thoughtful social observers.

Although they proliferate after the Kinks' late 1970s renaissance, lesser-known Kinks songs were not neglected by earlier cover artists in the 1960s. Between 1964 and 1970, still using "You Really Got Me" and "Lola" as the initial parameters, there are scattered throughout more obscure song covers: "I Took My Baby Home" by the Pickwicks is one of the earliest, and probably strangest, selections in 1964, released by Warner Brothers in Britain as a B side, considering that it didn't even chart for the Kinks.[7] Other curiosities include "So Mystifying" from Denmark in 1964; "Come on Now" from Spain; and "I Bet You Won't Stay" in 1965, from the American group the Cascades. There is a splash of "Just Can't Go to Sleep" covers from groups in the United States, Germany, and Norway in 1965, and a handful of others; rarely will one find even an isolated example of a more obscure song without one or two other releases around the same date. That said, the majority of 1960s covers, whether hits or deeper cuts, tend to be European with fewer American ones appearing after the 1965 ban.[8]

THIS STRANGE EFFECT   145

Although sixties hits are useful for a band to copy or to cash in on the Kinks' sound, even the obscure materials might prove successful for someone else. The Kinks, as did the Beatles and the Who, composed their own material; if their songwriters have demonstrable talent with commercial potential, that would surely mean that taking a risk on a B side or an obscure cut would be a safe bet. Certainly in the early days, Larry Page and others in the Kinks' management would encourage covers as well, as much money was to be made off the publishing rights to Ray's songs, regardless of their chart status.[9] Hence a number of these lesser-known songs were Ray Davies compositions written specifically with the idea of selling them to others: "I Go to Sleep" and "A House in the Country" are two examples—keeping in mind that in addition to grinding out songs for the Kinks' own assembly line, Ray had been incorporated as a songwriter for others in the mold of Lennon-McCartney (see chapter 3)—although it was only in 2016 that someone twigged with the idea of releasing a compilation of these particular releases (see the discography "Further Listening"). The idea of getting mileage out of publishing rights is, of course, a model that stretches back to Stephen Foster in the nineteenth century and Tin Pan Alley in the 1920s and 1930s, as the real money in the music business came from and still comes from sheet music and the composition itself, rather than the performance. Profits here go to the publisher, frequently to the detriment of not only the performer but also the actual composer who sells his songs on.

It is probably safe to say, given that the majority of the sixties covers are the hits or are those songs Ray composed for others, that early covers were not necessarily produced to associate oneself with any particular image of the Kinks (e.g., rebels with the loud, raucous stuff from the early sixties, or purveyors of Englishness and music-hall liveliness, a minor trend between 1966 and 1968); rather, record producers and managers produced the covers so their clients would provide a profit for the record company. Interpretations and originality were, for the most part, off the table: the Pickwicks' "I Took My Baby Home" and Gary Lewis and the Playboys' "All Day and All of the Night" followed closely the originals. The same holds true for many of these early covers, even the ones rendered into other (European) languages: French, Spanish, and Italian are well represented. Similarly, orchestral and instrumental versions of rock tracks were something of a novelty trend in the early sixties, with record labels cannibalizing their own acts: George Martin's orchestral versions of Beatles tracks filled out United Artists' release of *A Hard Day's Night*'s soundtrack, and the Larry Page Orchestra served up a generous helping of 1,001 "stringified" Kinks tunes with *Kinky Music* in 1965. Say the liner notes on the latter by Page, "The word 'Kink' now has a different meaning. It means hits! Ray Davies has the golden pen that seems to only write hit songs and I have selected here twelve of my personal favorites composed by him and/or his brother Dave." Stop reading now, and type "Larry Page Orchestra Kinks" into the YouTube search bar immediately. Are the vocals lines on "You Really Got Me" a sax or a kazoo? It doesn't matter, as the images conjured up are at once so painfully Austin Powers it's worth the price of admission.

The late sixties of *Village Green* and *Arthur* and the seventies stage shows did not inspire the same rush of covers as did the 1960s Pye hits, nor are they among the continued commercial releases of these particular top-ten chestnuts across the ensuing fifty years, demonstrating that at least among the professionals that the Kinks' covers or songs seem limited to a very particular set of songs. Many of these hits have long been at risk of overexposure due to endless oldies airplay and repackaging of the Kinks' catalog; new releases of complete Kinks albums by Sanctuary and Koch Records were welcomed by fans in the late 1990s as making available once again tracks that had languished in obscurity outside of the die-hard fan set, all lovingly remastered in glorious mono. Oddly enough, when the Kinks' American ban was lifted, two LPs of rarer and more obscure songs were released, *The Great Lost Kinks Album* and *The Kinks' Kronikles*, both with liner notes from journalist and Kinks enthusiast John Mendelssohn, who himself has championed releases of the more obscure stuff. Neither were big sellers, and the former was pulled from the shelves allegedly on Ray Davies's request.

The changes in cover choices begin to appear in the seventies when new bands who grew up as fans recorded their favorite tracks as their own rebellion against contemporary music trends, particularly in Britain when progressive rock and glam were all the rage. And yet while the Kinks may have profited from their renewed commercial success thanks to a cover of their ur-hit "You Really Got Me" by Van Halen, it is interesting that when the Jam and the Pretenders eschewed current trends and chose to record music from their childhood Mod and rock heroes respectively, they chose more obscure or less covered Kinks tracks, for example, "David Watts" for Paul Weller's group, and "I Go to Sleep" for Chrissie Hynde's. As for the Kinks as purveyors of nostalgia (by whatever definition one chooses) or Englishness, one sees covers of these typical songs much later in the day: for example, Kirsty McColl's iconic cover of "Days" dates only from 1989.[10] As a song now most associated with thoughtful reflection of the past, "Days" did not really take off as cover material until the early twenty-first century.

The free-for-all of covers of both well-visited and obscure tracks explodes with the Internet beginning in the late nineties, the availability of home-recording devices and software, and the advent of social media such as MySpace, Facebook, and YouTube. The latter especially has become, in its first decade, a major platform for sharing and distribution of covers. And because the Kinks have written songs about *everything*, covers of "Phenomenal Cat" populated with actual cats have been uploaded to the site. Even in the age of the Internet, however, covers of the hits proliferate among Kinks recorded versions. Many fans have a go at the hand-cramping power chords; the comments section, usually a vast wasteland in open media sites, tend to be fairly positive for the most part (and videos of the Kinks themselves frequently become thoughtful discussions among old and new fans). Ray himself is not above covering his own material, but he is keen to have it reinterpreted; he himself has given Kinks tracks choral treatment courtesy of the Crouch End Chorus. Numerous famous fans have reworked their favorite Kinks tunes as found, for example, on the album *This Is Where I Belong: The Songs of Ray Davies and the Kinks*. While Dave has always argued for moving forward and avoiding turning shows into what he calls "Karaoke Kinks," Ray is more thoughtful about the artist's role as a creator and allowing others to take his songs where they may.

The Internet has also created a platform in which fans old and new can communicate instantly (if not anonymously) among themselves and share material over social media. This includes uploading their own covers of songs and footage of live performance stretching from 1960s television shows to streaming live, albeit shaky phone footage of a concert, or simply blogging about their interpretation of a particular track as whimsy takes them. Hence both covers and the dialogue they create reinforce the theme raised at the start of this chapter: the accessibility of the music has increased reflection and engagement with the Kinks' music. Such communication has not only reinforced and shaped the Kinks' image more than the original marketers and promoters ever dreamed but also shaped the character of fan communities. Whatever songs Ray created, whether due to his contractual obligations, wrestling with his personal demons, or drawing off his family experiences, also shaped the experiences of a younger generation—experiences they now recapture through amateur performance or discussion of said performance. Some of the amateur covers may well simply be peacocking, but the sheer proliferation of them, and from all over the Kinks' catalog, demonstrates a characteristic that the fans themselves brought up repeatedly in the survey response: that the Kinks are versatile musically as a group, and there is a style to fit anyone. As one fan described them, "When you think of the Kinks . . . the tone of the lyrics [can be] sarcastic, sardonic, humorous, cynical, rebellious, intellectual, and even dark at times." The covers create a community—whether seeking out the original track, arguing over the cover's merits, or sharing their own memories and interpretation of the track. All of these individuals and outsiders are brought together by the different avatars of the same group, and the obscurity or exclusive factor makes these bonds even stronger.

Fandom's social unity through the music has affected the shape of the Kinks' image if not legacy. Certainly covers are a component of this, serving to engage the community into the merits of a cover or allowing participation of the music as a form of inclusion with the band. Covers exemplify an indirect relationship with the band; fandom itself takes many forms that run the gamut from admiration from afar to fans who claim to be part of the Kinks' intimate circle. Appreciation of and by fans and Kinks alike is a two-way street.

DAN'S A FAN: KINKS FAN CULTURE

A familiar phenomenon at a Kinks/Ray/Dave concert is of hundreds of people singing along to the chorus of "I'm not like everybody else!" The rebellious nature of Ray Davies's lyrics and Dave Davies's angry-young-man guitar-playing style has been a rallying point for the group's fans and an extension of their own self-expression since the band bust out on stage with early versions of "You Really Got Me" in 1964. Additionally, especially outside of England, tracks such as "A Well Respected Man," "Dedicated Follower of Fashion," and "Village Green Preservation Society" have presented to Anglophile fans an image of English humor and attitude. Even the commercial ban on the group from America for four years had a profound impact on fan culture, especially in the United States, as fans who doggedly managed to follow the band in these "lost years" sometimes see themselves as superior to fans who discovered the group in the wake of Van Halen's cover of "You Really Got Me." These and other aspects of Kinks fandom are examined in this section, supported by information provided by the fans themselves from a survey conducted worldwide (via the Internet) in April–May 2014. These fans were queried about their heroes and asked, among other things, what made them become fans of the Kinks and what made the group for them, personally, special. Most of the roughly two hundred people who answered the survey were white men from Western Europe and North America, with a majority in their sixties; most were fairly well educated with some college or higher degrees, and most held white-collar, professional jobs.

A common thread among the replies was the band's support of those who feel as if they're on the outside of society. The Kinks remain rock music's favorite underdogs, always coming in "fourth," and snubs of the band and Ray Davies are both a source of frustration and pride for the fans. Many of the fans surveyed commented on this aspect of the Kinks as one that was appealing about the band: "The Kinks helped me realize that I was an outsider, and that it was all right to be one. Being an individual is one of the greatest things I've gotten from them." Another noted, "They've stayed relatively unknown to the general public. That increased their cool factor for more hardcore music fans." Kinks fans are especially proud that their heroes suffered commercial obscurity because of their constant defiance of authority, management, and commercialism. Remarked one, "The Kinks were always different than other bands; they had a sound that was their own, [and] they wrote about the common man and his issues and weren't afraid to express it, knowing that it wouldn't be commercially successful."

The Kinks as underdog is also reinforced in newspaper and magazine articles and blogs about the Kinks; often such reports note the Kinks are always bridesmaids compared to the commercial juggernaut of their British Invasion counterparts, notably the holy trinity of the

Beatles, the Rolling Stones, and the Who. Argued a fan, "They are a 'thinking man's' group. Ray's lyrics were always ahead of his contemporaries. They weren't just lyrics for lyric sake. The lyrics meant something." Another commented, "The nature of the songwriting, its attitude, [and] the storytelling in just a few word[s] . . . there's a depth and meaning, humor and hubris . . . a craft to the words that there isn't with most bands." And while fans acknowledge that other composers, such as Pete Townshend of the Who, also wrote songs that contained social commentary, "Ray writes songs that sound like they *mean* something to him. Pete [Townshend] spins what he finds in his own soul into social commentaries and spiritual allegories, while Ray looks at the everyday world around him and finds his own soul there."

Critics and journalists often try to identify what made the Kinks outsiders, and many point to the ban as the critical point of the band's development and consequent commercial exclusion. The fans surveyed for this project had a different take on it, however, and they remarked that from the beginning the band projected from the stage and drew together with the audience a sense of inclusion among others who felt rejected. Said one, "It's how family is important to the band . . . in their books and in their songs, family is key. It, to me, is a reason the Kinks aren't as popular with people as [are] other British Invasion [groups]. . . . Critics, Kultists [*sic*], and bands inspired by them get it. The general public doesn't. I can be an outsider at times, and that's how the Kinks are." Another argued, "The Kinks . . . never 'played the game' . . . [they] are a working man's band. Everything they sing about is everyday life. I relate to the songs. I can't always relate to the Stones or any other ban like I do with the Kinks." For the fans, the ban did not define the group; it was simply one consequence of the band's already strongly defined character as misfits that appealed to their followers. [11]

So possibility the Kinks' obscurity seems to come from a desire to remain ordinary and avoid commercial success (whether intentionally or not remains a topic of conjecture). Regardless of the reasons for the Kinks' position as underdogs, it's a point of proprietary pride and camaraderie among their admirers; fans and critics alike want as many people as possible to know this. Considering then how *many* of these articles and reviews there are, especially whenever a Kinks milestone comes along, and how mainstream the media sources are that publish them (in addition to the usual *Mojo* and guitar magazine stories, articles and reviews on the Kinks regularly appear in *The Guardian*, *The Telegraph*, and for the more prurient reader's pleasure, the *Daily Mail*), rock and roll's best-kept secret is in serious peril of overexposure.

I AM IN PARADISE: FAN CULTURE AND ESCAPISM

Christopher Partridge has recently published a study on the connection between spiritual experience and the effects of performing onstage before an enthusiastic crowd.[12] In speaking to a number of performers, Partridge noted that many felt transformed on stage and that the rush of emotion during the performance became an almost addictive thing. To end the show was emotionally and physically a letdown. Ray has also described a number of times in interviews and in his own writing the vitality he draws off audiences and the strong sense of happiness and self-worth he has felt in performances, transformed completely into another person with an elevated sense of worth and belonging, only to crumble emotionally when the lights come back up and the crowd files out, the connection broken. This strong connection among identity, performance, and adulation as the defining attitudes of self-identification and self-worth became the basis of Ray's 1974 Granada Television play *Starmaker*: he plays an arrogant pop star who thrives on the adulation of fans and refuses to let the mundanity of the world offstage interfere with his self-purpose. Gradually his sense of worth erodes as he agrees to allow an ordinary bloke to switch places with him. Eventually Everyman rises to become the successful rock star and take everything the star has, reducing him to a silent, staring, blank face lost among the crowd of fans, embodied in the track "A Face in the Crowd."

Contact and relationships with fans started straight out of the gate for the Kinks' early tours, and travel up and down the country quickly resulted in the harem typical of a "girl in every port." Whereas Cynthia Lennon documents how female fans stalked the Beatles practically into hiding,[13] at least one of the Kinks was still a teen, and the others not much older, and still lived at home (if not nearby) at the start of their crazy fame. Both write at length about the madness of these fans—some of whom became friends in the early days and who offered accommodation and escape from life on the road and the endless screaming. Others, especially female fans, are described simply in terms of their appearance, physical attributes, and sexual appetites; they remain nameless and fulfilled simply a physical need or momentary whim. Even well into their fifties at the time of writing their autobiographies, both Davieses could describe looks and particular physical characteristics of many of their early conquests. Ray, for example, took great pride in "shaping" one girl into a great beauty on each successive visit to her port of call; and yet in *X-Ray*, his elder statesman avatar disgusts and embarrasses his younger self[14] with relentless descriptions of girls' breasts and blow jobs, asking, "Isn't this why you came here?"[15]

The Kinks have otherwise certainly appreciated their fans' support, especially the diehards who remained loyal through thick and thin. "Rock 'n' Roll Cities" is an example of fan appreciation if not a tribute to life on the road, and it is a paean to those fans who stuck with the band during their low period of the 1970s. The band has also demonstrated connectivity with fans since the days of the Kinks through to solo and tribute shows by initiating sing-alongs. Some fans complain that Ray puts on little more than cabaret, or as one fan noted on a message board, that Dave's 2013 US performances were little more than drunken karaoke.[16] One can't see the Davieses being particularly wounded by such assessments. The 1968 album *Live at Kelvin Hall* certainly reveals that even early in their career as a hipster band allegedly heralding the end of Western civilization, the shambolic singsong nature of the live performance belies camaraderie with their audience. During the 1970s, press reviews on both sides of the Atlantic praised the Kinks' connection to their audiences, even if their technical chops and offerings were lacking. As one fan noted for this project, "The Kinks line-up never forgot that the fan came first. No matter how tired, how difficult, how challenging life on the road was for any of them, when the house lights went down, and the stage lights went up, they gave you 1000%." Judging from the response on the surveys and from myriad professional reviews, such engagement remains one of the band's strongest attractions.

SO WHAT ABOUT FANDOM?

Fans come in all flavors and all intensities, including those who simply buy tickets for a show, have a good night out, and go home, that is, casual fans who recognize the hits. Then there are the diehards who collect all of the music, sleep on pavements to get tickets (or these days crash the website when the tickets go on sale), show up at the gigs an hour before the sound check, and linger by the stage door until hours after the performance. Casual fans view the diehards as a bit odd; diehards argue that "casual" is not in a real fan's vocabulary. Even the diehards have internal divisions: distinctive among Kinks fans are those who date themselves back to back in the sixties and those younger fans who came on board with the Kinks' commercial renaissance in the eighties; these groups are further stratified as to who is the "true fan" or not.[17] The band seems to make no distinction, showing appreciation for the quiet fans as well as acknowledging the diehards who stuck with the band even through the periods of their obscurity. Furthermore, the Kinks may well be the only band with a thriving tribute band made up of myriad former members who've left or been sacked, themselves easy and comfortable with the fans at gatherings and gigs.

The Kinks have been around long enough for famous fans to actually record music by invitation or actually hobnob with—if not almost marry—their heroes. One distinctive characteristic about the Kinks in particular, however, is how even the most ordinary fan feels somehow a part of the Kinks' circle, even if they too remain simply a face in the crowd. A common theme from the survey was the revelation that the Kinks were just "ordinary guys" and "fun" after seeing them in concert. The scary snarls heard on the radio turned out to come from "the kind of guys you could hang out and have a beer with." Said one simply, "It was a nice surprise to find out just how much fun they were in concert." Another comment on the down-to-earth quality of the band members was, "[Dave] walked right over to us ready to talk or see what we wanted . . . you know, kinda like a regular person would if someone called out their name." As for the distinct bond formed between the Kinks and their fans, and the in-concert vibe of other bands, a fan surveyed remarked, "[The Kinks] love to perform and fans are encouraged to participate. They always shake hands . . . and you feel that bond between the two. I know of no other artists that has created that type of relationship." Kinks fans thus form their own tribe with a distinct if not fluid hierarchy. Regardless of their internal politics, however, they strongly see themselves as distinct from both the "casual Kinks fans" and the fans of other (especially) more commercially successful bands.

The bond among the tribe is fueled partly by identification with the songs' lyrics and partly by the creation of alliances with like-minded fans (accelerated especially in the past fifteen or so years by the advent of social media online). [18]

While many respondents to the survey said that they were content to remain anonymous among the fandom, some diehards have taken advantage of the Internet and its instant communication on the one hand and its anonymity on the other to reinforce their own sense of identity by standing along the edges of the Kinks' own spotlight and having some of the glamour if not distinction of that fantasy world rub off on them. They have developed a superficial relationship with the band by being recognized, if not at shows, then as an online presence and, in extreme cases, believe that they truly are friends with the band. Indeed, the artificial intimacy of social media has led to a blurry distinction of the line between fan and Kink. It results in an uncomfortable objectification of the band evident from their earliest days, but the Internet has made all too obvious the loudest voices.

"Rock 'n' Roll Fantasy" explores such a Kinks fan. The track begins as a reflection of life as a rock star as the narrator reflects on the ordinary person he used to be and how he might want to break up his band and start a new life. A verse or two in, the verse describes the enthusiast Dan the Fan who has all of the albums and goes to all of the gigs; his loyalty knows no bounds. In the short story Ray wrote to accompany the song, this fan has no concept of social boundaries, approaching the celebrity in the story when he's just returning from a loved one's funeral. [19] The fan demands an autograph and asks the grieving artist about upcoming album releases and tours. Unlike Chuck Berry's paean to fandom, "Sweet Little Sixteen," Ray's depiction of the diehard is couched in loneliness and some resentment rather than indulgence. The fan shapes his life around the band's commercial milestones ("He's seen us low and he's seen us high") but fails to see that for the band, it's just another day's work. Dan the Fan idolizes the hero, not the man, and there are indeed several fans who claim with great pride that Ray wrote the song about them. But they neglect to pay attention to the repeated hooks of the song, where the singer protests that he doesn't *want* to be a rock-and-roll fantasy and that he doesn't want to spend the rest of his life hiding away his true character, lost behind the facade of celebrity. In celebrating the enthusiasm of a die-hard fan,

Ray's song reveals much loneliness, if not resentment, at being the object of such devotion. "Celluloid Heroes," discussed below, is another musical expression of the depression felt by a performer because of the price of fame, and these and other songs about fame demonstrate that the relationship between fan and performer is as much a facade as is the onstage persona.

IF MY FRIENDS COULD SEE ME NOW: THE PRICE OF FAME AND RECOGNITION

Did the Kinks like being famous? While they celebrate fans in song and included them in sing-alongs from the very beginning, one of their earliest songs reflects the difficulties of fame, as noted in chapter 3. Ray sings lead on "Where Have All the Good Times Gone?" and here he is, at only twenty years old, looking back "on all the good times we had" and wishing it could just be like yesterday; for a song released in October 1965, perhaps this is indicative of just how much stress and pressure the band had been through in only the fourteen months since "You Really Got Me" hit number one on the charts. Nearly ten years later, the Kinks released "Sitting in My Hotel" (September 1973). This track describes the loneliness of touring: the singer is dressed in his fancy stage clothes, he has the world handed to him by hangers-on, and he's driven about in a chauffeured limousine. He's hiding behind a locked door, however, seven stories up, isolated from the crowds. He's stuck in an anonymous hotel room, wondering if his friends would envy him his good fortune but fearing that they would mock him for selling out—a similar sentiment in "All of My Friends Were There," as the lazy performer fears mockery from his actual friends for a shoddy performance. The latter performer hides behind a false moustache to give his terrible show; the singer in "Sitting in My Hotel" copes with his fears by retreating to past comforts—he sits alone, watches old television shows, and is "writing songs for old-time vaudeville revues."

These themes of loneliness and isolation and of the glamorous facade versus mundane reality were most famously addressed in 1972's "Celluloid Heroes," sung by Ray in a fragile voice against a simple accompaniment. The song appears on the album *Everybody's in Show-Biz*, a divisive album among Kinks fans and some critics (who find its live side sloppy and self-indulgent), yet its studio side contains several thoughtful and provocative tracks. "Celluloid Heroes" sublimely illustrates the two-sided coin of fame and adoration by fans: the exterior, public facade created by the businessmen and consumed by the audience, and the internal isolation and fragility of the actual person. Fame and adulation of the fans brings immortality if not a transitory sense of being alive and important. What the audience devours and how they interpret that performer is frozen in time; the film, the painting, and the record become the physical, collectable avatar of the performer.

The cost of fame is tremendous: the real person must be sacrificed to become that object. The spiritual life force described by Partridge the sociologist and Ray Davies the performer takes a toll on the performer; they may appear tough as nails on stage and adored by millions, but the output and the image take on a life of their own—the actual person behind the creation is actually known by very few. In a number of respects, "Celluloid Heroes" works on the same level of the Homeric hymns: for the ancient Greeks, it was not enough to gain honor through one's deeds alone (*arête*); there had to be public recognition and acclamation of the deeds (*tîmê*). The hero wanted songs sung about him and an audience to listen and share; he became defined by his deeds and public behavior. Likewise does Ray describe the fragility of the performer and the sort of immortality that fame brings in "Celluloid Heroes." Not only do such performers remain strong in popular consciousness as the embodiment of a certain image (how many university freshmen in 2016 still hang on their dormitory walls iconic posters of Marilyn Monroe or James Dean?), but also their names are, as Ray sings, literally written in concrete—not marble or gold but plain, solid cement with a functional purpose: to be walked on by oblivious passersby. Such works not only ensure the immortality of and maintain a connection between the hero and the community but also reveal the human weakness even behind the most heroic of facades. "Celluloid Heroes" reflects on Greta Garbo's fragility and how it was motivation for her to work so hard to present a cool public face. While the men in the song stand strong even in death (Rudolph Valentino looks up the ladies' dresses; Bela Lugosi is apt to bite the ankles of strangers who step on his star), the women are lonely (Bette Davis) or "not very tough" and "flesh and blood" (Marilyn Monroe) in real life—an interesting dichotomy considering Ray's own association with feminine emotion and fragility (as discussed in chapter 5) in contrast to the cheeky chappies or hard-edged men who ran the music business. Real-life vulnerability stands in contrast to the image of princesses of the screen and the deceptive "iron or steel" persona presented to their fans. "Celluloid Heroes" represents a conflict that the Kinks, as well as any celebrity, seem to wrestle with: a need to be in the spotlight and to be adored by the fans as well as a human need to have a normal, quiet life among trusted friends and family. The quiet life itself, however, is one of loneliness and isolation—another phenomenon of the struggle between the desire for fame and the security of obscurity that has antecedents in antiquity. When Aeneas journeys to the underworld to ask advice of his father, he sees among the dead the great hero Achilles. Fanboy that he is (and seeming to ignore the fact that Achilles was among those whose attack on and destruction of Aeneas's hometown started him on his journey from Troy to Italy in the first place), Aeneas rushes over to speak to his hero. Achilles, famous for choosing a short life and an immortal, heroic reputation over a long, stable life that ends in obscurity, however, is merely a sorrowful shade of his earthly self: he now sadly wanders about the underworld as a shadow and asks Aeneas, "Do they still sing songs about me?"

With similar sentiment, 1987's "The Road" complements "Sitting in My Hotel"; as Ray noted in his 2014 stage show in support of *Americana*, people assume he's oh, so English, but in actuality, because he's been touring for nearly fifty years, he doesn't feel as if he has a home anywhere.[20] "The Road" reflects what was easily by then a lifetime of touring for the Kinks and is reflective by that point of their second wind in the United States. Again the song comes from the point of view of a narrator sitting lonely in an anonymous hotel room, reflecting back on life on the road: the dives, the bars, and the dubious characters he and his band have encountered. He remembers friends he's left behind—and he also marvels that after all of these years, he and the band are actually still touring at all. The song is autobiographical, as the narrator speaks wistfully of his younger self, heading out into Soho with a cheap, knock-off American guitar and inspired by the Rolling Stones to put together a band and to go out on the road with them. He describes the members of the original Kinks lineup, playing in—what would have been to the teenaged Kinks—exotic places such as Wigan in the UK. As with "Celluloid Heroes" the song addresses the victims of fame—both those who perished in its wake and those who are still doggedly performing, still needing the adulation of the crowd. The song also answers the question about the Kinks' complicated relationship with the music business as well as their fans: as long as the fans keep showing up for the gigs (albeit to hear the oldies, as Ray names "Dedicated Follower of Fashion [1966]," "A Well Respected Man" [1965], and "Come Dancing"), the band will continue to perform, despite the negative comments of the critics.

SO WHY KINKS? ARE THE SCHOLARS CORRECT? ARE THE KINKS REAL OR ARTIFICIAL MEN?

It's a complex situation: the majority of fans like the Kinks for being ordinary blokes and guys one feels ostensibly comfortable with and can identify with. The Kinks' own music expresses appreciation of the fans, but at the same time it expresses a longing to return to anonymity. The Kinks' appeal, that is, the world they created with their songs—whether English, working class, misfit, or happy families—strikes deeply a chord among their fans, even if said fans aren't English, rural, or working class. Instead it is their engagement that appeals; not only do they appeal literally to the audience with sing-alongs or meet and greets, but also they remain to the fans "authentic" and down to earth. Said one fan from Mexico that despite growing up in urban sprawl, with the music of the Kinks, "I was drawn into the comfort zone of its simpler world . . . I was 16 and the real world was too complicated. I enjoyed the world of village greens and nostalgia and of being, as far as I could tell, the only Kinks fan around." Another mused, "[Misfits] opened up an appreciation of how different we all really are and how I belonged to something bigger than the surrounding bullshit parts of my life at the time." Perhaps here is where the connection Ray felt with the older generation of his family, that they held together and remained happy even in the face of difficult times, becomes the catalyst of engagement between the Kinks and their fans. One British, female fan noted, "[It's] songwriting from the heart. Brutal honesty. Being able to express self-doubt and despair of all the world's ills. Also a sense of upbeat sensibility to go on and make the most of it despite it all." There is also a strongly ingrained sense of stubbornness that appeals: hard times can be overcome with familial solidarity; defiance is better than selling out.

A number of survey respondents remarked that part of the appeal of the Kinks was their approachability. For many, attending a performance was critical as it enhanced the emotional connection and identification already enjoined through the music. Most of the respondents had seen the Kinks live in some capacity, and for almost all of them, there was a connection felt that went beyond the music itself, although the desire to meet the band or be friends with them was *not* part of their relationship for the majority of them. Most people put on the brakes when it came to a desire to actually meet the band, but a few others have attempted to break through the wall between them and the group. The Kinks are admired for their *nobilitas*, a good descriptor of "Englishness." *Nobilitas* is a Roman virtue that describes one's ability to carry on through extraordinary and difficult times—the "stiff upper lip" image of the Briton who "keeps calm and carries on," especially if it's done with a dry, humorous understatement. As noted throughout this book, the Kinks were praised for their authenticity—that they describe real life and ordinary people; as one fan put it, "They speak to real people. They aren't singing about hot button social and political issues, but about real life." One might laugh at the thought of a huge group of fans singing along to "I'm Not Like Everybody Else," but many of the fans acknowledge the irony of the sentiment and comment that the recognition of ordinary individuals lifted them from their own feelings of isolation and loneliness: "'Life Goes On . . .' really made me felt that I was not alone," commented one.

In the 1960s, Ray and the Kinks' depiction of English life and ordinary people failed to chart commercially, but it did not stop record producers from hustling out covers of the Kinks' tried-and-true catalog. As the Kinks turned inward and sat out their American ban by becoming more and more introspectively English in content, a number of groups in the UK, Europe, and even the United States were still covering Kinks' top tens, such as "You Really Got Me" (especially) and their other key singles between 1964 and 1969. Reprise packaged the Kinks up as English working-class gentlemen on their return to the United States in 1969 with the "God Save the Kinks" campaign, complete with free samples of plastic grass distributed with a now-rather-coveted re-packaging of Kinks hits called *Kinks: Then and Now*. Village greens did not sell in the 1960s, and the Kinks briefly gave the people what they wanted during the late 1970s and 1980s with arena tours and album-oriented rock (AOR), but ultimately, at the end of the day what persists most strongly of the Kinks' character is a mash-up of the band as a group of misfit rebels, describing a very everyman-us-against-them as the journalists and reissuers package and repackage them as part of "English Heritage." They are funny, they are thoughtful. The Kinks are, as Andrew Tyler of the *New Music Express* remarked, "a thoroughly confusing phenomenon" as Ray is a "man of summer sandwiches and classless frippery" and the Kinks themselves, led by Dave's guitar, were "roughhewn as the junkiest pub band."[21] So what *are* the Kinks as others see them? Rebels? Misfits? English vaudevillians? Tea-drinking, working-class ruffians? Tick all that apply.

NOTES

INTRODUCTION

1. I. Spragg, *London's Underground's Strangest Tales* (London: Portico, 2013), 106.

2. A. Bellotti, "Ham and High: Ray and Dave Davies Interview," *Hampstead Theatre Online*, April 11, 2014, accessed January 30, 2015, http://www.hampsteadtheatre.com/.

1. AROUND THE DIAL

1. Ray Davies, *X-Ray* (New York: Overlook, 1995), 102.

2. See Carey Fleiner, "The Influence of Family and Childhood Experience on the Works of Ray and Dave Davies," *Popular Music and Society* 34, no. 3 (July 2011): 330n2. Peter Quaife was no different in the sixties, and he also wielded a wicked, if not inappropriate, sense of humor when it came to making comments to the press. For example, he once falsely told reporters that the Kinks were busy at work on a collection of Bob Dylan covers (Doug Hinman, *The Kinks: All Day and All of the Night; Day-by-Day Concerts, Recordings, and Broadcasts, 1961–1996* [San Francisco: Backbeat, 2004], 93). Another time, Quaife was escorted by machine-gun-wielding guards back onto a plane during a refueling stop in Moscow in response to his query if "Baldy" was still running the country (Thomas Kitts, *Ray Davies: Not Like Everybody Else* [New York: Routledge, 2008], 49).

3. Sean Michaels, "Ray Davies Wants to Reunite the Kinks," *Guardian*, September 25, 2008, accessed October 5, 2008, http://www.guardian.co.uk/.

4. Neville Marten and Jeffrey Hudson, *The Kinks: Well Respected Men* (Chessington, UK: Castle Communications, 1996), 14.

5. The closest one might get is the track "A Little Bit of Abuse," according to Kitts in his discussion of the albums *Give the People What They Want* and *State of Confusion*, in *Ray Davies*, 205.

2. SOMETHING BETTER BEGINNING

1. Interview with Dave Davies by Joe Lynch, "Dave Davies Reflects on the Kinks' Origins, Embracing Technology and Relationship with Ray," *Billboard*, February 20, 2015, accessed June 14, 2015, http://www.billboard.com/.

2. Interview with Dave Davies by Jeb Wight, "Dave Davies: There's Madness There!" Classic Rock Revisited, accessed June 14, 2015, http://www.classicrockrevisited.com/.

3. Keith Gildart, *Images of England through Popular Music: Class, Youth and Rock 'n' Roll, 1955–1976* (London: Palgrave MacMillan, 2013), 8–10; on live music in Britain during the postwar period through to the 1950s, see Simon Frith, Matt Brennan, Martin Cloonan, and Emma Webster, eds., *The History of Live Music in Britain*, vol. 1, *1950–1967 (From the Dance Hall to the 100 Club)* (London: Ashgate, 2013), 1–11.

4. Recommended reading includes Asa Briggs, *A Social History of England*, 3rd rev. ed. (London: Weidenfeld & Nicolson, 1994); E. Hopkins, *A Social History of the English Working Classes, 1815–1945* (London: Hodder Education, 1979); E. P. Thompson, *The Making of the English Working Class* (London: Penguin, 2013); Eric Hobsbawm, *The Age of Extremes: The Short Twentieth Century, 1914–1991* (London: Michael Joseph, 1994); P. Catterall and J. Obelkevich, eds., *Understanding Post-War British Society* (London: Routledge, 1994); and S. Todd, *The People: The Rise and Fall of the Working Class, 1910–2010* (London: John Murray, 2015).

5. See, for example, Keith Gildart, "Class, Nation and Social Change in the Kinks' England," in his *Images of England*, 128–47; D. Simonelli, *Working Class Heroes: Rock Music and British Society in the 1960s and 1970* (Lanham, MD: Lexington, 2013); Peter Frame, *The Restless Generation: How Rock Music Changed the Face of 1950s Britain* (London: Rogan House 2007); Adrian Horn, *Juke Box Britain: Americanisation and Youth Culture, 1945–1960* (Manchester, UK: Manchester University Press, 2009); Arthur Marwick, *The Sixties: Cultural Revolution in Britain, France, Italy, and the United States, c. 1958–c. 1974* (London: Bloomsbury Reader, 2012); Joanna Bourke, *Working-Class Cultures in Britain, 1890–1960: Gender, Class and Ethnicity* (London: Routledge, 1996); and Ross McKibbin, *Classes and Cultures: England 1918–1951*

(Oxford: Oxford University Press, 1998). On the Kinks themselves, see, for example, Thomas Kitts, *Ray Davies: Not Like Everybody Else* (New York: Routledge, 2008); Neville Marten and Jeffrey Hudson, *The Kinks: Well Respected Men* (Chessington, UK: Castle Communications, 1996), 38–43; Joseph G. Marotta, "The Loss of Identity and the Myth of Edenic Return in Ray Davies," in *Living on a Thin Line: Crossing Aesthetic Borders with the Kinks*, ed. Thomas M. Kitts and Michael J. Kraus, 68–77 (Rumford, RI: Rock 'n' Roll Research Press, 2002); Nick Baxter-Moore, "'This Is Where I Belong': Identity, Social Class, and the Nostalgic Englishness of Ray Davies and the Kinks," *Popular Music and Society* 29, no. 2 (2006): 145–65; and Keith Gildart, "From 'Dead End Streets' to 'Shangri-Las': Negotiating Social Class and Post-War Politics with Ray Davies and the Kinks," *Contemporary British History* 26, no. 3 (2012): 273–98.

6. Gildart's introductory survey on current scholarship is indispensable in *Images of England*, 5–12.

7. Much of the discussion of the Kinks' family and upbringing throughout this chapter is adapted from my article, "The Influence of Family and Childhood Experience on the Works of Ray and Dave Davies," *Popular Music and Society* 34, no. 3 (July 2011): 329–50. Other good discussions on the Kinks' formative years include Ray and Dave's own autobiographies, as well as the biographies by Jon Savage, *The Kinks: The Official Biography* (London: Faber & Faber, 1984); Marten and Hudson, *The Kinks*; and Kitts, *Ray Davies*, among the others noted in chapter 1.

8. Dave Davies, *Kink* (New York: Hyperion, 1996), 5; Kitts, *Ray Davies*, 1.

9. On "Dead End Street" influences, see Johnny Rogan, *The Complete Guide to the Music of the Kinks* (London: Omnibus, 1998), 17. A thoughtful exegesis of the song can be found in Kitts, *Ray Davies*, 75–78.

10. D. Davies, *Kink*, 6.

11. As noted by Kitts, *Ray Davies*, 2.

12. For "big picture" surveys on this period, see Dominic Sandbrook, *Never Had It So Good: A History of Britain from Suez to the Beatles* (London: Abacus, 2006); Peter Hennessy, *Having It So Good: Britain in the Fifties* (London: Penguin, 2007); D. Kynaston, *Austerity Britain, 1945–1951 (Tales of a New Jerusalem)* (London: Bloomsbury, 2008); D. Kynaston, *Family Britain: 1951–1957* (London: Bloomsbury, 2009); D. Kynaston, *Modernity Britain: Opening the Box, 1957–1959* (London: Bloomsbury, 2013); and P. Addison and H. Jones, eds., *A Companion to Contemporary Britain, 1939–2000* (Oxford, UK: Blackwell, 2005).

13. Marten and Hudson, *The Kinks*, 14. See also McKibbin, *Classes and Cultures*, 332–85 (sport), 386–418 (popular music and the *danse palais*), 419–56 (cinema), 457–76 (radio listening and the influence of the BBC). For a

contemporary sociological study on working-class pastimes and entertainments, see B. S. Rowntree and G. R. Lavers, *English Life and Leisure: A Social Study* (London: Longmans, Green, 1951). For a more recent evaluation, see Frith et al., *History of Live Music*, 1–35.

14. D. Davies, *Kink*, 9.

15. Ray Davies, *X-Ray* (New York: Overlook, 1995). On the lives of women in this period, see Bourke, *Working-Class Cultures*; and E. Roberts, *Women and Families: An Oral History, 1940–1970* (Oxford, UK: Blackwell, 1995).

16. D. Davies, *Kink*, 13.

17. See Deena Weinstein, "Relations in the Kinks: Familiar but Not Fully Familial," *Popular Music and Society* 29, no. 2 (2006): 167–87.

18. R. Davies, *X-Ray*, 38–39; D. Davies makes a similar comment (*Kink*, 13).

19. D. Davies, *Kink*, 9.

20. R. Davies, *X-Ray*, 38–39.

21. Many thanks to Dave Tillerton for supplying this list. Dave Davies's prelist show tends to mix Kinks tracks with more contemporary rock and roll and his current interests; many thanks to Rebecca G. Wilson for her kind help supplying tracks from Dave's more recent tours.

22. See Patricia Gordon Sullivan, "'Let's Have a Go at It': The British Music Hall and the Kinks," in Kitts and Kraus, *Living on a Thin Line*, 80–99.

23. While the sons have generally fond memories of Fred Davies, Kitts notes that outsiders were not always so generous in their description of him (Kitts, *Ray Davies*, 3).

24. Kitts, *Ray Davies*, 11.

25. Kitts, *Ray Davies*, 5; R. Davies, *X-Ray*, 39.

26. Ray Davies in interview with Terry Gross, "Naive, Yet Revolutionary: Ray Davies on 50 Years of the Kinks," *Fresh Air*, December 25, 2014, accessed 7 August 2015, http://www.npr.org/.

27. R. Davies, *X-Ray*, 32, 62–63.

28. On punk and music hall, see Royston Ellis, *The Big Beat Scene* (York, UK: Music Mentor, [1961] 2010), 73–86.

29. *Never Mind the Baubles* went out on BBC Four on December 26, 2013. See David Simpson, "Anarchy in Huddersfield: The Day the Sex Pistols Played Santa," *Guardian*, December 23, 2013, accessed January 15, 2015, http://www.theguardian.com/. The footage is also in Temple's 2000 film, *The Filth and the Fury*.

30. Or, as he put it, "I am not a musician. I am a ham." Quoted in E. Nuzum, *Parental Advisory: Music Censorship in America* (New York: Perenniel, 2001), 243. A transcript of the original interview, conducted by David Gans while touring with the band in January 1982, can be found at "Ozzy

Osbourne," Levity, January 10, 1982, accessed January 25, 2015, http://www. levity.com/.

31. John Cleese, *So, Anyway . . .* (London: Random House, 2014), 257.

32. D. Davies, *Kink*, 107.

33. Ibid., 16–17. On buying the guitar on the "never-never," see, for example, C. Vinnicombe, "Dave Davies Talks Guitars, Self Expression, and 'You Really Got Me,'" MusicRadar, June 2, 2014, accessed June 30, 2014, http:// www.musicradar.com/.

34. R. Davies, *X-Ray*, 83, 157.

35. Many of which are used as illustrations for the band's early history in Savage, *The Kinks*.

36. See M. J. Roberts, *Tell Tchaikovsky the News: Rock 'n' Roll, the Labor Question, and the Musicians' Union, 1942–1968* (Durham, NC: Duke University Press, 2014), 96–98, on the guitar as an instrument of rage and expression for the working classes.

37. Marten and Hudson, *The Kinks*, 15; D. Davies, *Kink*, 10; R. Davies, *X-Ray*, 35.

38. D. Davies, *Kink*, 10.

39. Kitts, *Ray Davies*, 21.

40. D. Davies, *Kink*, 16.

41. Peter Frame discusses radio airplay and the subterfuge of offshore and European radio stations, such as Radio Luxembourg (*Restless Generation*, 216–18).

42. On the impact of rock-and-roll cinema in Britain, especially Elvis Presley's films, see ibid., 161–65, 170–74.

43. Ibid., 218–19, on producer Jack Good and the impact of *The Six-Five Special*.

44. Ibid., 154.

45. See Adrian Horn's *Juke Box Britain* on the interpolation of and resistance to American music and culture both in the 1950s and 1960s.

46. See Frith et al., *History of Live Music*, 11–26.

47. Ibid., 32. See 29–53 for a discussion of the regulations of and the effects on live music by the state from the Victorian period through to the 1960s in Britain, and the social demarcation created if not reinforced by such legislation.

48. R. Davies, *X-Ray*, 32–33.

49. Frame, *Restless Generation*, 118.

50. See Frith and colleagues on the changing shape of music venues, especially in London, as an effect of a younger demographic frequenting live performances (*History of Live Music*, 170–80), and the mutual effects of audience behavior and the control of the promoter on this behavior (180–84). On the

nuanced effect of the younger generation on the creation of a specifically "young" live music scene, see 122–26, 131–35.

51. Such snobbery has very commercial and economic overtones, as the definition of music as "art" or "entertainment" affected the wages of professional musicians during this era, especially in the context of unions and live versus recorded performances in both Britain and America; see Roberts, *Tell Tchaikovsky*, 2–14, 113–65, and in particular 135–37, on the conflicts among professional musicians themselves over what constitutes art versus entertainment.

52. Frame's *Restless Generation* provides detailed context throughout, underscoring the discussion of Donegan and the skiffle scene, as well as the evolution of the coffee bars' music scene through this period; see also Savage's brief review of the scene, *The Kinks*, 11–13. Frith and colleagues also discuss the skiffle scene with a consideration of both its amateur enthusiasts and also how the genre was commercially exploited (*History of Live Music*, 87–116).

53. R. Davies, *X-Ray*, 53–54, 76–77.

54. Ibid., 70–71.

3. MARKETING AND THE MONEY-GO-ROUND

1. Ray and the Kinks made their debut on *Ready, Steady, Go!* February 7, 1964, quoted in Ray Davies, *X-Ray* (New York: Overlook, 1995), 105.

2. George Harrison, during an interview for *The Beatles Anthology* in 1995, quote taken from BeatlesQuotes.com, accessed June 8, 2014, http://beatlesquotes.com/.

3. Ray Davies, *Americana : The Kinks, The Road and the Perfect Riff* (London: Virgin, 2013), 108.

4. See, for example, Robin Morgan and Ariel Leve, *1963: The Year of the Revolution; How Youth Changed the World with Music, Art, and Fashion* (New York: itbooks, 2013); and Shawn Levy's *Ready Steady Go! The Smashing Rise and Giddy Fall of Swinging London* (London: Doubleday, 2002).

5. Bill Wyman is quoted in *1963* as noting how the band was aware vaguely that "stuff was happening," but no one was really aware of how significant the social changes were at the time. As he puts it, "It was amateur hour. We just took it day by day. We didn't plan to be rebels" (Morgan and Leve, *1963*, 109).

6. For a contemporary look at the beat scene in Britain and the rise of the new music professionals, see Royston Ellis, *The Big Beat Scene* (York, UK: Music Mentor, [1961] 2010); and Peter Frame's *Restless Generation: How Rock Music Changed the Face of 1950s Britain* (London: Rogan House, 2007).

Frame discusses Larry Parnes throughout this work; for other recent discussion of Parnes and his business model, see Simon Frith, Matt Brennan, Martin Cloonan, and Emma Webster, eds., *The History of Live Music in Britain*, vol. 1, *1950–1967 (From the Dance Hall to the 100 Club)* (London: Ashgate, 2013), 121–37; and Simon Napier-Bell's essential *Black Vinyl, White Powder* (London: Ebury, 2002), esp. 41–44 on Parnes. Billy Fury's home page includes interviews with Parnes as well as how Fury's image and career was shaped by him ("Larry Parnes," billyfury.com, accessed June 17, 2014, http://www.billyfury.com/parnes).

7. On the birth of Beatlemania, see the Beatles' original (and authorized) biographer, Hunter Davies, *The Beatles: The Authorized Biography* (New York: Dell, 1968), 202–12; and Cynthia Lennon, *A Twist of Lennon* (New York: Avon, 1978). Steven D. Stark explains the impact of the Beatles within the cultural context of 1963 Britain in *Meet the Beatles: A Cultural History of the Band that Shook Youth, Gender, and the World* (New York: HarperCollins, 2005), 138–47. On the Beatles' image and its creation in American media and culture, see M. R. Frontani, *The Beatles: Image and the Media* (Jackson: University of Mississippi Press, 2007).

8. Peter Quaife, *Veritas, Volume 2* (unpublished manuscript, 2014), 106–7.

9. It is unlikely anyone in the Beatles' camp would have sensationalized the band to get coverage: as Tony Barrow notes, "Brian [Epstein] anyway would have been against such stunts. We never used any and we never had to." Quoted in H. Davies, *The Beatles*, 203.

10. Morgan and Leve, *1963*, 177–81.

11. Arthur Howes is quoted by Hunter Davies as remarking that the life expectancy of a group was about five years—by which time the artists' fans would have grown up and a new generation of artists have captured the lucrative market (H. Davies, *The Beatles*, 238–39). Keith Richard's outlook in 1963 was even more pessimistic: "There was also a feeling of doom, that feeling that if you got a recording contract, a recording career lasted only two years." Quoted in Morgan and Leve, *1963*, 111.

12. Quoted in Alan Clayson, *Beat Merchants: The Origins, History, Impact and Rock Legacy of the British Pop Groups* (London: Blandford, 1995), 224.

13. Quoted by Steve Roller, "Let's Write a Swimming Pool!" American Writers and Artists Inc., February 17, 2012, accessed June 9, 2014, http://www.awaionline.com/. Variations on this quote appear elsewhere ("Now, let's write a swimming pool!").

14. See Napier-Bell on the greed and exploitation rampant in the early days of British rock and roll; he notes, for example, the abysmal contracts Brian Epstein negotiated for the Beatles and how others cashed in by exploiting loopholes Epstein overlooked (*Black Vinyl*, 54–57); for an introduction on how

music publishing and promotion changed in Britain in the postwar period (and thus context for understanding the issues surrounded the Kinks' contracts and management), see Frith et al., *History of Live Music*.

15. The poster boys here are Dave Clark, of the Dave Clark 5, and Peter Noone of Herman's Hermits. See Napier-Bell, *Black Vinyl*, 67–68; and (on Clark) Clayson, *Beat Merchants*, 224–25.

16. Hunter Davies's biography of the Quarrymen, the "pre-Beatles" as it were, certainly supports this particular phenomenon; Hunter Davies, *The Quarrymen* (London: Omnibus, 2001).

17. Doug Hinman, *The Kinks : All Day and All of the Night; Day-by-Day Concerts, Recordings, and Broadcasts, 1961–1996* (San Francisco: Backbeat, 2004), 9.

18. Ibid., 11–17.

19. See, for example, Deena Weinstein, "Relations in the Kinks: Familiar but Not Fully Familial," *Popular Music and Society* 29, no. 2 (2006): 167–87; and Carey Fleiner, "The Influence of Family and Childhood Experience on the Works of Ray and Dave Davies," *Popular Music and Society* 34, no. 3 (July 2011): 346n2.

20. One story recounts that it was "Rave On" and Wace knocking out a tooth on a microphone that led to Ray taking over the vocals. Another is that the audience was comprised of working-class kids who sang along with Wace in a mockingly posh accent until Dave took over. As with all legends, however, the details vary from teller to teller.

21. Hinman, *The Kinks*, 15; Dave Hunter, "Comeback Kink," *Guitar Magazine*, January 1999, accessed June 30, 2014, http://www.davedavies.com/. Or as Ray put it recently, "My brother was 17 and did what 17-year-old people do." Ray Davies in interview with Terry Gross, "Naive, Yet Revolutionary: Ray Davies on 50 Years of the Kinks," *Fresh Air*, December 25, 2014, accessed August 7, 2015, http://www.npr.org/.

22. See D. Brackett, "The British Art School Blues," in *The Pop, Rock, and Soul Reader: Histories and Debates*, ed. D. Brackett, 227–32 (Oxford: Oxford University Press, 2006).

23. Hinman, *The Kinks*, 15.

24. On the changes wrought in the promotion of live music in Britain after the war, see Frith et al., *History of Live Music*, 1–28.

25. Hinman, *The Kinks*, 14; R. Davies, *X-Ray*, 95–96.

26. On Page and the Kinks, see Jon Savage, *The Kinks: The Official Biography* (London: Faber & Faber, 1984), 17–19; Johnny Rogan, *The Kinks: A Mental Institution* (New York: Proteus, 1984), 13–15; more recently there is Thomas Kitts's *Ray Davies: Not Like Everybody Else* (New York: Routledge, 2008), which introduces Page at page 33; and Nick Hasted's *Story of the Kinks:*

You Really Got Me (London: Omnibus, 2011). Savage also wrote a detailed biography of Page on the latter's website, "Larry Page: The Man Who Rewrote Pop History," Larry Page Productions, accessed July 10, 2014, http://www. larrypageproductions.com/; the web page also contains a link to a section on Page's work with the Kinks.

27. For a discussion of Talmy not colored specifically by a Kink or one of their biographers, see David N. Howard, *Sonic Alchemy: Visionary Music Producers and Their Maverick Recordings* (New York: Hal Leonard, 2004), 91–114; and Richie Unterberger, *Urban Spacemen and Wayfaring Strangers: Overlooked Innovators and Eccentric Visionaries of '60s Rock* (London: Backbeat, 2000), 148–59. Succinctly, Talmy "bullshitted [his] way into [the scene] in London," fibbed to all and sundry about hit records he hadn't actually worked on, and managed to be in the right place (England) at the right time (when the British pop music industry wanted the "American sound"). Talmy quoted in Andrew Loog Oldham, *Stoned* (London: Vintage, 2001), 139–40. Talmy told a similar tale of his break into the British music scene and working with the Kinks to an interviewer for *Music and Sound Output* in 1985, quoted almost in its entirety in W. Wadhams, *Inside the Hits: The Seduction of a Rock and Roll Generation* (Boston: Berklee, 2001), 180–83.

28. The Teddy Boys were a 1950s subculture of young men so called because of their "Edwardian" fashions (narrow trousers, bootlace ties, and long hair slicked into "Tony Curtis"–style coifs); they were keen on rock-and-roll music and could be rough customers in the dance halls. See R. Ferris and J. Lord, *Teddy Boys: A Concise History* (London: Milo, 2012), for a brief overview of the culture.

29. Savage, "Larry Page."

30. Ray describes the colorful relationship the Kinks had with Carter as he attempted to create a diamond out of their rough in *X-Ray*, 139–43.

31. Gross, "Naive, Yet Revolutionary."

32. On hiding John's marriage, see H. Davies, *The Beatles*, 173–74. Ray describes the days around his own wedding in *X-Ray*, 191–95.

33. R. Davies, *X-Ray*, 228–29.

34. Dave Davies, *Kink* (New York: Hyperion, 1996), 42.

35. Ray in conversation with David Simpson, "Ray Davies: I'm Not the Godfather of Britpop . . . More a Concerned Uncle," *Guardian*, July 16, 2015, accessed August 9, 2015, http://www.theguardian.com/.

36. On the subject of recording contracts, see Hinman, *The Kinks*, 17–19.

37. Ray once mentioned in an interview that the song should have been sung by Dave, and Kitts concurs that Dave may have injected the vocals with more giddy abandonment (*Ray Davies*, 36).

38. The "safe" song was "How Do You Do It" by Mitch Murray—a song the Beatles considered too cissy, and indeed, they did a number of fruity takes on it before George Martin gave up and allowed the group to record the Lennon-McCartney composition "Love Me Do" as their first single. Gerry and the Pacemakers went to the top with "How Do You Do It" as their debut single in 1963.

39. Hinman, *The Kinks*, 29. Ray also felt that the band finally connected with their audience with this song, and despite management's reservations, he wanted very much to record "You Really Got Me" as a consequence (ibid., 27).

40. On the Beatles' version of "Long Tall Sally," see Ian MacDonald, *Revolution in the Head : The Beatles Records and the Sixties*, 2nd rev. ed. (London: Pimlico, 2005), 112–14. Part of the song's energy comes from Paul singing in a higher key than Little Richard as well as channeling the group's Hamburg days.

41. A version of the clip could be found on YouTube at the time of this writing at Javier Ochagavía, "The Kinks: Cavern Club 1964," October 25, 2008, accessed August 5, 2016, https://www.youtube.com/watch?v=ACauqjzqyk4. The energy is there but held in check.

42. Allegedly, "Long Tall Sally" only charted due to "aggressive advertising" on the part of Pye and Talmy (Collins is quoted by Kitts that Pye may have shipped deliberately an excess of records into the shops; Kitts, *Ray Davies*, 36). This isn't particularly sensational or unusual; payola operated in a similar fashion in the United States from the 1920s through to the end of the 1950s; Napier-Bell notes that artists also paid the offshore pirate station Radio Caroline to get their records played (*Black Vinyl*, 63–64). In the Kinks' case, however, "Long Tall Sally" sank off the charts without a trace in about a week.

43. Johnny Rogan, *The Complete Guide to the Music of the Kinks* (London: Omnibus, 1988), 59. Rogan recommends the UK pressing of the record rather than Reprise's *Live Kinks*; Doug Hinman, *The Kinks Part One: You Really Got Me; An Illustrated World Discography of the Kinks, 1964–1993* (London: Backbeat, 1994), 63.

44. The details and anecdotes about the Kinks and their tours in 1964 and 1965 can be found in various flavors and points of view in their own memoirs as well as in all of the principle biographies; for a straightforward, month-by-month account, Hinman's *The Kinks* is indispensable.

45. R. Davies, *X-Ray*, 104–5.

46. Ibid., 219.

47. Kitts, *Ray Davies*, 42–43. For an additional commentary on recording the song, see Hinman, *The Kinks*, 29. Ray's folkloric telling of the song's creation is "The Third Single," on his 1998 solo release, *Storyteller*.

48. On Ray's recollection of creating and recording "You Really Got Me," see his *X-Ray*, 146–52.

49. The "UK Singles Charts: September 1964," Demondaveuk, accessed February 4, 2012, http://demondaveuk.bravepages.com/.

50. On the influence and immediate effects of "You Really Got Me," see Kitts, *Ray Davies*, 42–43.

51. IBC engineer Alan Florence, who was one of the two engineers on the final recording that day, made his comments online in response to a *Rolling Stone* article about the BBC Two documentary on July 11, 2014. J. Blistein, "Kinks Refute BBC Doc Saying Jimmy Page Played on 'You Really Got Me,'" *Rolling Stone*, July 10, 2014, accessed May 10, 2016, http://www.rollingstone.com/.

52. Quoted in Morgan and Leve, *1963*, 66–67.

53. "Shot of a lifetime!" was the catchphrase of Harry Goodwin, the official BBC photographer for *Top of the Pops*. Ray describes his character and encounter with the Kinks in *X-Ray*, 326–37.

54. Ibid., 203. Dave also notes what happens when the songs fall off the charts: when the Kinks were in the top ten, he was allowed to load up on free clothes from shops in Carnaby Street, but once the hits stopped coming in the later 1960s, Dave was accused, in the same store and by the same owner, of shoplifting (D. Davies, *Kink*, 111–12).

55. In 1886, the Berne Convention established that the *physical* aspects of recorded music were held in copyright, that is, the actual records themselves, or the published music therein recorded (see, for example, N. Parker, *Music Business: Infrastructure, Practice, and Law* [Andover, UK: Sweet & Maxwell, 2004], 60). One can view the document that added Great Britain as a signatory to the convention (the "International Copyright Act," London, 1886) at "Primary Sources on Copyright (1450–1900)," accessed August 5, 2016, http://www.copyrighthistory.org/.

56. R. Davies, *X-Ray*, 179–81. Ray speculates that Kassner's empty greed may well have been a means to recover what he himself had lost during the war, including his personal wealth and his capacity for empathy.

57. Dave describes at some length the conditions of the Kinks' early contracts with understandable bitterness and frustration in *Kink* (32–37). On the complexities of not only these labyrinthine contracts but also the subsequent lawsuit against Kassner Music, see Rogan, *The Kinks*, 56–64.

58. For an excellent overview of the conflict between the American Federation of Musicians and British musicians in the early sixties, see M. J. Roberts, *Tell Tchaikovsky the News: Rock 'n' Roll, the Labor Question, and the Musicians' Union, 1942–1968* (Durham, NC: Duke University Press, 2014), 167–200. For a Kinks-centric discussion of the two 1965 tours and the ban,

Hinman (*The Kinks*) covers the chronology, Kitts (*Ray Davies*), Jon Savage (*The Kinks: The Official Biography* [London: Faber & Faber, 1984]), Rogan (*The Kinks: A Mental Institution*), and Hasted (*Story of the Kinks*) describe the events, and Ray and Dave provide a personal spin in their respective autobiographies.

4. HUMOR AND THE KINKS

1. Ray Davies to Loraine Alterman, "Who Let the Kinks In?" *Rolling Stone Magazine*, December 18, 1969, KindaKinks.net, accessed August 3, 2015, http://www.kindakinks.net/.

2. Simon Napier-Bell, *Black Vinyl, White Powder* (London: Ebury, 2002), 71.

3. On humor and British rock and roll, see Iain Ellis, *Brit Wits: A History of British Rock Humor* (Bristol, UK: Intellect, 2012), 1–10, in general and on the Kinks specifically, 39–41.

4. John Wilson, "Ray Davies: Words Were My Weapons," *BBC News*, November 27, 2012, accessed January 23, 2015, http://www.bbc.co.uk/.

5. George Orwell, "Charles Dickens," in *Shooting an Elephant and Other Essays*, ed. Jeremy Paxman, 49–114 (London: Penguin, 2009), 109.

6. Ibid., 110.

7. Kate Fox, *Watching the English: The Hidden Rules of English Behaviour* (London: Hodder & Stoughton, 2004); Jeremy Paxman, *The English : A Portrait of a People* (London: Penguin, 1999); Bill Bryson, *Notes from a Small Island* (New York: HarperCollins, 1996); Andrew Collins, *Where Did It All Go Right? Growing Up Normal in the '70s* (London: Ebury, 2003); Tim Moore, *You Are Awful (But I Like You): Travels through Unloved Britain* (London: Vintage, 2013). *The Trip* was written by Steve Coogan and directed by Michael Winterbottom; it was first transmitted on BBC Two as a six-part series in August 2013. *A Child's Christmases in Wales* was a one-off special written by Mark Watson and directed by Chris Gernon, transmitted December 24, 2009 on BBC Four.

8. Numerous collections of Peter Cook's writing are still in print. Michael Palin, *The Python Years: Diaries, 1969–1979*, vol. 1 (London: W & N, 2014); and John Cleese, *So, Anyway . . .* (London: Random House, 2014).

9. For academic studies on Ealing, see S. Muir, *Studying Ealing Studios* (London: Auteur, 2010); and Mark Duguid and Lee Freeman, *Ealing Revisited* (London: British Film Institute, 2012).

10. As an example of what makes these films "English," note that the ending of *The Lavender Hill Mob* had to be changed in order to sell the film to

American distributors: in the original script, Alec Guinness's character Henry Holland gets away with his daring robbery and enjoys luxurious retirement away from drab Britain in colorful Rio. In the released version, Henry is in Rio telling his tale to the policeman who has come to arrest him and remand him to prison in Britain—the Americans' Hayes Code wouldn't allow a criminal to escape to live happily ever after.

11. Robert Sellers, *Don't Let the Bastards Grind You Down: How One Generation of British Actors Changed the World* (London: Preface, 2011). A number of the actors featured in Sellers's book are also part of the circle of movers and shakers profiled in Shawn Levy's *Ready Steady Go! The Smashing Rise and Giddy Fall of Swinging London* (London: Doubleday, 2002).

12. H. Carpenter, *The Angry Young Men: A Literary Comedy of the 1950s* (London: Allen Lane, 2001); H. Carpenter, *That Was Satire That Was: The Satire Boom of the 1960s* (London: Phoenix, 2000).

13. Scripts of *Beyond the Fringe* are readily in print as are off-air recordings and official records, even if their video survival in the BBC archive is limited.

14. Colin Wilson, *The Angry Years: The Rise and Fall of the Angry Young Men* (London: Robson, 2007).

15. Wilson, a working-class playwright who went to university on a scholarship and deliberately choose to live in poverty in his early career, wrote his memoir in reaction to what he saw as inaccuracies in Carpenter's survey (ibid., xx).

16. Ibid., xv–xvi.

17. Ibid., xvi. An older but useful collection of academic essays on English satire is James Sutherland, *English Satire: The Clarke Lectures, 1956* (Cambridge: Cambridge University Press, 1962). Sutherland concludes with a chapter on the history of satire in the theater, but only from the eighteenth century up through to Shaw; although he doesn't address the issue of the Angry Young Men, he does begin this chapter noting that "satire has always been unwelcome to people in authority" (133).

18. Wilson compares his time of living rough (by choice) and writing in the Reading Room of the British Library to Marx's experiences a century earlier (*Angry Years*, xvi–xviii on Rousseau; on Wilson's "rough-living," 2–3), which ignores Marx's comfortable middle-class background—as well as the working-class background of some of the satirists whom he scorns, including Alan Bennett, a working-class student on a university scholarship (Bennett is quoted as describing his upbringing as working-class in Carpenter, *That Was Satire*, 19).

19. Orwell, "Charles Dickens," 111.

20. Jon Savage, *The Kinks: The Official Biography* (London: Faber & Faber, 1984), 55.

21. Ellis, *Brit Wits*, 40.

22. R. Davies, *X-Ray* (New York: Overlook, 1995), 85.

23. A "wide boy" is a petty criminal, and "Jack the Lad" is a name applied to a brash and cocky young man.

24. Parts of this section are adapted from my article "The Influence of Family and Childhood Experience on the Works of Ray and Dave Davies," *Popular Music and Society* 34, no. 3 (July 2011): 329–50.

25. "Eels," *The Mighty Boosh*, written by Julian Barratt and Noel Fielding, directed by Paul King, transmitted on November 15, 2007, on BBC Three. Fielding makes reference to borrowing his grandfather's mannerisms and Cockney speech patterns on the DVD commentary for the *Boosh* episode.

26. "Last among Equals: Why Fry Wasn't First Choice as QI Host," *Chortle*, December 21, 2006, accessed January 24, 2015, http://www.chortle.co.uk/. Another example is the BBC's 2008 "Children in Need" special edition of *QI*; middle-class comedian David Mitchell commented on how excited the audience got suddenly to hear a snippet of "My Old Man's a Dustman"—he joked that the greater British public had no interest in an intellectual quiz show and what they really wanted was a "good knees'-up," that is, a typical working-class sing-along round the family piano (or in the pub). ("Families," *QI*, directed by Ian Lorimer, transmitted on November 14, 2008, on BBC Two).

27. Parts of this section on siblings in popular music is adapted from my chapter "Siblings in American Music," in *Music in American Life*, ed. J. Edmonson, 4:1054–56 (Santa Barbara, CA: ABC-CLIO, 2013).

28. Johnny Rogan, *The Complete Guide to the Music of the Kinks* (London: Omnibus, 1998), 162.

29. R. Cooke, "Ray Davies: I'm Easy to Love . . . But Impossible to Live With," *Guardian*, May 1, 2011, accessed January 24, 2014, http://www.theguardian.com/.

30. Jeff Slate, "A Kinks Reunion? Ray and Dave Are Talking," *Daily Beast*, January 18, 2015, accessed January 21, 2015, http://www.thedailybeast.com/.

31. David Simpson, "Ray Davies: I'm Not the Godfather of Britpop . . . More a Concerned Uncle," *Guardian*, July 16, 2015, accessed August 9, 2015, http://www.theguardian.com/.

32. Doug Hinman, *The Kinks : All Day and All of the Night; Day-by-Day Concerts, Recordings, and Broadcasts, 1961–1996* (San Francisco: Backbeat, 2004), 318–19.

33. Ibid., 317. As of this writing (January 13, 2015), the performance is on YouTube: "The Kinks: Hatred (A Duet)," August 9, 2010, http://www.youtube.com/.

34. The British point with their middle fingers, but who knows; Ray and Dave are certainly Americanophiles and know the gesture's alternate meaning.

35. Parts of this section are adapted from my article "Influence of Family" and several conference papers given between 2012 and 2014 on the Kinks and English identity.

36. Dave Davies, *Kink* (New York: Hyperion, 1996), 7; R. Davies, *X-Ray*, 20–21.

37. Ray was very close to his niece; being the only black child on a London street in the 1950s, she'd had to cope with jibes from neighbors as well as her own cousins. He notes that one of the first songs he wrote was for her, when she was feeling sad (*X-Ray*, 67). As a teenager, she went on with her friends to create the first Kinks fan club (105). The racial troubles the family experienced would be explored as a subplot in the musical *Come Dancing*.

38. Ibid., 21.

39. Parts of this following section on "A Well Respected Man" is adapted from my article "A Well Respected Man," *Songlexikon* (Albert-Ludwigs-Universitat, Freiburg), April 2012, last updated October 2013, accessed January 25, 2015, http://www.songlexikon.de/. See also Nick Baxter-Moore, "'This Is Where I Belong': Identity, Social Class, and the Nostalgic Englishness of Ray Davies and the Kinks," *Popular Music and Society* 29, no. 2 (2006): 156–57.

40. Thomas Kitts, *Ray Davies : Not Like Everybody Else* (New York: Routledge, 2008), 63.

41. On the genesis and his own explanation of the song, see R. Davies, *X-Ray*, 262–66; on context and analysis of "A Well Respected Man" as social satire, see Kitts, *Ray Davies*, 57–67.

42. Hinman, *The Kinks*, 61.

43. Ibid., 65.

44. Ray noted in an interview in mid-1965 that the Kinks were becoming more interested in storytelling songs (quoted in Hinman, *The Kinks*, 65).

45. Johnny Rogan, *The Kinks: A Mental Institution* (New York: Proteus, 1984), 160.

46. Cleese, *So, Anyway*, 260. He makes similar comments on the freshness of the antiauthority sketches on television shows *Beyond the Fringe* (149–51) and *That Was the Week That Was* (163–64) as inspiration to his own early work for the Cambridge Footlights.

47. See M. J. Roberts on blues and rock-and-roll stars who became heroes of the working class because they actively *avoided* work and celebrated their laziness in song in *Tell Tchaikovsky the News: Rock 'n' Roll, the Labor Question, and the Musicians' Union, 1942–1968* (Durham, NC: Duke University Press, 2014), 48–82.

48. R. Davies, *X-Ray*, 288–29.

49. In real life, the band limited themselves to chasing down the street after a press conference a reporter with whom they disagreed (Roberts, *Tell Tchaikovsky*, 189).

50. "Heart of Gold" was written in response to the three-ringed press circus that surrounded his then-partner Chrissie Hynde's labor and subsequent trip to the hospital. He mentions a similar intrusion of privacy in *Americana*: this volume of his autobiography is framed around the time he was shot by a mugger in New Orleans, and he mentions how peaceful it was at first, not to be recognized, and how disappointed he was the first time a medical worker, having recognized him, requested his autograph (Ray Davies, *Americana: The Kinks, The Road and the Perfect Riff* [London: Virgin, 2013], 185–86).

51. Hinman, *The Kinks*, 318.

52. Cleese notes that his father was interested in Cleese's budding career in entertainment but also slightly disappointed that he didn't marry a duchess and improve the family's fortunes (*So, Anyway . . .*, 250).

53. *A Fish Called Wanda*, written by John Cleese and directed by Charles Crichton (Beverly Hill, CA: MGM, 1988).

54. Ray described Hawaii as his best holiday in a *Rolling Stone* interview, quoted in Hinman, *The Kinks*, 61; cf. R. Davies, *X-Ray*, 255–56.

55. A similar fish-out-of-water class joke is played in *A Hard Day's Night* when Paul's grandfather steals Ringo's invitation to a baccarat club. When the Beatles finally catch up with him and learn the damages owed by "Lord McCartney," the Beatles' manager sputters, "A hundred and eighty pounds?!" only to be corrected smugly by the maître d', "That's *guineas*, sir." One hundred eighty-nine guineas in 1964 would be worth roughly £3,455 in 2015 according to the This Is Money website; Ray's ukulele clocks in at a mere £524.33. Richard Browning, "Historic Inflation Calculator: How the Value of Money Has Changed since 1900," accessed January 25, 2015, http://www.thisismoney.co.uk/.

56. Although Ray has said on occasion that he doesn't like family, see, for example, Jim Sullivan's "Dave Davies Talk About His New Solo Album, Possibilities for a Kinks' Reunion," ARTery, November 16, 2014, accessed January 24, 2015, http://artery.wbur.org/.

57. Fox, *Watching the English*, 63–64.

5. I KNOW WHAT I AM, AND I'M GLAD
I'M A MAN

1. Cf. Carey Fleiner, "Heroes and Villains: The Medieval Guitarist and Modern Parallels," in *The British Museum Citole: New Perspectives*, British

Museum Research Publication, ed. James Robinson and Naomi Speakman, 51–60 (London: British Museum, 2015).

  2. This is the case especially with black artists and performers. See E. Nuzum, *Parental Advisory: Music Censorship in America* (New York: Perenniel, 2001), 149–61; and P. Blecha, *Taboo Tunes: A History of Banned Bands and Censored Songs* (San Francisco: Backbeat, 2004), 85–122. On UK censorship, see M. Cloonan, *Banned! Censorship of Popular Music in Britain, 1967–92*, Popular Culture Studies 9 (London: Arena, 1996), who provides a brief history of censorship of British music as well as legal and broadcasting regulatory context.

  3. Ian MacDonald, *Revolution in the Head: The Beatles' Records and the Sixties*, 2nd rev. ed. (London: Pimlico, 2005), 8.

  4. Dominic Sandbrook, *Never Had It So Good: A History of Britain from Suez to the Beatles* (London: Abacus, 2006), xvi.

  5. See Clive Irving's contemporary book on the scandal, *Anatomy of a Scandal: A Study of the Profumo Affair* (New York: M. S. Mill, 1963); and "The Four Phases of the Profumo Affair," dated from June 9, 1963, which is included in R. Connolly's anthology, *In the Sixties* (London: Pavilion, 1995), 46–50. See also R. P. T. Davenport-Hines, *An English Affair: Sex, Class and Power in the Age of Profumo* (London: Harper, 2013) (more a cultural retrospective on the fiftieth anniversary of the scandal than an academic work); or the sensational A. Summers and S. Dorril, *Honeytrap: The Secret Worlds of Stephen Ward* (London: Weidenfeld & Nicolson, 1987), and P. Knightely and C. Kennedy, *An Affair of State: The Profumo Case and the Framing of Stephen Ward* (London: J. Cape, 1987).

  6. S. Levy, *Ready Steady Go! The Smashing Rise and Giddy Fall of Swinging London* (London: Doubleday, 2002). Robin Morgan and Ariel Leve, *1963: The Year of the Revolution; How Youth Changed the World with Music, Art, and Fashion* (New York: itbooks, 2013), traces the changes in popular culture through a collection and synthesis of interviews with many key players from the contemporary scene in Britain; S. Millward's *Changing Times: Music and Politics in 1964* (London: Matador, 2013) complements Morgan and Leve with an overview on the effects of similar cultural changes in the United States especially in the wake of the British Invasion. See also Arthur Marwick, *The Sixties: Cultural Revolution in Britain, France, Italy, and the United States, c. 1958–c. 1974* (London: Bloomsbury Reader, 2012), esp. 3–223, which covers the period 1958 through to 1963 on matters of art, morality, and social relations. Another survey of social changes in the period between 1958 and 1963 is Sandbrook, *Never Had It So Good*, and Joanna Bourke, *Working-Class Cultures in Britain, 1890–1960: Gender, Class and Ethnicity* (London: Routledge, 1996), 27–61.

7. Nik Cohn, *Awopbop-Aloobop-Alopbam-Boom: Pop from the Beginning* (London: Pimlico, 2004), 58.

8. Charles Hamblett and Jane Deverson, *Generation X* (London: Anthony Gibbs, 1964).

9. Wyman felt secure with the ephemeral lifestyle of a pop star because of his National Service experience and his up-to-date engineering credentials—unlike the rest of the Stones who were much younger and scrounging off Mick Jagger's student grant (Wyman quoted in Robin Morgan and Ariel Leve, *1963: The Year of the Revolution; How Youth Changed the World with Music, Art, and Fashion* [New York: itbooks, 2013], 113).

10. R. Davies, *X-Ray* (New York: Overlook, 1995), 266.

11. Cohn, *Awopbop*, 195.

12. Select sources on the Mod scene include Cohn, *Awopbop*; P. Hewitt, ed. *The Sharper Word: A Mod Anthology*, rev. and updated (London: Helter Skelter, 1999); R. Weight, *Mod! A Very British Style* (London: Bodley Head, 2013); T. Rawling's illustrated *Mod: Clean Living under Difficult Circumstances—A Very British Phenomenon* (London: Omnibus, 2000); Stan Hawkins on Mod music, culture, and masculinity in *The British Pop Dandy: Male Identity, Music, and Culture* (London: Ashgate, 2009), 1–36; and J. E. Perone, *Mods, Rockers, and the Music of the British Invasion* (Westport, CT: Praeger, 2009). For a case study of the archetypical Mod, see Mark Patress's "day in the life" of Mark Bolan in Hewitt, *Sharper Word*, 54–63.

13. R. Barnes, "Mods," in Hewitt, *Sharper Word*, 40–41.

14. See H. David, *On Queer Street: A Social History of British Homosexuality, 1895–1995* (London: HarperCollins, 1997). For a contemporary discussion of homosexuality in Britain with particular emphasis on changes to its legal status, see H. Montgomery Hyde, *The Love that Dared Not Speak Its Name: A Candid History of Homosexuality in Britain* (Boston: Little, Brown, 1970).

15. Cohn, *Awopbop*, 187.

16. Barnes, "Mods," 41. See Keith Gildart, *Images of England through Popular Music: Class, Youth and Rock 'n' Roll, 1955–1976* (London: Palgrave MacMillan, 2013), 108–27, for a discussion of how young working-class men in particular embraced Mod culture and its spread from London and into the local provincial scene.

17. Alan Clayson, *Beat Merchants: The Origins, History, Impact and Rock Legacy of the British Pop Groups* (London: Blandford, 1995), 177.

18. Quoted by Barnes, "Mods," 43.

19. Barnes, "Mods," 43. On the role of gay men and feminization of male fashion in the sixties, see R. Dyer, *The Culture of Queers* (London: Routledge, 2002), 63–69.

20. Nik Cohn, "Carnaby Street," in Hewitt, *Sharper Word*, 49–51.

21. Ibid., 51.

22. See Dyer, *Culture of Queers*, 49–62.

23. Perone, *Mods, Rockers*, 102–6, on the Who and the Kinks. See also Hawkins, *British Pop Dandy*, 47–52, on the Kinks and the Mods. On the cultural context of the Mods in the early 1960s with case studies in particular on the Who and the Kinks, see Gildart, *Images of England*, 87–148.

24. See Gildart, *Images of England*, 144, for a brief discussion of "kinky fashion" and the Kinks' own English distinction among the PVC, zips, and male makeup.

25. Neville Marten and Jeffrey Hudson, *The Kinks: Well Respected Men* (Chessington, UK: Castle Communications, 1996), 57; Dave Davies, *Kink* (New York: Hyperion, 1996), 89, 167.

26. For additional discussion of "Dedicated Follower of Fashion," see Thomas Kitts, *Ray Davies: Not Like Everybody Else* (New York: Routledge, 2008), 67–69; Marten and Hudson, *The Kinks*, 72–74; and Doug Hinman, *The Kinks: All Day and All of the Night; Day-by-Day Concerts, Recordings, and Broadcasts, 1961–1996* (San Francisco: Backbeat, 2004), 74.

27. Kitts sees the song as the singer drawing on his past for comfort and security (Kitts, *Ray Davies* 116), but Hawkins sees it as a complementary satire to "Dandy" and Ray's cruel send-up of himself as a performer (Hawkins, *British Pop Dandy*, 49).

28. Hawkins, *British Pop Dandy*, 49.

29. Gildart, *Images of England*, 136.

30. Cf. R. Davies, *X-Ray*, 238; and Ray Davies, *Americana : The Kinks, The Road and the Perfect Riff* (London: Virgin, 2013), 45.

31. Clayson, *Beat Merchants*, 167.

32. Ibid.

33. Ibid.

34. Ibid., 168.

35. Gildart, *Images of England*, 135.

36. See A. August, "Gender and 1960s Youth Culture: The Rolling Stones and the New Woman," *Contemporary British History* 23, no. 1 (2009): 79–100.

37. On Dave, see R. Davies, *X-Ray*, 140; on Proby, see Cohn, *Awopbop*, 211–17. Proby got away with the trouser splitting a couple times but finally ended up banned and boycotted in the British music industry, and the backlash against his campy, burlesque performances proved brutal (Cohn, *Awopbop*, 215).

38. R. Davies, *X-Ray*, 93–96.

39. Hyde, *Love that Dared Not*, 6–8.

40. For a brief introduction to British camp and entertainment as a creative outlet for homosexual actors, see Dyer, *Culture of Queers*, 49–69. As Hyde notes, not all actors were gay, but many homosexual men felt safer in the world of theater and entertainment simply because it was a more tolerant and less judgmental profession (*Love that Dared Not*, 18–19). See also Dan Rebellato, *1956 and All That: The Making of Modern British Drama* (London: Routledge, 1999), 156–92, on the "hidden" world of homosexuality in British theater.

41. Kitts, *Ray Davies*, 69. D. Davies, *Kink*, 53, on his relationships with men in the group's early days.

42. Marten and Hudson, *The Kinks*, 57; R. Davies, *X-Ray*, 219. Ray claims this is when the American "character assassination" of the Kinks began.

43. R. Davies, *X-Ray*, 257–58.

44. Cohn, *Awopbop*, 214.

45. Ibid., 211–17, on Proby.

46. B. Hadleigh, *The Vinyl Closet: Gays in the Music Industry* (San Diego: Les Hombres, 1991), 164–66.

47. Cohn, *Awopbop*, 162.

48. See Martin King, *Men, Masculinity and the Beatles* (London: Ashgate, 2013), which complements M. R. Frontani's *The Beatles: Image and the Media* (Jackson: University of Mississippi Press, 2007), 20–69; and Steven D. Stark's *Meet the Beatles: A Cultural History of the Band that Shook Youth, Gender, and the World* (New York: HarperCollins, 2005), esp. 122–37. All three provide an excellent starting point on the Beatles' gender-bending image and the impact their image had on both British and especially American men.

49. See R. Ferris and J. Lord, *Teddy Boys: A Concise History* (London: Milo, 2012). A more academic discussion of the Teddy Boys against the general social climate of Britain in the late fifties and early sixties is Gildart, *Images of England*, 19–86.

50. Ian MacDonald, *Revolution in the Head: The Beatles' Records and the Sixties*, 2nd rev. ed. (London: Pimlico, 2005), 85.

51. See Amy Shillinglaw's analysis of the feminine and homosexual subtext found in the imagery and dialogue of the film in "'Give Us a Kiss': Queer Codes, Male Partnering, and the Beatles," in *The Queer Sixties*, ed. P. J. Smith, 127–43 (London: Routledge, 1999).

52. The film shows the Beatles as four lads keeping close together in male solidarity, but the novel presents George, for example, as thoughtfully longing after the schoolgirls the Beatles serenade on the train to London as he wistfully longs for that special girl who would love him truly for himself and not just for his fame. See John Burke, *The Beatles in A Hard Day's Night* (New York: Dell, 1964), 59, 119–27.

53. On recollection of their experiences with Watts, see R. Davies, *X-Ray*, 319–22; and D. Davies, *Kink*, 93–96.

54. R. Davies, *X-Ray*, 319.

55. D. Davies, *Kink*, 94.

56. Ibid.

57. Ibid., 95.

58. Ibid.

59. Of course, as fond as Dave was of Watts, he was dismayed to learn that Ray had traded his brother's virtue in exchange for Watts's magnificent house (D. Davies, *Kink*, 95–96; R. Davies, *X-Ray*, 320).

60. R. Davies, *X-Ray*, 321.

61. See J. Bellman, "Indian Resonances in the British Invasion, 1965–1968," *Journal of Musicology* 15, no. 1 (Winter 1997): 116–36.

62. On the title change and the implications of "friend" as queer code, see, for example, Marten and Hudson, *The Kinks*, 69–70; and Johnny Rogan, *The Kinks: A Mental Institution* (New York: Proteus, 1984), 59.

63. M. Geldart, "Persona and Voice in the Kinks' Songs of the Late 1960s," *Journal of the Royal Music Association* 128, no. 2 (2003): 218, esp. n59. On other discussion of the song and its meaning by Kinks scholars, see, for example, Kitts, *Ray Davies*, 51, 69–70, which puts the song in the context of the Kinks' (and the Davieses') love of camp and theater; Marten and Hudsen, *The Kinks*, 72–74. Ray and Dave have discussed the song in myriad interviews since 1965; the song is mentioned in their autobiographies *X-Ray*, 275–77; and *Kink*, 74–75.

64. R. Davies, *X-Ray*, 276.

65. See Jon Savage, *The Kinks : The Official Biography* (London: Faber & Faber, 1984), 60, where Ray recalls telling his young wife that if it weren't for her, he would probably be gay.

66. R. Davies, *X-Ray*, 276.

67. Geldart, "Persona and Voice," 218–20.

68. Savage, *The Kinks*, 115.

69. Ibid.

70. Kinks scholarship on "Lola" includes Kitts, *Ray Davies*, 97–99; Johnny Rogan, *The Kinks: A Mental Institution* (New York: Proteus, 1984), 109–10; Hinman, *The Kinks*, 142; and Marten and Hudsen, *The Kinks*, 105–7.

71. Savage, *The Kinks*, 115.

72. Rogan, *The Kinks*, 110.

73. Marten and Hudsen, *The Kinks*, 115. Dave Davies argues to the contrary (J. Charlton, "Two Oldies but Goodies: The Kinks, Dave Davies and Joe D'Allesandro," Janet Charlton's Hollywood, July 21, 2014, accessed July 24, 2014, http://www.janetcharltonshollywood.com/).

74. R. Davies, *Americana*, 108.

75. Ray Davies remarked that record-plugger Johnny Wise was instrumental in drawing attention to "Lola," making it a "crucial and virtually career-saving" record (Hinman, *The Kinks*, 142).

76. Perone, *Mods, Rockers*, 115.

77. Rogan, *The Kinks*, 110–11.

6. HERE COMES MR. FLASH

1. Ray Davies at the Fulcrum Festival, University of Southampton, April 24, 2015.

2. Bob Dawbarn, "Ray: The Patriot Kink," *Melody Maker*, April 16, 1966, quoted in Rogan, *The Kinks*, 73.

3. Simon Price, "Ray Davies, Royal Albert Hall, London," *Independent*, October 7, 2012, accessed October 22, 2014, http://www.independent.co.uk/.

4. Numerous news outlets reported on the incident at the time including the *Telegraph* on July 31, 2013, "Fracking: Chrissie Hynde and Ray Davies' Daughter Natalie Arrested in Balcombe after Superglue Protest," accessed October 22, 2014, http://www.telegraph.co.uk/.

5. The "£10 Pommie" scheme refers to opportunities for working-class English to escape dead-end jobs and austerity for better opportunities in Australia, which, after the war, was actively recruiting labor of all sorts to the continent. The £10 refers to the cheap tickets made available for sailing Down Under for those in Britain, and "Pommie" is Australian slang for the English, specifically soldiers. This scheme started in 1947, as Australia sought migrant workers to rebuild its economy after the war. While the scheme benefitted Australia, it was also a boon to working-class Britons as a chance to escape poverty and acquire property, land, and prosperity that would have been unattainable back home. For a popular overview, see L. Matthews, "The £10 Ticket to Another Life," *BBC Timewatch*, January 31, 2008, accessed October 22, 2014, http://news.bbc.co.uk/. For a more academic study, see A. James Hammerton and A. Thomson, *Ten Pound Poms: Australia's Invisible Migrants* (Manchester, UK: Manchester University Press, 2005).

6. Ray Davies in interview with Terry Gross, "Naive, Yet Revolutionary: Ray Davies on 50 Years of the Kinks," *Fresh Air*, December 25, 2014, accessed August 7, 2015, http://www.npr.org/.

7. Dave Davies, *Kink* (New York: Hyperion, 1996), 100. On other analyses of the track, see Thomas Kitts, *Ray Davies: Not Like Everybody Else* (New York: Routledge, 2008), 75–76); Johnny Rogan, *The Kinks : A Mental Institution* (New York: Proteus, 1984), 73–75; and Neville Marten and Jeffrey Hud-

son, *The Kinks: Well Respected Men* (Chessington, UK: Castle Communications, 1996), 82–83.

8. Dominic Sandbrook's synthesis of the period includes *State of Emergency: The Way We Were; Britain, 1970–1974* (London: Penguin, 2011); and *Seasons in the Sun: The Battle for Britain, 1974–1979* (London: Penguin, 2013).

9. An afternoon's trawl though Foyles bookshop in Charing Cross Road turned up books ranging from, for example, Andy Beckett's *When the Lights Went Out: What Really Happened to Britain in the Seventies* (London: Faber & Faber, 2009); and Alwyn W. Turner, *Crisis? What Crisis? Britain in the 1970s* (London: Aurum, 2008), featuring the leads from the 1970s British television drama *The Sweeney* on the cover; to myriad books on bubbly pop culture such as R. Opie, *The 1970s Scrapbook* (London: PI Global, 1999); S. Webb's *A 1970s Teenager: From Bell-Bottoms to Disco Dancing* (London: History Press, 2013); and D. Tait, *A 1970s Childhood: From Glam Rock to Happy Days* (London: History Press, 2011).

10. On Heath, see, for example, P. Ziegler, *Edward Heath: The Authorised Biography* (London: HarperPress, 2010); and Edward Heath, *The Course of My Life* (London: Hodder & Stoughton, 1998). Stuart Ball and Anthony Seldon have edited a series of essays that reassess the prime minister's career in *The Heath Government, 1970–1974: A Reappraisal* (London: Longman, 1996). More recent academic studies, too numerous to include here, reappraise Heath's role in British economy, the "special relationship" between America and Britain, and the search for stability in Britain's relationship with Northern Ireland. While not the most objective of British newspapers, the *Mirror*'s provocative story "Edward Heath: The Prime Minister Other Tories Want Erased from History . . . " (Kevin Maguire, *Mirror*, May 18, 2014, accessed October 19, 2014, http://www.mirror.co.uk/) illustrates that even thirty-five years later, Heath's policies can still elicit ire from the laboring class.

11. Sandbrook, *Seasons in the Sun*, 92–93. This exhibition had such an impact on the general public that the Victoria & Albert revisited it in a lecture by Sir Roy Strong and others on November 15, 2014, in a daylong workshop course (accessed October 19, 2014, http://www.vam.ac.uk/). Sandbrook notes that one result of the exhibition, which vividly illustrated the loss of old country houses and manors, was a rise in the "Disneyfication" of estates and country houses (92).

12. Ibid., 76–96.

13. For general overviews, see A. Booth, *The British Economy in the Twentieth Century* (New York: Palgrave, 2001); N. W. C. Woodward, *The Management of the British Economy, 1945–2001* (New York: Palgrave, 2004); and Sidney Pollard, *The Development of the British Economy, 1914–1980* (Balti-

more: E. Arnold, 1983). On the connection between the British economy and society in the twentieth century, see F. Carnevali and J. M. Strange, eds., *20th Century Britain: Economic, Cultural, and Social Change*, 2nd ed. (London: Routledge, 2007).

14. See N. W. C. Woodward, "Inflation," in *The British Economy since 1945*, ed. N. F. R. Crafts and N. W. C. Woodward (Oxford, UK: Claredon, 1991), 180–212.

15. See, for example, Eric Hobsbawm, *Age of Extremes: The Short Twentieth Century, 1914–1991* (London: Michael Joseph, 1994); and his posthumously published *Fractured Times: Culture and Society in the Twentieth Century* (London: Abacus, 2014).

16. In general, see Arthur Marwick's *British Society since 1945*, 4th ed. (London: Penguin, 2003); and P. Addison and H. Jones, eds., *A Companion to Contemporary Britain, 1939–2000* (Oxford, UK: Blackwell, 2005). Other general studies consulted for creating this chapter included L. Black, *Reassessing 1970s Britain* (Manchester, UK: Manchester University Press, 2013), R. Coopey and N. W. C. Woodward, *Britain in the 1970s: The Troubled Decade* (New York: St. Martin's, 1996); B. Jackson and R. Saunders, eds., *The Making of Thatcher's Britain* (Cambridge: Cambridge University Press, 2012); and J. Tomlinson, *The Politics of Decline: Understanding Post-War Britain* (Harlow, UK: Longman, 2001). Popular music and politics in Britain are old bedfellows; see M. Cloonan, *Popular Music and the State in the UK: Culture, Trade or Industry?* (London: Ashgate, 2007).

17. This essay can be found in the Penguin edition of Orwell's essays: George Orwell and Bernard Crick, *Essays* (London: Penguin, 2000). See also B. Clarke, "Orwell and Englishness," *Review of English Studies* 57, no. 228, New Series (February 2006): 83–105.

18. See, for example, Kate Fox's humorous *Watching the English: The Hidden Rules of English Behaviour* (London: Hodder & Stoughton, 2004); Jeremy Paxman, *The English: A Portrait of a People* (London: Penguin, 1999); and A. Marr, *A History of Modern Britain* (London: Pan, 2009).

19. See A. Travis, "UK Migrants to Face 'Patriotic' Citizenship Test," *Guardian*, July 1, 2012, accessed October 19, 2014, http://www.theguardian.com/; "UK Citizenship Test 'to Cover Britain's Greats,'" *BBC News*, January 28, 2013, accessed October 19, 2014, http://www.bbc.co.uk/; and P. Wintour, "David Cameron Joins Calls for Promoting 'British Values' in Schools," *Guardian*, June 15, 2014 (the anniversary of the signing of Magna Carta, not completely coincidentally), accessed October 19, 2014, http://www.theguardian.com/.

20. See, for example, Sandbrook, *Seasons in the Sun*, 76–104; H. Sounes, *The Seventies: The Sights, Sounds, and Ideas of a Brilliant Decade* (London: Pocket, 2007), which covers the "serious art" of the 1970s and eschews discus-

sion of the world of *Top of the Pops*; and J. A. Walker, *Left Shift: Radical Art in 1970s Britain* (London: I. B. Taurus, 2002). For an interesting collection of recent essays to place against the context of the so-called intellectual artists, see B. Bebber, ed., *Leisure and Cultural Conflict in Twentieth-Century Britain* (Manchester, UK: Manchester University Press, 2012).

21. Good overviews of Pink Floyd and David Bowie's music include M. Blake, *Comfortably Numb: The Inside Story of Pink Floyd* (Cambridge, MA: Thunder's Mouth, 2008); and J. E. Perone, *The Words and Music of David Bowie* (Westport, CT: Praeger, 2007).

22. On the trial, see briefly, Kitts, *Ray Davies*, 112, and Rogan, *The Kinks*, 56–64, as well as other references in chapter 3 of this book.

23. Ray Davies, *X-Ray* (New York: Overlook, 1995), 344.

24. Ibid., 339–49 (344).

25. Ibid., 346.

26. Ibid., 343.

27. Ibid.

28. Ibid., 344.

29. The album's title is a play on Muswell Hill, London, where Ray, Dave, and Pete grew up, and the vocals on a number of the songs reflected Ray's ever-increasing predilection for mimicking Johnny Cash's singing voice. On the album itself and discussion of the band's new (American-facing) direction with RCA, see Kitts, *Ray Davies*, 159–62; and Nick Hasted, *The Story of the Kinks: You Really Got Me* (London: Omnibus, 2011), 170–78.

30. As the BBC found out in 1973, the idea of the British Empire provoked strongly *negative* reactions in the 1970s. See Sandbrook, *Seasons in the Sun*, 82–83.

31. See M. Kurlansky, *1968: The Year that Rocked the World* (London: Vintage, 2005); Ger-Reiner Horn, *The Spirit of '68: Rebellion in Western Europe and North America, 1956–1976* (Oxford: Oxford University Press, 2007); and M. Klimke and J. Scharloth, eds., *1968 in Europe: A History of Protest and Activism, 1956–1977* (New York: Palgrave, 2008), which look at the roots of the 1968 protest movements in America, Britain, and Europe.

32. R. Cooke, "Ray Davies: I'm Easy to Love . . . But Impossible to Live With," *Guardian*, May 1, 2011, accessed January 24, 2014, http://www.theguardian.com/.

33. The idea of new towns in Britain in the postwar era and the effects and disruption of social networks from the 1970s through to the 1990s is explored in several monographs including J. Grindrod, *Concretopia: A Journey around the Rebuilding of Postwar Britain* (Brecon, UK: Old Street, 2013).

34. See Johnny Rogan's assessment on what Ray seemed to be trying (and failing) to achieve with his "experimental dream" in *The Kinks*, 141–42. For

additional analysis, see Kitts, *Ray Davies*, 187–212; and Hasted's extensive discussion in *Story of the Kinks*, 186–87, 190–209. Alex DiBlasi's academic lecture on "The Kinks: Preservation," given at The Public School, New York, May 4, 2013, http://thepublicschool.org/, can be found on Dave Emlen's website KindaKinks.net, accessed October 30, 2014, http://www.kindakinks.net/.

35. See Sandbrook, *State of Emergency*, 92–133, for the 1926 strike and its legacy in general; and M. J. Roberts, *Tell Tchaikovsky the News: Rock 'n' Roll, the Labor Question, and the Musicians' Union, 1942–1968* (Durham, NC: Duke University Press, 2014), 11, 21–25, on the effects of the unions and the strikes in the music industry in the 1920s (which would eventually have repercussions on the Kinks' folderol with the American unions in 1965).

36. A recent book explores, with dry humor, Mary Whitehouse's crusade to preserve the sanctity of British morality: Ben Thompson, ed., *Ban This Filth! Letters from the Mary Whitehouse Archive* (London: Faber & Faber, 2012).

37. Johnny Rogan, *The Complete Guide to the Music of the Kinks* (London: Omnibus, 1998), 101.

38. Hasted refers to the role of the Kinks in these productions as being "fully integrated into Ray's freak show" (*Story of the Kinks*, 209).

39. On Dave's frustration with *Preservation* and *Starmaker*, see D. Davies, *Kink*, 166.

40. In a recent documentary by Julien Temple, John Lydon argued the Sex Pistols were pure music hall; it must be noted that this charity concert was for the children of striking fire-brigade workers (David Simpson, "Anarchy in Huddersfield: The Day the Sex Pistols Played Santa," *Guardian*, December 23, 2013, accessed January 15, 2015, http://www.theguardian.com/). On the other hand, Ozzy Osbourne, whose "shock rock" engendered complaints by authorities in the 1970s and 1980s, once defended himself to a critic by exclaiming, "I am not a musician; I'm a ham." Quoted in E. Nuzum, *Parental Advisory: Music Censorship in America* (New York: Perenniel, 2001), 243.

41. W. Glinga, *Legacy of Empire: A Journey through British Society* (Manchester, UK: Manchester University Press, 1986), 68.

42. See R. Taylor, "The Rise and Disintegration of the Working Classes," in *A Companion to Contemporary Britain, 1939–2000*, ed. P. Addison and H. Jones, 371–87 (Oxford, UK: Blackwell, 2005). For contemporary viewpoints and interviews, see L. McNeil and G. McCain, *Please Kill Me: The Uncensored Oral History of Punk* (London: Little, Brown, 1996); and Jon Savage, *England's Dreaming: Sex Pistols and Punk Rock* (London: Faber & Faber, 1991). An excellent study on the punk scene and its cultural impact, written as half reference book, half ransom, see Nick Rombes, *The Cultural Dictionary of Punk, 1974–1982* (London: Continuum, 2009). As Rombes notes, punk presents a challenge to critics and scholars if not its followers, as it is a genre

that was never meant to be tamed or categorized. Additionally useful is R. Sabin, *Punk Rock, So What? The Cultural Legacy of Punk* (London: Routledge, 1999).

43. On Blondie, see C. Heylin, *From the Velvets to the Voidoids: The Birth of American Punk Rock* (Chicago: Chicago Review Press, 2005), 155–65.

44. By the nineties, punk had become part of London's tourist industry— even some punkers of the time are now embarrassed about their own political naïveté. Said Don Letts in an interview in the *Independent* (October 2004), in the punk generation, "We . . . all got into the music [to be] anti-establishment. It seems to me nowadays that people get into music today to be a part of the establishment." Quoted in "The Clash's 30 Best Songs," *Uncut*, March 13, 2015, accessed August 4, 2015, http://www.uncut.co.uk/. The quote is a variation of a statement Letts made in an interview for the *Independent* in October 2004.

45. Rombes, *Cultural Dictionary*, 263–64.

46. Ibid., 119–20.

47. Ibid., 36.

48. Ibid., 36–37, 74–77.

49. Ibid., 55–56.

50. See Nick Rombes, *Ramones' Ramones*, 33 1/3 (series) (London: Continuum, 2005).

51. Rombes, *Cultural Dictionary*, 12, 31.

52. Marten and Hudson, *The Kinks*, 14.

53. Rogan, *Complete Guide*, 115. Although to be fair, Rogan's comment on *Sleepwalker* is in response to the commercially friendly, straightforward album-oriented rock (AOR) material the band delivered in the wake of the previous years of "grandiloquent concept albums."

54. Ray was asked in a 2014 interview if it was only him, and not all of the Kinks, performing in the Olympics; his response was, "[The Olympic Committee] only asked me. I think more than anything else they wanted the song." J. Rees, "Ray Davies, Interview: I Can't Play as the Kinks," *Telegraph*, October 24, 2004, accessed October 26, 2014, http://www.telegraph.co.uk/.

7. I MISS THE VILLAGE GREEN

1. Ray Davies, quoted by James McNair, "Ray Davies' Well-Respected Legacy," *Independent*, June 18, 2009, accessed January 16, 2016, http://www. independent.co.uk/.

2. Eric Hobsbawm, *The Age of Extremes: The Short Twentieth Century, 1914–1991* (London: Michael Joseph, 1994).

3. D. Simonelli, *Working Class Heroes: Rock Music and British Society in the 1960s and 1970* (Lanham, MD: Lexington, 2013), 57.

4. Ibid., 56–57. On the Kinks in general, 55–58.

5. See R. G. H. Burns, "Depicting the 'Merrie': Historical Imagery in English Folk-Rock," *Music in Art* 35, nos. 1/2, *Rethinking Music in Art: New Directions in Music Iconography* (Spring–Fall 2010): 105–17; N. Green, "Songs from the Wood and Sounds of the Suburbs: A Folk, Rock and Punk Portrait of England, 1965–1977," *Built Environment* (1978–) 31, no. 3, *Music and the City* (2005): 255–70; and T. K. Ramnarine, "Imperial Legacies and the Politics of Musical Creativity," *World of Music* 46, no. 1, *Contemporary British Music Traditions* (2004): 91–108.

6. C. Bray has a recent overview of 1965 as a pivotal year of change in the midst of what is called "the long decade." *1965: The Year Modern Britain Was Born* (London: Simon & Schuster, 2014), 9.

7. G. P. Garrett et al., *Film Scripts Four: Darling, A Hard Day's Night, The Best Man* (New York: Irvington, 1989), 49.

8. See Joseph G. Marotta, "The Loss of Identity and the Myth of Edenic Return in Ray Davies," in *Living on a Thin Line: Crossing Aesthetic Borders with the Kinks*, ed. Thomas M. Kitts and Michael J. Kraus, 68–77 (Rumford, RI: Rock 'n' Roll Research Press, 2002); and Nick Baxter-Moore, "'This Is Where I Belong': Identity, Social Class, and the Nostalgic Englishness of Ray Davies and the Kinks," *Popular Music and Society* 29, no. 2 (2006): 145–65.

9. Simonelli, *Working Class Heroes*, 56.

10. B. Martin, "The Sacralization of Disorder: Symbolism in Rock Music," *Sociological Analysis* 40, no. 2 (Summer 1979): 109. See also Christopher Partridge's monograph that discusses rock-and-roll rebellion against societal sacred cows and the reaction of ecclesiastical and secular authorities: *The Lyre of Orpheus: Popular Music, the Sacred, and the Profane* (Oxford: Oxford University Press, 2014), 102–4.

11. Partridge, *Lyre of Orpheus*, 100–103.

12. The week prior to the University of Southampton talk, Ray gave a talk at the Southbank Centre in London on music and politics. Recalling it at Southampton, he chuckled and rolled his eyes, asking, "What do *I* know about politics?" He suggested to the enrapt crowd that if they wanted a message, they should simply send a telegram.

13. Hans Jauss refereed to this phenomenon in his discussion of reception theory in his seminal *Towards an Aesthetic of Literary Reception* (Minneapolis: University of Minnesota Press, 1982). A discussion of how the meaning of a Kinks song changes depending on the context and experience of the listener merits its own dissertation.

14. Ray Davies in interview with Terry Gross, "Naïve, Yet Revolutionary: Ray Davies on 50 Years of the Kinks," *Fresh Air*, December 25, 2014, accessed August 7, 2015, http://www.npr.org/.

15. P. Gruner, "Academic Gown for a Dedicated Follower of Fashion: Kinks Legend Ray Davies Honoured by London Met," *Islington Tribune*, August 1, 2014, accessed August 7, 2014, http://www.islingtontribune.com/.

16. Thomas Kitts, *Ray Davies: Not Like Everybody Else* (New York: Routledge, 2008), 3.

17. Dave Davies, *Kink* (New York: Hyperion, 1996), 5–6.

18. There are an increasing number of studies appearing on the importance of wives and mothers in British family life in the 1940s and 1950s as housewives and family providers; a number not only examine solidarity experienced from living through the post-war period but also feature case studies of people who discuss the strong influence of mothers and grandmothers within the household. See, for example, V. Nicholson, *Millions Like Us: Women's Lives during the Second World War* (London: Penguin, 2012); and E. Roberts, *Women and Families: An Oral History, 1940–1970* (Oxford, UK: Blackwell, 1995).

19. D. Davies, *Kink*, 4, 107.

20. See, for example, N. Lannamann, "The Creepiest Love Songs of All Time," *Portland Mercury*, February 9, 2012, accessed February 10, 2012, http://www.portlandmercury.com/.

21. See Keith Gildart, *Images of England through Popular Music: Class, Youth and Rock 'n' Roll, 1955–1976* (London: Palgrave MacMillan, 2013), 135–36, on "Two Sisters" as an example of the Kinks' more nuanced reading of gender.

22. Simonelli, *Working Class Heroes*, 56–57.

23. For a discussion of the symbolism of this rite of rebellious passage and the influence of rock music and performers on rebellion against the symbols and codes of "expected behavior," see Martin, "Sacralization of Disorder," 87–124.

24. Ibid., 109–13. The examples she gives include tribalism among teens (in fashion, for example).

25. Ibid., 88, 102–4. On the working-class ideology of the counterculture in Britain, Simonelli offers a concise overview (*Working Class Heroes*, 139–55).

26. Martin, "Sacralization of Disorder," 94–95. Martin notes the work of contemporary sociologist David Matza, who pointed out that even as the younger generation transforms the cultural norms of society, they also mirror the symbols and social system of their parents.

27. Simonelli, *Working Class Heroes*, 56. The Beatles may have outraged some with the award of their MBE, but certainly official recognition for ser-

vices to the country cemented their position within the cultural establishment. As for the bad boys of rock and roll, the Stones carefully plotted, blocked, and rehearsed for hours what would amount to two and a half minutes of outrage on a television performance (Martin, "Sacralization of Disorder," 103–4).

28. S. Turner, *A Hard Day's Write: The Stories behind Every Beatles Song* (London: Carlton, 2005), 125–26.

29. Ray Davies, *X-Ray* (New York: Overlook, 1995), 137.

30. Martin, "Sacralization of Disorder," 91.

31. Bray, *1965*, 247–52. The plot was subverted in a Monty Python sketch in which the apparently illiterate northerner is in fact an award-winning playwright, and his suited and booted son wants nothing more than to go down the mines. The son chastises his father for subjecting his mother to the exhausting stress of "meeting film stars, attending premieres and giving gala luncheons," while his father berates him: "What do you know about getting up at five o'clock in t'morning to fly to Paris . . . back at the Old Vic for drinks at twelve, sweating the day through press interviews, television interviews and getting back here at ten to wrestle with the problem of a homosexual nymphomaniac drug-addict involved in the ritual murder of a well-known Scottish footballer. That's a full working day, lad, and don't you forget it!" In Luke Dempsey's *Monty Python's Flying Circus: All The Bits, Complete and Annotated* (New York: Black Dog and Leventhal, 2012), 40–41.

32. Jon Savage, *The Kinks: The Official Biography* (London: Faber & Faber, 1984), 102–4.

33. D. Davies, *Kink*, 227. Jon Savage includes in his biography a photograph of Uncle Frank beside a photo of Ray from the video; the resemblance is startling (*The Kinks*, 160).

34. Cf. Johnny Rogan, *The Kinks: A Mental Institution* (New York: Proteus, 1984), 155.

35. R. Davies, *X-Ray*, 30–31.

36. Ibid., 62–63.

37. Ibid., 33.

38. D. Davies, *Kink*, 2.

39. Ibid., 101–12.

40. Savage, *The Kinks*, 48.

8. THIS STRANGE EFFECT

1. Fan Dave Tillerton's comment in response to a survey for this project.

2. Recommended readings to start with on music fandom and effects on fame include D. Calvicchi, *Tramps Like Us: Music and Meaning among*

Springsteen Fans (Oxford: Oxford University Press, 1998); D. R. Shumway, *Rock Star: The Making of Musical Icons from Elvis to Springsteen* (Baltimore: Johns Hopkins University Press, 2014); and Sheila Whiteley, *Too Much Too Young: Popular Music, Age, and Gender* (London: Routledge, 2005). On fandom in general as a means to social connections, there is an embarrassment of riches available; a good starting place are the collections edited by Jonathan Gray, *Fandom: Identities and Communities in a Mediated World* (New York: New York University Press, 2007); and M. Duffett, *Understanding Fandom: An Introduction to the Study of Media Fan Culture* (London: Bloomsbury Academic, 2013).

3. Enjoy: https://www.youtube.com/watch?v=jyy78nxV1aQ (accessed 24 May 2015).

4. Emlen's work follows as its printed source the formidable work done by Doug Hinman (with Jason Brabazon) in his *Kinks Part One: You Really Got Me; An Illustrated World Discography of the Kinks, 1964–1993* (London: Backbeat, 1994). Hinman has compiled a catalog of Davies's compositions by others (including illustrations of record sleeves and labels; 471–503). I highly recommended Hinman's text if you can find a copy.

5. Official source: my 1979 ninth-grade classmate Ruby who *refused* to believe that some "old guys" were actually responsible for the song.

6. For the record, at least according to Emlen's site, this is the first cover to appear by an American band, in 1965, by Gary Lewis and the Playboys. Enjoy, if still available, at the following: HermansHermitsMusic, "Gary Lewis and the Playboys: All Day and All of the Night," YouTube, December 23, 2010, accessed April 28, 2015, https://www.youtube.com/watch?v=qGEnjRy35dc. It's the perkiest and most clean-cut, sexually obsessed lament by the politest angry young man ever recorded.

7. Of course it's on YouTube, at least at the time of this writing (flatop47, "The Pickwicks: I Took My Baby Home," July 23, 2012, accessed April 28, 2015, https://www.youtube.com/watch?v=W1MiB7PY2Ys). Check it out to hear young session musician Jimmy Page on lead guitar.

8. American covers *do* appear throughout the ban, but they are restricted to the British Top Ten hits—excluding the really *British* ones. "Autumn Almanac," widely covered in Europe in the sixties, doesn't appear as an American cover until over a decade later.

9. Cf. Hinman, *The Kinks*, 471.

10. There are one or two 1960s covers of the song, including one by Petula Clark and an early 1970s by fans Flo and Eddie (whose alter ego, the Turtles, had had an album produced by Ray Davies at around the same time).

11. Oddly, the ban is the battle cry for fans who feel the exclusion cost the Kinks their popularity (see, for example, J. Kurp, "The Frustrating Reason the

Kinks Were Never as Popular as the Rolling Stones," Uproxx Music, May 1, 2015, accessed 4 May 2015, http://uproxx.com/. This article, and others like it, breaks no new ground in any fashion, remarking only vaguely on the ban, even though quite a bit of information is available on the circumstances around it—what *is* important in yet another rehashing of the story is how Kinks fans have this particular rallying cry when defending their heroes' lack of space on the multinational corporate brand that the Stones and Beatles enjoy. That said, one imagines there would be utter outrage were the Kinks to be suddenly elevated to that same status.

12. Christopher Partridge, *The Lyre of Orpheus: Popular Music, the Sacred, and the Profane* (Oxford: Oxford University Press, 2014).

13. Cynthia Lennon, *A Twist of Lennon* (New York: Avon, 1978), 103–5, 124–27, and elsewhere.

14. *X-Ray* is presented as a science-fiction story in which a younger version of Ray, raised and corrupted by the "corporation," is sent to interview the older version of Ray who provides the story of the Kinks.

15. See, for example, R. Davies, *X-Ray* (New York: Overlook, 1995), 8–12.

16. "Last summer I saw Dave Davies (guitarist and sometimes vocalist for The Kinks). He sang about as well as the worst, drunkest karaoke singers you'll ever hear." "A Weak Pit: Singers/Groups Touring 30–40 Years Later," Straight Dope Message Board, February 27, 2014, accessed March 2, 2014, http://boards.straightdope.com/.

17. A number of "famous fans" refused to contribute to this project as they argued that I wasn't "known" among the fandom. For a fan base that takes great pride in being outsiders, there is somewhat of a suspicious streak that runs through the so-called inner circle of superfans.

18. While online activity and connections proliferate, there is no shortage of Kinks fan meetings, especially the annual one in London, as well as activities on the Continent. The West End's *Sunny Afternoon* has also proven a popular connection point for a certain segment of the fan population as well.

19. Ray Davies, "Rock and Roll Fantasy," in *Waterloo Sunset*, 19–34 (London: Penguin, 1997).

20. Discussion from a concert to support *Americana* at the Union Chapel, Islington, March 4, 2014. Throughout the book, Ray ponders his Englishness in the context of living and touring in America; cf. *Americana: The Kinks, The Road and the Perfect Riff* (London: Virgin, 2013), 149.

21. Andrew Tyler, quoted in Doug Hinman, *The Kinks: All Day and All of the Night; Day-by-Day Concerts, Recordings, and Broadcasts, 1961–1996* (San Francisco: Backbeat, 2004), 176.

BIBLIOGRAPHY

Abrams, Mark Abrams, et al., eds. *Values and Social Change in Britain*. Basingstoke, UK: MacMillan, 1985.

Addison, P., and H. Jones, eds. *A Companion to Contemporary Britain, 1939–2000*. Oxford, UK: Blackwell, 2005.

Allen, D. "Feelin' Bad This Morning: Why the British Blues?" *Popular Music* 26, no. 1, Special Issue on the Blues in Honour of Paul Oliver (January 2007): 141–56.

Alterman, Loraine. "Who Let the Kinks In?" *Rolling Stone Magazine*, December 18, 1969. KindaKinks.net. Accessed August 3, 2015. http://www.kindakinks.net/.

August, A. "Gender and 1960s Youth Culture: The Rolling Stones and the New Woman." *Contemporary British History* 23, no. 1 (2009): 79–100.

Auslander, P. "I Wanna Be Your Man: Suzi Quatro's Musical Androgyny." *Popular Music* 23, no. 1 (January 2004): 1–16.

Ball, Stuart, and Anthony Seldon, eds. *The Heath Government, 1970–1974: A Reappraisal*. London: Longman, 1996.

Baranczak, S. "How to Translate Shakespeare's Humor? (Reflections of a Polish Translator)." *Performing Arts Journal* 14, no. 3 (September 1992): 70–89.

Barfe, L. *Where Have All the Good Times Gone? The Rise and Fall of the Record Industry*. London: Atlantic, 2004.

Barnes, R. "Mods." In *The Sharper Word: A Mod Anthology*, edited by P. Hewitt. Rev. and updated. London: Helter Skelter, 1999.

Barratt, J., and N. Fielding. "Eels." *The Mighty Boosh*. BBC Three, November 15, 2007.

Baxter-Moore, Nick. "'This Is Where I Belong': Identity, Social Class, and the Nostalgic Englishness of Ray Davies and the Kinks." *Popular Music and Society* 29, no. 2 (2006): 145–65.

BBC News. "Ray Davies Keen for Kinks Reunion." September 23, 2008. Accessed October 5, 2008. http://news.bbc.co.uk/.

———. "'Strictly' Most Watched." November 10, 2008. Accessed November 19, 2008. http://news.bbc.co.uk/.

———. "UK Citizenship Test 'to Cover Britain's Greats.'" January 28, 2013. Accessed October 19, 2014. http://www.bbc.co.uk/.

Bebber, B., ed. *Leisure and Cultural Conflict in Twentieth-Century Britain*. Manchester, UK: Manchester University Press, 2012.

Beckett, Andy. *When the Lights Went Out: What Really Happened to Britain in the Seventies*. London: Faber & Faber, 2009.

Bellman, J. "Indian Resonances in the British Invasion, 1965–1968." *Journal of Musicology* 15, no. 1 (Winter 1997): 116–36.

Bellotti, A. "Ham and High: Ray and Dave Davies Interview." *Hampstead Theatre Online*, April 11, 2014. Accessed January 30, 2015. http://www.hampsteadtheatre.com/.

Berger, A. A. *Ads, Fad, and Consumer Culture: Advertising's Impact on American Character and Society*. 4th ed. Lanham, MD: Rowman & Littlefield, 2011.

Black, L. *Reassessing 1970s Britain*. Manchester, UK: Manchester University Press, 2013.

Blake, M. *Comfortably Numb: The Inside Story of Pink Floyd*. Cambridge, MA: Thunder's Mouth, 2008.

Blecha, P. *Taboo Tunes: A History of Banned Bands and Censored Songs*. San Francisco: Backbeat, 2004.

Blistein, J. "Kinks Refute BBC Doc Saying Jimmy Page Played on 'You Really Got Me.'" *Rolling Stone*, July 10, 2014. Accessed May 10, 2016. http://www.rollingstone.com/.

Booth, A. *The British Economy in the Twentieth Century*. New York: Palgrave, 2001.

Bourke, Joanna. *Working-Class Cultures in Britain, 1890–1960: Gender, Class and Ethnicity*. London: Routledge, 1996.

Brackett, D. "The British Art School Blues." In *The Pop, Rock, and Soul Reader: Histories and Debates*, edited by D. Brackett, 227–32. Oxford: Oxford University Press, 2006.

Bradley, D. *Understanding Rock 'n' Roll: Popular Music in Britain, 1955–1964*. Buckingham, UK: Open University Press, 1992.

Bray, C. *1965: The Year Modern Britain Was Born*. London: Simon & Schuster, 2014.

Brendon, P. *The Decline and Fall of the British Empire, 1781–1997*. New York: Knopf, 2008.

Briggs, Asa. *A Social History of England*. 3rd rev. ed. London: Weidenfeld & Nicolson, 1994.

Bryson, Bill. *Notes from a Small Island*. New York: HarperCollins, 1996.

Burke, John. *The Beatles in A Hard Day's Night*. New York: Dell, 1964.

Burns, R. G. H. "Continuity, Variation, and Authenticity in the English Folk-Rock Movement." *Folk Music Journal* 9, no. 2 (2007): 192–218.

———. "Depicting the 'Merrie': Historical Imagery in English Folk-Rock." *Music in Art* 35, nos. 1/2, *Rethinking Music in Art: New Directions in Music Iconography* (Spring–Fall 2010): 105–17.

Butler, S. "Don't Get Me Wrong: We're Protecting, Not Protesting, Says Chrissie Hynde's Activist Daughter." *Evening Standard*, August 1, 2013. Accessed October 26, 2014. http://www.standard.co.uk/.

Buttkereit, H. *40 Years of the Kinks*. 2004. KindaKinks.net. Accessed August 11, 2015. http://www.kindakinks.net/.

Calvicchi, D. *Tramps Like Us: Music and Meaning among Springsteen Fans*. Oxford: Oxford University Press, 1998.

Cant, B., and S. Hemmings. *Radical Records: Thirty Years of Lesbian and Gay History, 1957–1987*. London: Routledge, 1998.

Carnevali, F., and J. M. Strange, eds. *20th Century Britain: Economic, Cultural, and Social Change*. 2nd ed. London: Routledge, 2007.

Carpenter, H. *The Angry Young Men: A Literary Comedy of the 1950s*. London: Allen Lane, 2001.

———. *That Was Satire That Was: The Satire Boom of the 1960s*. London: Phoenix, 2000.

Carr, J., and L. Greeves. *The Naked Jape: Uncovering the Hidden World of Jokes*. London: Penguin, 2007.

Cashmere, Paul. "Another Kinks Reunion Rumour Surfaces and Is Dismissed." *Undercover*, September 25, 2008. Accessed October 5, 2008. http://www.undercover.com.au/.

Catterall, P., and J. Obelkevich, eds. *Understanding Post-War British Society*. London: Routledge, 1994.

Cavicchi, D. "Loving Music: Listeners, Entertainments, and the Origins of Music Fandom in Nineteenth-Century America." In *Fandom: Identities and Communities in a Mediated World*, edited by Jonathan Gray, 235–49. New York: New York University Press, 2007.

Charlton, J. "Two Oldies but Goodies: The Kinks, Dave Davies and Joe D'Allesandro." *Janet Charlton's Hollywood*, July 21, 2014. Accessed July 24, 2014. http://www.janetcharltonshollywood.com/.

Clarke, B. "Orwell and Englishness." *Review of English Studies* 57, no. 228, New Series (February 2006): 83–105.

Clayson, Alan. *Beat Merchants: The Origins, History, Impact and Rock Legacy of the British Pop Groups*. London: Blandford, 1995.

Cleese, John. *So, Anyway . . .* London: Random House, 2014.

Cloonan, M. *Banned! Censorship of Popular Music in Britain, 1967–92*. Popular Culture Studies 9. London: Arena, 1996.

———. *Popular Music and the State in the UK: Culture, Trade or Industry?* London: Ashgate, 2007.

Cohn, Nik. *Awopbop-Aloobop-Alopbam-Boom: Pop from the Beginning*. London: Pimlico, 2004.

———. "Carnaby Street." In *The Sharper Word: A Mod Anthology*, edited by P. Hewitt. Rev. and updated. London: Helter Skelter, 1999.

Collins, Andrew. *Where Did It All Go Right? Growing Up Normal in the '70s*. London: Ebury, 2003.

Collins, N. "Introduction: Not Necessarily 'English Music'; Britain's Second 'Golden Age.'" *Leonardo Music Journal* 11 (2001): 1–3.

Connolly, R. *In the Sixties*. London: Pavilion, 1995.

Cook, Matt, ed. *A Gay History of Britain: Love and Sex between Men since the Middle Ages*. Oxford, UK: Greenwood World, 2007.

Cooke, R. "Ray Davies: I'm Easy to Love . . . But Impossible to Live With." *Guardian*, May 1, 2011. Accessed January 24, 2014. http://www.theguardian.com/.

Coopey, R., and N. W. C. Woodward. *Britain in the 1970s: The Troubled Decade*. New York: St. Martin's, 1996.

Coppa, F. "A Perfectly Developed Playwright: Joe Orton and Homosexual Reform." In *The Queer Sixties*, edited by P. J. Smith, 87–104. London: Routledge, 1999.

Crafts, N. F. R., and N. Woodward, eds. *The British Economy since 1945*. Oxford, UK: Clarendon, 1991.

"Dave Davies Message Board." Dave Davies Website, September 23, 2008. Accessed September 11, 2009. http://www.davedavies.com/.

Davenport-Hines, R. P. T. *An English Affair: Sex, Class and Power in the Age of Profumo*. London: Harper, 2013.

David, H. *On Queer Street: A Social History of British Homosexuality, 1895–1995*. London: HarperCollins, 1997.

Davies, Dave. *Kink*. New York: Hyperion, 1996.

Davies, Hunter. *The Beatles: The Authorized Biography*. New York: Dell, 1969.

———. *The Quarrymen*. London: Omnibus, 2001.

Davies, Matt. "The Kinks Back at the Clissold Arms, Just." *Haringey* (blog), March 16, 2008. Accessed November 12, 2009.http://mattdaviesharingey.blogspot.com/.

Davies, Ray. *Americana: The Kinks, The Road and the Perfect Riff*. London: Virgin, 2013.

———. "Rock and Roll Fantasy." In *Waterloo Sunset*, 19–34. London: Penguin, 1997.

———. *X-Ray*. New York: Overlook, 1995.

Dawbarn, Bob. "Ray: The Patriot Kink." *Melody Maker*, April 16, 1966.

Dempsey, Luke. *Monty Python's Flying Circus: All The Bits, Complete and Annotated*. New York: Black Dog and Leventhal, 2012.

DiBlasi, Alex. "The Kinks: Preservation." Lecture given at The Public School, New York, May 4, 2013. http://thepublicschool.org/. On KindaKinks.net. Accessed October 30, 2014. http://www.kindakinks.net/.

Duffett, M., ed. *Understanding Fandom: An Introduction to the Study of Media Fan Culture*. London: Bloomsbury Academic, 2013.

Duguid, Mark, and Lee Freeman. *Ealing Revisited*. London: British Film Institute, 2012.

Dyer, R. *The Culture of Queers*. London: Routledge, 2002.

Easier Lifestyle. "Muswell Hill Pub Receives New Lease of Life." February 28, 2008. Accessed November 12, 2009. http://www.easier.com/.

Ellis, Iain. *Brit Wits: A History of British Rock Humor*. Bristol, UK: Intellect, 2012.

Ellis, Royston. *The Big Beat Scene*. York, UK: Music Mentor, [1961] 2010.

Emlen, Dave. "News and Rumours: You Decide." KindaKinks.net, April 2, 2007. Accessed November 12, 2009. http://www.kindakinks.net/.

"Families." *QI*. Directed by Ian Lorimer. BBC Two, November 14, 2008.

Ferris, R., and J. Lord. *Teddy Boys: A Concise History*. London: Milo, 2012.

Feydri, Alain. *The Kinks: Une histoire anglaise*. Bègles, France: Le Castor Astral, 2013.

Fleiner, Carey. "Heroes and Villains: The Medieval Guitarist and Modern Parallels." In *The British Museum Citole: New Perspectives*, British Museum Research Publication, edited by James Robinson and Naomi Speakman, 51–60. London: British Museum, 2015.

———. "The Influence of Family and Childhood Experience on the Works of Ray and Dave Davies." *Popular Music and Society* 34, no. 3 (July 2011): 329–50.

———. "'Rosy, Won't You Please Come Home': Family, Home, and Cultural Identity in the Music of Ray Davies and the Kinks." In *Mad Dogs and Englishness: Popular Music and English Identity*, edited by Mark Donnelly, Lee Brooks, and Richard Mills. London: Bloomsbury, forthcoming, 2017.

———. "Siblings in American Music." In *Music in American Life*, edited by J. Edmonson, 4:1054–56. Santa Barbara, CA: ABC-CLIO, 2013.

———. "A Well Respected Man." *Songlexikon* (Albert-Ludwigs-Universitat, Freiburg), April 2012. Last updated October 2013. Accessed January 25, 2015. http://www.songlexikon.de/.

Floud, R., and P. Johnson, eds. *The Cambridge Economic History of Modern Britain*. Vol. 3, *Structural Change and Growth, 1939–2000*. Cambridge: University of Cambridge Press, 2004.

Fox, Kate. *Watching the English: The Hidden Rules of English Behaviour*. London: Hodder & Stoughton, 2004.

"Fracking: Chrissie Hynde and Ray Davies' Daughter Natalie Arrested in Balcombe after Superglue Protest." *Telegraph*, July 31, 2013. Accessed October 22, 2014. http://www.telegraph.co.uk/.

Frame, Peter. *The Restless Generation: How Rock Music Changed the Face of 1950s Britain*. London: Rogan House, 2007.

Frith, S. *The Sociology of Rock*. London: Constable, 1978.

Frith, Simon, Matt Brennan, Martin Cloonan, and Emma Webster, eds. *The History of Live Music in Britain*. Vol. 1, *1950–1967 (From the Dance Hall to the 100 Club)*. London: Ashgate, 2013.

Frith, Simon, and Andrew Goodwin, eds. *Rock, Pop, and the Written Word: On the Record*. London: Routledge, 1990.

Frontani, M. R. *The Beatles: Image and the Media*. Jackson: University of Mississippi Press, 2007.

Gans, David. "Ozzy Osbourne." Levity, January 10, 1982. Accessed January 25, 2015. http://www.levity.com/.

Garbáty, T. J. "Satire and Regionalism: The Reeve and His Tale." *Chaucer Review* 8, no. 1 (Summer 1973): 1–8.

Garrett, G. P., et al. *Film Scripts Four: Darling, A Hard Day's Night, The Best Man*. New York: Irvington, 1989.

Geldart, M. "Persona and Voice in the Kinks' Songs of the Late 1960s." *Journal of the Royal Music Association* 128, no. 2 (2003): 200–241.

Gildart, Keith. "From 'Dead End Streets' to 'Shangri-Las': Negotiating Social Class and Post-War Politics with Ray Davies and the Kinks." *Contemporary British History* 26, no. 3 (2012): 273–98.

———. *Images of England through Popular Music: Class, Youth and Rock 'n' Roll, 1955–1976*. London: Palgrave MacMillan, 2013.

Glinga, W. *Legacy of Empire: A Journey through British Society*. Manchester, UK: Manchester University Press, 1986.

Gracyk, T. A. "Romanticizing Rock Music." *Journal of Aesthetic Education* 27, no. 2 (Summer 1993): 43–58.

Gray, Jonathan, ed. *Fandom: Identities and Communities in a Mediated World*. New York: New York University Press, 2007.

Green, N. "Songs from the Wood and Sounds of the Suburbs: A Folk, Rock and Punk Portrait of England, 1965–1977." *Built Environment* (1978–) 31, no. 3, *Music and the City* (2005): 255–70.

Grindrod, J. *Concretopia: A Journey around the Rebuilding of Postwar Britain*. Brecon, UK: Old Street, 2013.

Gross, Terry. "Naive, Yet Revolutionary: Ray Davies on 50 Years of the Kinks." *Fresh Air*, December 25, 2014. Accessed August 7, 2015. http://www.npr.org/.

Grost, Mike. "A Guide to 1980's Music Video Directors." MikeGrost.com. Accessed October 18, 2009. http://mikegrost.com/.

Gruner, P. "Academic Gown for a Dedicated Follower of Fashion: Kinks Legend Ray Davies Honoured by London Met." *Islington Tribune*, August 1, 2014. Accessed August 7, 2014. http://www.islingtontribune.com/.

Hadleigh, B. *The Vinyl Closet: Gays in the Music Industry*. San Diego: Les Hombres, 1991.

Hamblett, Charles, and Jane Deverson. *Generation X*. London: Anthony Gibbs, 1964.

Hammerton, A. James, and A. Thomson. *Ten Pound Poms: Australia's Invisible Migrants*. Manchester, UK: Manchester University Press, 2005.

Harris, T., and M. O'Brien Castro, eds. *Preserving the Sixties: Britain and the "Decade of Protest."* London: Palgrave, 2014.

Hasted, Nick. *The Story of the Kinks: You Really Got Me*. London: Omnibus, 2011.

Hawkins, Stan. *The British Pop Dandy: Male Identity, Music, and Culture*. London: Ashgate, 2009.

Heath, Edward. *The Course of My Life*. London: Hodder & Stoughton, 1998.

Hennessy, Peter. *Having It So Good: Britain in the Fifties*. London: Penguin, 2007.

Hewitt, P., ed. *The Sharper Word: A Mod Anthology*. Rev. and updated. London: Helter Skelter, 1999.

Heylin, C. *From the Velvets to the Voidoids: The Birth of American Punk Rock*. Chicago: Chicago Review Press, 2005.

Hinman, Doug. *The Kinks: All Day and All of the Night; Day-by-Day Concerts, Recordings, and Broadcasts, 1961–1996*. San Francisco: Backbeat, 2004.

———. *The Kinks Part One: You Really Got Me; An Illustrated World Discography of the Kinks, 1964–1993*. London: Backbeat, 1994.

———. *You Really Got Me: Supplement*. Rumford, RI: Doug Hinman, 1997.

Hobsbawm, Eric. *Age of Extremes: The Short Twentieth Century, 1914–1991*. London: Michael Joseph, 1994.

———. *Fractured Times: Culture and Society in the Twentieth Century*. London: Abacus, 2014.

Hopkins, E. *A Social History of the English Working Classes, 1815–1945*. London: Hodder Education, 1979.

Horn, Adrian. *Juke Box Britain: Americanisation and Youth Culture, 1945–1960*. Manchester, UK: Manchester University Press, 2009.

Horn, Ger-Reiner. *The Spirit of '68: Rebellion in Western Europe and North America, 1956–1976*. Oxford: Oxford University Press, 2007.

Horsfall, A. "Battling for Wolfenden." In *Radical Records: Thirty Years of Lesbian and Gay History, 1957–1987*, edited by B. Cant and S. Hemmings, 10–21. London: Routledge, 1998.

Howard, David N. *Sonic Alchemy: Visionary Music Producers and Their Maverick Recordings*. New York: Hal Leonard, 2004.

Howes, K. *Broadcasting It: An Encyclopaedia of Homosexuality on Film, Radio, and TV in the UK, 1923–1993*. London: Cassell, 1993.

Hudd, Roy. *Roy Hudd's Book of Music-Hall, Variety and Showbiz Anecdotes*. London: Robson, 1998.

———. *Roy Hudd's Cavalcade of Variety Acts: A Who Was Who of Light Entertainment, 1945–60*. London: Robson, 1998.

Hunter, Dave. "Comeback Kink." *Guitar Magazine*, January 1999. Accessed June 30, 2014. http://www.davedavies.com/.

Hyde, H. Montgomery. *The Love that Dared Not Speak Its Name: A Candid History of Homosexuality in Britain*. Boston: Little, Brown, 1970.

h2g2. "The Kinks: The Band 1971 Onwards." August 4, 2006. Accessed November 13, 2009. http://www.bbc.co.uk/.

Irving, Clive. *Anatomy of a Scandal: A Study of the Profumo Affair*. New York: M. S. Mill, 1963.

Jackson, B., and R. Saunders, eds. *The Making of Thatcher's Britain*. Cambridge: Cambridge University Press, 2012.

Jauss, Hans. *Towards an Aesthetic of Literary Reception*. Minneapolis: University of Minnesota Press, 1982.

Jennings, P. "British Humour." *Journal of the Royal Society of Arts* 118, no. 5164 (March 1970): 169–78.

Johnson, A. *This Boy: A Memoir of a Childhood*. London: Transworld, 2014.

Jones, A. R. *Fads, Fetishes, and Fun: A Sociological Analysis of Pop Culture*. San Diego: Cognella, 2009.

Jovanovic, Rob. *God Save the Kinks: A Biography*. London: Aurum, 2013.

King, Martin. *Men, Masculinity and the Beatles*. London: Ashgate, 2013.

Kitts, Thomas. *Ray Davies: Not Like Everybody Else*. New York: Routledge, 2008.

Klimke, M., and J. Scharloth, eds. *1968 in Europe: A History of Protest and Activism, 1956–1977*. New York: Palgrave, 2008.

Knightely, P., and C. Kennedy. *An Affair of State: The Profumo Case and the Framing of Stephen Ward*. London: J. Cape, 1987.

Kraus, Michael J. "Revelations, Revisions, and Reinventions: Davies Interviews as Essential Works in the Kinks' Canon." In *Living on a Thin Line: Crossing Aesthetic Borders with the Kinks*, edited by Thomas M. Kitts and Michael J. Kraus, 257–66. Rumford, RI: Rock 'n' Roll Research Press, 2002.

———. "Unfinished Business: The Evolving Artistry of David Russell Gordon Davies." In *Living on a Thin Line: Crossing Aesthetic Borders with the Kinks*, edited by Thomas M. Kitts and Michael J. Kraus, 120–30. Rumford, RI: Rock 'n' Roll Research Press, 2002.

Krause, P. *The Kinks: A Rock and Roll Fantasy*. Berlin: Parthas, 2006.

Kurlansky, M. *1968: The Year that Rocked the World*. London: Vintage, 2005.

Kurp, J. "The Frustrating Reason the Kinks Were Never as Popular as the Rolling Stones." Uproxx Music, May 1, 2015. Accessed 4 May 2015. http://uproxx.com/.

Kynaston, D. *Austerity Britain, 1945–1951 (Tales of a New Jerusalem)*. London: Bloomsbury, 2008.

———. *Family Britain, 1951–1957*. London: Bloomsbury, 2009.

———. *Modernity Britain: Opening the Box, 1957–1959*. London: Bloomsbury, 2013.

Lahr, J. *The Orton Diaries*. New York: Da Capo, 1996.

Lannamann, N. "The Creepiest Love Songs of All Time." *Portland Mercury*, February 9, 2012. Accessed February 10, 2012. http://www.portlandmercury.com/.

"Last among Equals: Why Fry Wasn't First Choice as QI Host." *Chortle*, December 21, 2006. Accessed January 24, 2015. http://www.chortle.co.uk/.

Lennon, Cynthia. *A Twist of Lennon*. New York: Avon, 1978.

LeRoy, Dan. *The Greatest Music Never Sold: Secrets of Legendary Lost Albums*. New York: Backbeat, 2007.

Levy, Shawn. *Ready Steady Go! The Smashing Rise and Giddy Fall of Swinging London*. London: Doubleday, 2002.

Lynch, Joe. "Dave Davies Reflects on the Kinks' Origins, Embracing Technology and Relationship with Ray." *Billboard*, February 20, 2015. Accessed June 14, 2015. http://www.billboard.com/.

MacDonald, Ian. *Revolution in the Head: The Beatles' Records and the Sixties*. 2nd rev. ed. London: Pimlico, 2005.

Maguire, Kevin. "Edward Heath: The Prime Minister Other Tories Want Erased from History . . ." *Mirror*, May 18, 2014. Accessed October 19, 2014. http://www.mirror.co.uk/.

Marmion, Patrick. "Cheers Ray, You Nearly Got Me Going." *DailyMail.com*, September 25, 2008. Accessed November 19, 2008. http://www.dailymail.co.uk/.

Marotta, Joseph G. "The Loss of Identity and the Myth of Edenic Return in Ray Davies." In *Living on a Thin Line: Crossing Aesthetic Borders with the Kinks*, edited by Thomas M. Kitts and Michael J. Kraus, 68–77. Rumford, RI: Rock 'n' Roll Research Press, 2002.

Marr, A. *A History of Modern Britain*. London: Pan, 2009.

Marsh, Dave. *The Beatles' Second Album*. New York: Rodale, 2007.

Marten, Neville, and Jeffrey Hudson. *The Kinks: Well Respected Men*. Chessington, UK: Castle Communications, 1996.

Martens, James W. "And Still He Walks the Streets of the Big Black Smoke: Ray Davies' Working Class." In *Living on a Thin Line: Crossing Aesthetic Borders with the Kinks*, edited by Thomas M. Kitts and Michael J. Kraus, 38–43. Rumford, RI: Rock 'n' Roll Research Press, 2002.

Martin, B. "The Sacralization of Disorder: Symbolism in Rock Music." *Sociological Analysis* 40, no. 2 (Summer 1979): 87–124.

Marwick, Arthur. *British Society since 1945*. 4th ed. London: Penguin, 2003.

———. *The Sixties: Cultural Revolution in Britain, France, Italy, and the United States, c. 1958–c. 1974*. London: Bloomsbury Reader, 2012.

Matthews, L. "The £10 Ticket to Another Life." *BBC Timewatch*, January 31, 2008. Accessed October 22, 2014. http://news.bbc.co.uk/.

McCarron, K. "Pilgrims or Tourists? Rock Music and 'Shrines' in England." *Critical Survey* 7, no. 2, *Heritage: Textual Landscapes* (1995): 165–71.

McKibbin, Ross. *Classes and Cultures: England 1918–1951*. Oxford: Oxford University Press, 1998.

McNair, James. "Ray Davies' Well-Respected Legacy." *Independent*, June 18, 2009. Accessed January 16, 2016. http://www.independent.co.uk/.

McNeil, L., and G. McCain. *Please Kill Me: The Uncensored Oral History of Punk*. London: Little, Brown, 1996.

Mendelssohn, John. *The Kinks Kronikles*. New York: Quill, 1985.

Michaels, Sean. "Ray Davies Wants to Reunite the Kinks." *Guardian*, September 25, 2008. Accessed October 5, 2008. http://www.guardian.co.uk/.

Miller, A. *The Kinks Are the Village Green Preservation Society*. 33 1/3 (series) 4. London: Continuum, 2003.

Millward, S. *Changing Times: Music and Politics in 1964*. London: Matador, 2013.

Moore, Tim. *You Are Awful (But I Like You): Travels through Unloved Britain*. London: Vintage, 2013.

Morgan, Robin, and Ariel Leve. *1963: The Year of the Revolution; How Youth Changed the World with Music, Art, and Fashion*. New York: itbooks, 2013.

Muir, S. *Studying Ealing Studios*. London: Auteur, 2010.

Napier-Bell, Simon. *Black Vinyl, White Powder*. London: Ebury, 2002.

Newman, Sarah. "Kinks Mourn the Loss of Their 'Shrine' as Another British Boozer Bites the Sawdust." *Independent*, March 24, 2007. Accessed November 12, 2009. http://www.independent.co.uk/.

Nicholson, V. *Millions Like Us: Women's Lives during the Second World War*. London: Penguin, 2012.

Nott, J. J. *Music for the People: Popular Music and Dance in Interwar Britain*. Oxford: Oxford University Press, 2002.

Nuzum, E. *Parental Advisory: Music Censorship in America*. New York: Perennial, 2001.

Obelkevich, James, and Peter Catterall. *Understanding Post-War British Society*. London: Routledge, 1994.

Oldham, Andrew Loog. *Stoned*. London: Vintage, 2001.

Opie, R. *The 1970s Scrapbook*. London: PI Global, 1999.

Orwell, George. "Charles Dickens." In *Shooting an Elephant and Other Essays*, edited by Jeremy Paxman, 49–114. London: Penguin, 2009.

Orwell, George, and Bernard Crick. *Essays*. London: Penguin, 2000.

Palin, Michael. *The Python Years: Diaries, 1969–1979*. Vol. 1. London: W & N, 2014.

Parker, N. *Music Business: Infrastructure, Practice, and Law*. Andover, UK: Sweet & Maxwell, 2004.

Partridge, Christopher. *The Lyre of Orpheus: Popular Music, the Sacred, and the Profane*. Oxford: Oxford University Press, 2014.

Paxman, Jeremy. *Empire: What Ruling the World Did to the British*. London: Viking, 2011.

———. *The English: A Portrait of a People*. London: Penguin, 1999.

Perone, J. E. *Mods, Rockers, and the Music of the British Invasion*. Westport, CT: Praeger, 2009.

———. *The Words and Music of David Bowie*. Westport, CT: Praeger, 2007.

Pollard, Sidney. *The Development of the British Economy, 1914–1980*. Baltimore: E. Arnold, 1983.

Price, Simon. "Ray Davies, Royal Albert Hall, London." *Independent*, October 7, 2012. Accessed October 22, 2014. http://www.independent.co.uk/.

Quaife, Peter. *Veritas*. Vol. 1. Hertfordshire, UK: Hiren, 2011.

———. "Veritas." Vol. 2. Unpublished manuscript, 2014.

Ramnarine, T. K. "Imperial Legacies and the Politics of Musical Creativity." *World of Music* 46, no. 1, *Contemporary British Music Traditions* (2004): 91–108.

Rawling, T. *Mod: Clean Living under Difficult Circumstances—A Very British Phenomenon*. London: Omnibus, 2000.

Rebellato, Dan. *1956 and All That: The Making of Modern British Drama*. London: Routledge, 1999.

Rees, J. "Ray Davies, Interview: I Can't Play as the Kinks." *Telegraph*, October 24, 2004. Accessed October 26, 2014. http://www.telegraph.co.uk/.

Reynolds, S. *Retromania: Pop Culture's Addiction to Its Own Past*. London: Faber & Faber, 2011.

Roberts, E. *Women and Families: An Oral History, 1940–1970*. Oxford, UK: Blackwell, 1995.

Roberts, M. J. *Tell Tchaikovsky the News: Rock 'n' Roll, the Labor Question, and the Musicians' Union, 1942–1968*. Durham, NC: Duke University Press, 2014.

Rogan, Johnny. *The Complete Guide to the Music of the Kinks*. London: Omnibus, 1998.

———. *The Kinks: A Mental Institution*. New York: Proteus, 1984.

———. *The Kinks: The Sound and the Fury*. London: Elm Tree, 1984.

Roller, Steve. "Let's Write a Swimming Pool!" American Writers and Artists Inc., February 17, 2012. Accessed June 9, 2014. http://www.awaionline.com/.

Rombes, Nick. *The Cultural Dictionary of Punk, 1974–1982*. London: Continuum, 2009.

———. *Ramones' Ramones*. 33 1/3 (series). London: Continuum, 2005.

Rowntree, B. S., and G. R. Lavers. *English Life and Leisure: A Social Study*. London: Longmans, Green, 1951.

Sabin, R. *Punk Rock, So What? The Cultural Legacy of Punk*. London: Routledge, 1999.

Sandbrook, Dominic. *Never Had It So Good: A History of Britain from Suez to the Beatles*. London: Abacus, 2006.

———. *Seasons in the Sun: The Battle for Britain, 1974–1979*. London: Penguin, 2013.

———. *State of Emergency: The Way We Were; Britain, 1970–1974*. London: Penguin, 2011.

———. *White Heat: A History of Britain in the Swinging Sixties*. London: Little, Brown, 2006.

Savage, Jon. *England's Dreaming: Sex Pistols and Punk Rock*. London: Faber & Faber, 1991.

———. *The Kinks: The Official Biography*. London: Faber & Faber, 1984.

———. "Larry Page: The Man Who Rewrote Pop History." Larry Page Productions. Accessed July 10, 2014. http://www.larrypageproductions.com/.

Schruers, Fred. "The Kinks Resurgence Continues." *Rolling Stone*, February 4, 1982.

Seago, A. "'Where Hamburgers Sizzle on an Open Grill Night and Day'(?): Global Pop Music and Americanization in the Year 2000." *American Studies* 41, nos. 2/3, *Globalization, Transnationalism, and the End of the American Century* (Summer/Fall 2000): 119–36.

Sellers, Robert. *Don't Let the Bastards Grind You Down: How One Generation of British Actors Changed the World*. London: Preface, 2011.

Shillinglaw, Ann. "'Give Us a Kiss': Queer Codes, Male Partnering, and the Beatles." In *The Queer Sixties*, edited by P. J. Smith, 127–43. London: Routledge, 1999.

Shumway, D. R. *Rock Star: The Making of Musical Icons from Elvis to Springsteen*. Baltimore: Johns Hopkins University Press, 2014.

Simonelli, D. *Working Class Heroes: Rock Music and British Society in the 1960s and 1970*. Lanham, MD: Lexington, 2013.

Simpson, David. "Anarchy in Huddersfield: The Day the Sex Pistols Played Santa." *Guardian*, December 23, 2013. Accessed January 15, 2015. http://www.theguardian.com/.

———. "Ray Davies: I'm Not the Godfather of Britpop . . . More a Concerned Uncle." *Guardian*, July 16, 2015. Accessed August 9, 2015. http://www.theguardian.com/.

Singh, Anita. "Ray Davies Plans Kinks Reunion." *Telegraph*, September 23, 2008. Accessed October 5, 2008. http://www.telegraph.co.uk/.

Slate, Jeff. "A Kinks Reunion? Ray and Dave Are Talking." *Daily Beast*, January 18, 2015. Accessed January 21, 2015. http://www.thedailybeast.com/.

Somma, R. "Rock Theatricality." *Drama Review: TDR* 14, no. 1 (Autumn 1969): 128–38.

Sounes, H. *The Seventies: The Sights, Sounds, and Ideas of a Brilliant Decade*. London: Pocket, 2007.

Spragg, I. *London's Underground's Strangest Tales*. London: Portico, 2013.

Stark, Steven D. *Meet the Beatles: A Cultural History of the Band that Shook Youth, Gender, and the World*. New York: HarperCollins, 2005.

Sterling Time. "The Ovaltineys." June 28, 2008. http://www.sterlingtimes.co.uk/.

Stevens, A., and F. Moore. *Liberation: The Unofficial and Unauthorised Guide to Blake's 7*. Tolworth, UK: Telos, 2003.

Sullivan, Jim. "Dave Davies Talk About His New Solo Album, Possibilities for a Kinks' Reunion." ARTery, November 16, 2014. Accessed January 24, 2015. http://artery.wbur.org/.

Sullivan, Patricia Gordon. "'Let's Have a Go at It': The British Music Hall and the Kinks." In *Living on a Thin Line: Crossing Aesthetic Borders with the Kinks*, edited by Thomas M. Kitts and Michael J. Kraus, 80–99. Rumford, RI: Rock 'n' Roll Research Press, 2002.

Summers, A., and S. Dorril. *Honeytrap: The Secret Worlds of Stephen Ward*. London: Weidenfeld & Nicolson, 1987.

Sutherland, James. *English Satire: The Clarke Lectures, 1956*. Cambridge: Cambridge University Press, 1962.

Tait, D. *A 1970s Childhood: From Glam Rock to Happy Days*. London: History Press, 2011.

Taylor, R. "The Rise and Disintegration of the Working Classes." In *A Companion to Contemporary Britain, 1939–2000*, edited by P. Addison and H. Jones, 371–87. Oxford, UK: Blackwell, 2005.

Thompson, Ben. *Ban This Filth! Letters from the Mary Whitehouse Archive*. London: Faber & Faber, 2012.

Thompson, E. P. *The Making of the English Working Class*. London: Penguin, 2013.

Thompson, Gordon. *Please Please Me: Sixties British Pop, Inside Out*. Oxford, UK: University Press, 2008.

Todd, S. *The People: The Rise and Fall of the Working Class, 1910–2010*. London: John Murray, 2015.

Tomlinson, J. *The Politics of Decline: Understanding Post-War Britain*. Harlow, UK: Longman, 2001.

Travis, A. "UK Migrants to Face 'Patriotic' Citizenship Test." *Guardian*, July 1, 2012. Accessed October 19, 2014. http://www.theguardian.com/.

Turner, Alwyn W. *Crisis? What Crisis? Britain in the 1970s*. London: Aurum, 2008.

Turner, S. *A Hard Day's Write: The Stories behind Every Beatles Song*. London: Carlton, 2005.

Uncut. "The Clash's 30 Best Songs." March 13, 2015. Accessed August 4, 2015. http://www.uncut.co.uk/.

Unterberger, Richie. *Urban Spacemen and Wayfaring Strangers: Overlooked Innovators and Eccentric Visionaries of '60s Rock*. London: Backbeat, 2000.

Vinnicombe, C. "Dave Davies Talks Guitars, Self Expression, and 'You Really Got Me.'" MusicRadar, June 2, 2014. Accessed June 30, 2014. http://www.musicradar.com/.

Vivalabeat. "Waterloo Sunset's Fine." *Muswell Hillbilly Girl* (blog), May 19, 2015. Accessed May 24, 2015. https://vivalabeat.wordpress.com/.

Wadhams, W. *Inside the Hits: The Seduction of a Rock and Roll Generation*. Boston: Berklee, 2001.

Walker, J. A. *Left Shift: Radical Art in 1970s Britain*. London: I. B. Taurus, 2002.

Walker, Tim. "First Night: Come Dancing, Theatre Royal, Stratford East: Davies Proves He Can Really Get Them Going." *Independent*, September 25, 2008. Accessed November 19, 2008. http://www.independent.co.uk/.

Watson, A. "Self-Deception and Survival: Mental Coping Strategies on the Western Front, 1914–18." *Journal of Contemporary History* 41, no. 2 (April 2006): 247–68.

Webb, S. *A 1970s Teenager: From Bell-Bottoms to Disco Dancing*. London: History Press, 2013.

Weight, R. *Mod! A Very British Style*. London: Bodley Head, 2013.

Weinstein, Deena. "Relations in the Kinks: Familiar but Not Fully Familial." *Popular Music and Society* 29, no. 2 (2006): 167–87.

Whiteley, Sheila. *Too Much Too Young: Popular Music, Age, and Gender*. London: Routledge, 2005.

Wight, Jeb. "Dave Davies: There's Madness There!" Classic Rock Revisited. Accessed June 14, 2015. http://www.classicrockrevisited.com/.

Wilson, Colin. *The Angry Years: The Rise and Fall of the Angry Young Men*. London: Robson, 2007.

Wilson, John. "Ray Davies: Words Were My Weapons." *BBC News*, November 27, 2012. Accessed January 23, 2015. http://www.bbc.co.uk/.

Wintour, P. "David Cameron Joins Calls for Promoting 'British Values' in Schools." *Guardian*, June 15, 2014. Accessed October 19, 2014. http://www.theguardian.com/.

Woodward, N. W. C. "Inflation." In *The British Economy since 1945*, edited by N. F. R. Crafts and N. W. C. Woodward, 180–212. Oxford, UK: Claredon, 1991.

———. *The Management of the British Economy, 1945–2001*. New York: Palgrave, 2004.

Young, G. "'So Slide over Here': The Aesthetics of Masculinity in Late Twentieth-Century Australian Pop Music." *Popular Music* 23, no. 2 (May 2004): 173–93.

Youngs, Ian. "The Kinks Start to Work on a Comeback." *BBC News*, November 5, 2008. Accessed November 19, 2008. http://news.bbc.co.uk/.

Ziegler, P. *Edward Heath: The Authorised Biography*. London: HarperPress, 2010.

FURTHER READING

Addison, P., and H. Jones. *A Companion to Contemporary Britain, 1939–2000*. Oxford, UK: Blackwell, 2005. Blackwell has produced a number of useful "Companions" to various historical and cultural eras. The essays found in this volume provide a useful starting place for locating the Kinks and their output socially and culturally.

Baxter-Moore, Nick. "'This Is Where I Belong': Identity, Social Class, and the Nostalgic Englishness of Ray Davies and the Kinks." *Popular Music and Society* 29, no. 2 (2006): 145–65. One of a number of excellent articles in a Kinks-themed issue of *PMS*.

Clayson, Alan. *Beat Merchants: The Origins, History, Impact and Rock Legacy of the British Pop Groups*. London: Blandford, 1995. Funny and thoughtful memoir—useful for context for the Kinks' formative years.

Davies, Dave. *Kink*. New York: Hyperion, 1996. Dave's autobiography: cheerful, funny, and reflective. Lots of sex and drugs and rock 'n' roll.

Davies, Ray. *Americana: The Kinks, The Road and the Perfect Riff*. London: Virgin, 2013. Part 2 of Ray's memoirs, more conventionally written than *X-Ray*; the latter part of Ray's life and career framed around being shot by a mugger in New Orleans in 2001. If *X-Ray* is Ray's grappling with the music industry and its effects on his creativity, *Americana* explores his love-hate relationship with the United States and identity as English.

———. *X-Ray*. New York: Overlook, 1995. Ray's strange science-fictionalized autobiography where a decrepit version of himself teases and torments a fictionalized younger version of himself sent to interview him in a grim, dystopian future England.

Ellis, I. *Brit Wits: A History of British Rock Humor*. Bristol, UK: Intellect, 2012. Neglected area of study for British rock and roll; the Kinks have only a short section in one chapter, but Ellis's study is useful for understanding the expression of rock-and-roll rebellion, British style, through humor, as well as for a general survey on a critical aspect of what makes the English English.

Frame, Peter. *The Restless Generation: How Rock Music Changed the Face of 1950s Britain*. London: Rogan House, 2007. Along with Clayson, another excellent overview of the popular music scene during the Kinks' youth and formative years.

Frith, Simon, Matt Brennan, Martin Cloonan, and Emma Webster, eds. *The History of Live Music in Britain*. Vol. 1, *1950–1967 (From the Dance Hall to the 100 Club)*. London: Ashgate, 2013. Recommended especially in tandem with Roberts, below, for those who have far greater capacity than I to grasp the context behind the Kinks' ban on performance in the United States for four years in the 1960s. Frith and colleagues' well-written study may also unravel the mystery behind *Top of the Pops* performances: are they partially live, completely live, or lip-synched? Yes, no, or all three at once?

Gildart, K. *Images of England through Popular Music: Class, Youth and Rock 'n' Roll, 1955–1976.* London: Palgrave MacMillan, 2013. Gildart has studied the effects of social class on the works of Ray Davies and the Kinks. This work complements D. Simonelli's *Working Class Heroes: Rock Music and British Society in the 1960s and 1970* (Lanham, MD: Lexington, 2013) as examples of how the Kinks fit into studies of cultural and social history of mid-twentieth-century Britain.

Hamblett, Charles, and Jane Deverson. *Generation X.* London: Anthony Gibbs, 1964. Widely selling book in 1964 and, up until about twenty years ago, ubiquitous in charity and secondhand bookshops. Essential reading for anyone who thinks *Austin Powers* is a documentary. The book is a series of interviews conducted with Britain youth between the ages of sixteen and twenty-five, revealing that the "Swinging Sixties" happened really only to a small part of the population and that most British youth were keen on finding jobs, getting married, and having families, following in the traditions and values of their parents' generation.

Hasted, Nick. *The Story of the Kinks: You Really Got Me.* London: Omnibus, 2011. Fast-moving biography of the Kinks; picks up with the postband years and solo careers of the principles. Hasted had access to members of the band for interviews.

Hinman, D. *The Kinks: All Day and All of the Night; Day-by-Day Concerts, Recordings, and Broadcasts, 1961–1996.* San Francisco: Backbeat, 2004. Exhaustive and impressive volume; exactly as it says in the title—a detailed diary of Kinks milestones, concerts, recordings, and broadcasts, 1961 through to 1996. Invaluable resource for the book in hand. Hinman plumbed the depths of visual and written media to support this catalog.

———. *The Kinks Part One: You Really Got Me; An Illustrated World Discography of the Kinks, 1964–1993.* London: Backbeat, 1994. Another top reference tool. Followed by a short supplement a year or so later. Complements Hinman's other work on the Kinks.

Kitts, Thomas. *Ray Davies: Not Like Everybody Else.* New York: Routledge, 2008. Partly biography, partly a study of Ray Davies's word and music in a social and cultural context. An academic monograph accessible to the general fan and highly recommended.

Kitts, Thomas M., and Michael J. Kraus, eds. *Living on a Thin Line: Crossing Aesthetic Borders with the Kinks.* Rumford, RI: Rock 'n' Roll Research Press, 2002. A collection of analytical and academic essays with illustrations by Pete Quaife. Variety of topics covered including sections of essays on influences on the Kinks' work, recurring themes, theatrical aspects of the band's concept albums, solo work, and comparisons between aspects of the Kinks' output and that of other musical and literary artists. Published by Rock 'n' Roll Research Press, it's sometimes a bit hard to find but is a good read for fans who want some depth to their interpretation and understanding of the context behind the Kinks' work.

Levy, Shawn. *Ready Steady Go! The Smashing Rise and Giddy Fall of Swinging London.* London: Doubleday, 2002. A good complement to *Generation X* (as is Frith's book on live music in Britain—especially for those who ingenuously assume that London equals all of Britain). Levy covers the key movers and shakers of early 1960s music, photography, art, and theater.

Marten, Neville, and Jeffrey Hudson. *The Kinks: Well Respected Men.* Chessington, UK: Castle Communications, 1996.

Mendelssohn, J. *The Kinks Kronikles.* New York: Quill, 1985. Great read from a journalist and devoted Kinks' fan. It's all about his adventures with the band in the 1970s as well as a fan's take on the history of the band and its influence on him.

Miller, A. *The Kinks Are the Village Green Preservation Society.* 33 1/3 (series) 4. London: Continuum, 2003. Tidy book covering the creation and cultural context for *Village Green*. Miller provides a succinct history of the band as well as context for the lead-up to the pastoral and storytelling songs on the album. The Kinks' only entry in the 33 1/3 series, mainly because Bloomsbury keeps shortlisting me and then choosing other works, sadly.

Quaife, Peter. *Veritas.* Vol. 1. Hertfordshire, UK: Hiren, 2011. Pete Quaife's version of the Kinks' story, about a fictional band's rise to fame. Volume 1 goes back a generation earlier and establishes the story and context of the band's parents before describing the childhood and formative years of the band's members. The volume draws to a close having seen the band finally reach number one on the charts and experience the madness of the commercial machine of the industry. It's witty and knowing but sadly also difficult to find owing to some legal issues surrounding the illustration on the book's sleeve. Volume 2, which covers the trials and tribulations of the fictional post–hit maker, is in private and limited circulation only as the Quaife estate searches for a suitable publisher, although it may be released as an eBook in 2016.

Roberts, M. J. *Tell Tchaikovsky the News: Rock 'n' Roll, the Labor Question, and the Musicians' Union, 1942–1968.* Durham, NC: Duke University Press, 2014. The Kinks' version of the Schleswig-Holstein Question is the reasons for their ban from touring and broadcasting performances for four years in the United States; of the three people who know the answer, one is dead, one has gone mad, and one has forgotten all about it. Much of the answer lies within the complexities of the demented marriage among popular music, performance rights, and the unions that exist in both Britain (see Frith's book above) and the United States. The laws and regulations gets only more demented when performers from each country attempt to perform in the other. Roberts manfully tackles the issue from the American side of things and writes so elegantly that I, who failed maths in both secondary school and at university, *almost* grasp the issue. Highly recommended.

Rogan, Johnny. *The Complete Guide to the Music of the Kinks.* London: Omnibus, 1998. Succinct and useful digest of the Kinks' UK canon.

———. *The Kinks: The Sound and the Fury.* London: Elm Tree, 1984. The second Kinks biography to appear in 1984. As with Savage, it is written without fanboy claptrap if you want to read about the band at the height of their US renaissance.

Savage, Jon. *The Kinks: The Official Biography.* London: Faber & Faber, 1984. Highly recommended and lavishly illustrated. Savage had access to the Davieses' mother and family for his interviews. Accessible but serious history of the band. Long out of print, and Savage has not been able to update it due to contractual folderol.

FURTHER LISTENING

Note: The Kinks released nearly three dozen official albums between 1964 and 1996. The list below covers only these official releases as they are one of the most overpackaged and reissued bands in pop music; that includes exploitation by their own labels and label subsidiaries during their Kinks heyday, a practice that actually undermined the sales of the official releases. There is no way to include every repackaged or reissued album or CD, but since the late 1990s, there have been high-quality reissues of the original Pye and RCA Kinks' albums via Castle and Sanctuary. Also within the last ten years there have appeared compilations that dig a bit deeper than the usual assortment of singles and greatest hits. These releases include alternate takes, BBC-only performances, demos, and previously unreleased tracks. There are also plenty of bootleg live performances out there, not to mention all of the post-1996 solo work from Ray and Dave Davies individually (and the rumor that Ray is sitting on as much unreleased, unheard music in Konk Studios than the Kinks produced officially over their thirty-two-year career). The titles listed below are UK releases (which is the scheme Sanctuary recording studio follows for the Kinks' Pye Records years). If this list doesn't satisfy you (and, for the sake of my sanity, it is necessarily limited), Doug Hinman rides to the rescue with two exhaustive works:

Hinman, D. *The Kinks Part One: You Really Got Me; An Illustrated World Discography of the Kinks, 1964–1993*. London: Backbeat, 1994.
———. *You Really Got Me: Supplement*. Rumford, RI: Doug Hinman, 1997.This short (sixty-four pages) supplement also includes corrections and addenda.

After 1997, you're on your own for any comprehensive list of solo releases. You can piece some together from Dave Emlen's "Unofficial
Kinks Web Site" KindaKinks.net as well as Ray's and Dave's own web-
sites (which are not always kept up to date.) KindaKinks.net has new
releases and discography on it, mostly related to the Kinks rather than
solo endeavors. Your best bet is to hit up *Wikipedia* where the fans and
fanatics maintain the lists of solo works on the Davieses' individual
pages. Johnny Rogan's *Complete Guide to the Music of the Kinks* (1998)
is a good digest that succinctly covers all of their official UK-released
singles, EPs, and albums.

THINKING VISUALLY

Check out *Alan's Album Archives*, which includes a page of the Kinks
surviving TV appearances between 1964 and 1995: http://
alansalbumarchives.blogspot.co.uk/.

COMPILATIONS

Not every Kinks hit is found on one of their official releases, as British
practice in the 1960s was to release hits (and potential hits) on singles or
EPs. British teens in the sixties didn't have as much money as their
American counterparts, and they would have been cross to buy albums
that were merely collections of the singles. That said, if you want to dip
into the Kinks' greatest hits without wiping out your bank account, try
The Kinks: The Ultimate Collection (London: Sanctuary, 2004; 2 discs).
This sift through the hits provides no surprises for the superfan but is a
good introduction for the casual listener (and probably more than one,
"Oh, right, the Kinks do this one!"). Loads of Dave Davies's stuff is
included on this one as well, which tends to get overlooked outside of
"Death of a Clown" on the other compilations.

The Kinks: Picture Book. London: Sanctuary, 2008 (6 discs). Whereas most compilations
    hover around the Pye years of the 1960s or focus exclusively on the hits, *Picture Book*
    covers the Kinks' entire output and includes deeper cuts and demos/alternate takes.
The BBC Sessions, 1964–1977. London: Sanctuary, 2012 (6 discs). Again mostly from the Pye
    era, but the BBC had the Kinks perform live for radio transmission, and as most of their
    1960s television performances have been wiped, it's a nice chance to have a listen to these

tracks performed off the cuff (and a number of their BBC appearances would have been lip-synched anyway). This set also has some interview bits from the Kinks' earliest days.

The Kinks' Anthology, 1964–1971. London: Sanctuary, 2014 (5 discs). The usual hits but loads of more obscure early releases and deeper cuts from the Kinks' heyday (according to purists).

Sunny Afternoon: The Very Best of the Kinks. London: Sanctuary, 2015 (2 discs). Gah, how many times can the Kinks' be repackaged? Crikey, loads; this little selection doesn't even scratch the surface. Anyway, the hook on this compilation is two pronged: the track list here is primarily the studio releases of the songs performed in Joe Penhall and Ray Davies's staged *nachleben* of the Kinks' story, *Sunny Afternoon* (not to be confused with the Official Cast Recording version of *Sunny Afternoon*, published by BMG Management, 2014). Second, the remaining songs that fill out the play's music and the remaining tracks on the CD are handpicked by Ray as his favorites and best-ofs, allegedly the only compilation out of the thirty-six kabillion where any of the Kinks have had any say on what ought to be included. Also includes sessions and interviews from the Kinks at the BBC between 1964 and 1967 and an American TV station.

Kinked! Kinks Songs and Sessions, 1964–1971. London: Ace Records, 2016. Twenty-six covers of Kinks' tracks from mostly the 1960s, when Ray was shackled to his writing desk not only to produce more songs for the Kinks but also to sell on to other artists. The Kinks did record some of these titles, but a number of the ones performed by these other artists have been difficult to find in their original singles form. It's a cracking fun compilation and high time these tracks got a proper airing. Alec Palao's liner notes are well worth a read as he discusses the artists and the recordings. I was sold with the chance to actually have a clean copy of Dave Berry's "This Strange Effect."

STUDIO ALBUMS (UK TITLES)

Kinks. Mitcham, UK: Pye, 1964. First studio album, thrown together quickly following on the heels of "You Really Got Me" hitting number one in the UK charts. Moody sleeve photo of the band in their red jackets. The tracks include concert staples as well as their first failed Pye single (get the Sanctuary CD for the second failed single, included as a bonus track, because last time I checked the original was going for about £450 on eBay—which is why my copy is in a safety deposit box!). Aside from "You Really Got Me," this album also contains "Stop Your Sobbing" and a fun cover of Bo Diddley's "Cadillac."

Kinda Kinks. Mitcham, UK: Pye, 1965. Another hastily assembled album, recorded in a few days following an exhausting world tour. The suits were determined to squeeze their money's worth out of the band while they lasted. Nevertheless, among the covers and rhythm and blues are some lovely bits and thoughtful songwriting: "Tired of Waiting" showed that the band wasn't all power chords. "Something Better Beginning" is wistful sweetness.

The Kink Kontroversy. Mitcham, UK: Pye, 1965. Another rushed album—a whole week in the studio. Well-known tracks include "Til the End of the Day" and "Where Have All the Good Times Gone?" Also found here are "I'm on an Island," a bit of pseudo-calypso from Ray. Many of the songs on these first three albums reflect the Kinks' blues and rhythm-and-blues influences.

Face to Face. Mitcham, UK: Pye, 1966. The beginnings and blossoming of Kinks' tracks as character and storytelling songs. "A Well Respected Man" was released as a single a year before this album, and if Ray discovered his Englishness with that project, it begins to come to fruition here. The songs were meant to be linked by sound effects that precede a number of the tunes on the album—a ringing phone for "Party Line" (which is about a shared phone line as people had in those days and *not* about a sex hotline, as so many modern bloggers seem to think!), faux Bach for "Session Man," and rags swirled in a bucket to mimic the surf for "Holiday in Waikiki." All of the songs here are Davies originals, and this is the one that contains "Sunny Afternoon." As with all of the Pye releases, Sanctuary's reissue of this album includes as extra tracks the key singles released at this time as well, including "Dead End Street" and "Big Black Smoke."

Something Else by the Kinks. Mitcham, UK: Pye, 1967. Another stab at a concept album, thwarted because the songs were not arranged on the album in the order that Ray wanted—and one that is much stronger again on the reissue thanks to Sanctuary's inclusion of contemporary singles. Virtually no throwaway tracks here and a very English album both thematically and musically—it kicks off with the homoerotic schoolboy lament "David Watts" and ends with "Waterloo Sunset." In between are songs that evoke English folk music ("Two Sisters"), music hall ("Harry Rag"), and country-western music ("Death of a Clown"). Together with its singles, it also represents a strong showing from Dave, with "Death of a Clown," "Love Me 'til the Sun Shines," and "Susannah's Still Alive." As for the title, it's pretty much all you need to know about how Ray felt about the grind of the music machine to which he was subject.

The Kinks Are the Village Green Preservation Society. Mitcham, UK: Pye, 1968. "You have to remember that North London was my village green, my version of the countryside. The street [and district] I grew up in was called Fortis Green, and then there was Waterlow Park and the little lake. I sang in the choir at St James's Primary School until I was about 10, then I trained myself to sing out of tune so I could hang around with a gang called the Crooners instead. Our Scottish singing teacher Mrs. Lewis said, 'Never mind, Davies—I hear crooners are making a lot of money these days.'" James McNair, "Ray Davies' Well-Respected Legacy," *Independent*, June 18, 2009, accessed January 16, 2016, http://www.independent.co.uk/.

Arthur (or the Decline and Fall of the British Empire). Mitcham, UK: Pye, 1969. Structured loosely around the story of the Davieses' sister and her family's emigration to a new life in Australia. It was written originally for a television program that fell through, leaving only the music. Poorly promoted at the time, it's now considered among the Kinks' finest work on Pye, including the tracks "Victoria," "Young and Innocent Days," and "Shangri-la"—and is about as antiwar as the Kinks would ever get.

Lola versus Powerman and the Moneygoround, Part One. Mitcham, UK: Pye, 1970. Ray's blistering satire of the music industry, based on the experiences of the band in the early days of their career. The best-known track, "Lola," was banned off the BBC not because it's a song about a transvestite but because the original lyrics mentioned Coca-Cola, breaking the BBC policy of no named productions allowed across the airwaves. (Paul Simon's "Kodachrome" was banned for the same reason.) "Lola" was the Kinks' last top-ten single until "Come Dancing" in 1982.

Muswell Hillbillies. New York: RCA Victor, 1971. The Kinks' first album on RCA, and it's a solid one too. The Kinks reinvent themselves—some country-western flavoring as well as adding a brass section in the Mike Cotton Sound. Nevertheless, a very "English" collection of songs focusing on working-class angst (even if Ray seems a bit flippant about it at times). Kicks off with the brilliant "20th Century Man." Englishness abounds in "Have a Cuppa Tea," "Oklahoma, U.S.A.," and "Muswell Hillbillies."

Percy. Mitcham, UK: Pye, 1971. The Kinks provided the soundtrack for a film about the world's first penis transplant. If you have to see it, Amazon carries it (region 1 only). Look for the EP instead, as the album is mostly instrumentals from the film, but the EP (Pye7NX 8001) includes Ray's four thoughtful tracks "God's Children," "The Way Love Used to Be," "Moments," and "Dreams." Yes, it's out of print, but what's life without a challenge? I just found one on eBay for £3.99.

Everybody's in Show-Biz. New York: RCA Victor, 1972. Half live album (which the fans hate) and half studio album—the latter focusing on life on the road and the loneliness of stardom, epitomized in "Celluloid Heroes."

Preservation Act 1. New York: RCA Victor, 1973. The first of a dystopian trilogy, filled with paranoia, fears of the loss of identity, and terror of the materialistic future, the *Preservation* story is actually a funny, flamboyant stage performance for those who were lucky enough to see the Kinks romps through it (I was only eight years old at the time, so no luck) or see it revived, as it is occasionally. Both *Preservations* and *Schoolboys* are woefully underrated by fans and critics and are only recently getting the appreciation they deserve.

Preservation Act 2. New York: RCA Victor, 1974. The one where the band wasn't having much fun anymore. Johnny Rogan notes that many feel this is more of a Ray show than a Kinks album. It didn't sell well, and critics had no idea what to do with it.

Schoolboys in Disgrace. New York: RCA Victor, 1975. The third in the *Preservation* trilogy— even if the theatricals aren't your cup of tea, the Kinks were prettier in their schoolboy gear than Angus Young (who of course pioneered the look in the previous year).

Soap Opera. New York: RCA Victor, 1975. The Kinks' studio version of Ray's *Starmaker*.

Sleepwalker. New York: Arista, 1977. A new label, loads of publicity, and the Kinks' return to their old rock-and-roll form—albeit with plenty of tracks about paranoia, working-man's blues, and Ray's predilection for character songs, with a few Dave songs allowed along for the ride. The next set of albums would reflect the Kinks' return to commercial success (especially in the United States) in the wake of newer bands covering their back catalog and would see arena tours and album-oriented rock (AOR) from the band.

Misfits. New York: Arista, 1978. Fan and critical favorite (Rogan describes the previous LP as "cold" if not antiseptic). High points are the eponymous opening track, and "Rock 'n' Roll Fantasy"—the latter the one that the super-fanboys just don't get (it's *not* a compliment to be Dan the Fan!).

Low Budget. New York: Arista, 1979. Still ascending a renewed peak; lively and raucous. The Kinks were still more popular in the United States at the time of release. Key hits off this album are "(Wish I Could Fly Like) Superman" and "Low Budget," the latter still an encore staple at Ray's solo shows.

Give the People What They Want. New York: Arista, 1981. More AOR and arena-tour-supported work in America. Contains lots of callbacks to the Kinks' earlier catalog in "Destroyer." "Art Lover" is a reflective piece by Ray about his children (which the creepier fanboys assume is about pedophilia. Sigh.)

State of Confusion. New York: Arista, 1983. Released in the United States before the UK as a way of thanking American fans for their support of the band. "Come Dancing" and "Don't Forget to Dance" were both written about the Daviesies' sisters and memories of their love of music and the "danse palais"; fitting tributes to the band's almost-twentieth anniversary. "Come Dancing" received ubiquitous airplay on MTV, and Julien Temple directed the video.

Word of Mouth. New York: Arista, 1984. The Kinks crashed and burned during and after this one, but "Do It Again" and Dave's "Living on a Thin Line" are standout tracks. Several tracks here are from Ray's solo project *Return to Waterloo*, which was a source of contention among the band.

Think Visual. London: London Records, 1986. Sort of a complement to *Lola*, as a number of the songs are about the pitfalls of the music industry (especially "Working at the Factory" and the eponymous track).

UK Jive. London: London Records, 1988. Sadly barely charted; the Kinks didn't tour to promote it. Some cracking tunes here, though, including "War Is Over" and "Down all the Days (till 1992)." Couple of brilliant tunes from Dave—"Perfect Strangers," which is lovely, and "Dear Margaret," which sadly wasn't revisited when Thatcher died.

Did Ya? New York: Columbia, 1991. Not an album but a five-song EP. "Did Ya" itself is a nifty bit of Ray skewering the rosy-colored contemporary craze for all things Swinging Sixties.

Phobia. New York: Columbia, 1993. Well supported by Columbia and the Daviesies doing publicity, but the album again didn't sell very well, a sad state of affairs considering that at this time all of the Britpop groups were banging on about how influential the Kinks were to their own work. Still, this is the one with the country-flavored "Hatred: A Duet"— check out Ray and Dave on Jay Leno's nighttime chat show, and see if it was all in jest or not.

LIVE ALBUMS

Live at Kelvin Hall. Mitcham, UK: Pye, 1968. Recorded at a Kinks' concert in 1967, Pye held off releasing it until early 1968 so that it didn't come into commercial conflict with *Something Else*. As so much footage of 1960s-era Kinks have been wiped, this is a rare chance to hear the madness underscoring an early live performance. The US version has no breaks between songs, so might be worth looking for.

One for the Road. New York: Arista, 1980.

Live: The Road. London: London Records, 1988.

To the Bone. London: Konk/Grapevine, 1994. One last recording: a stripped-down live set in front of a small, invited audience.

TWO ODDS AND SODS

Kinks Kronikles. New York: Reprise, 1972. American release of singles, B sides, and assorted, previously unreleased tracks from between 1966 and 1970. An essential album according to journalist and Kinks' fan John Mendelsohn and one that was shamefully ignored at the time of release as he felt it filled in many gaps for American fans who were only just rediscovering the band after their touring ban of the United States.

Great Lost Kinks Album. New York: Reprise, 1973.Another American release by Reprise, this one of unreleased material recorded between 1966 and 1970. Released without the Kinks' knowledge (they found out only when it charted on *Billboard*), Ray Davies sued Reprise, and the album was withdrawn. The tracks eventually made their way onto official releases after 1998 as Sanctuary tidied them up and included them on several CD reissues of Kinks' work (including the *BBC Sessions 1964–1977* [2001], the deluxe reissue of *Village Green* [2004], and *The Kinks Anthology, 1964–1971* [2014]).

INDEX

ABOUT THE AUTHOR

Carey Fleiner is senior lecturer in classical and early medieval history and programme leader in classical studies in the Department of History, and part-time contributor to popular music studies pathway at the University of Winchester in Winchester, UK. Her formal studies include Roman and medieval history, Latin, and classical guitar at the University of Delaware and postgraduate studies in Carolingian and Roman history. She has written, spoken, and published academic pieces on the Kinks as well as other topics including the reputation of popular musicians in the Middle Ages, siblings in rock and roll, and the somewhat tempestuous relationship between the Emperor Nero and his mother Agrippina the Younger. She lives on the south coast of England.

CPSIA information can be obtained
at www.ICGtesting.com
Printed in the USA
BVOW03*0513170217
476065BV00003B/3/P